15

Annika Kahrs

OFF SCORE

Hamburger Bahnhof

Nationalgalerie der Gegenwart

Für die / For the Nationalgalerie –
Staatliche Museen zu Berlin
herausgegeben von / edited by
Sam Bardaouil & Till Fellrath

SilvanaEditoriale

Nationalgalerie
Staatliche Museen zu Berlin

Inhalt / Content

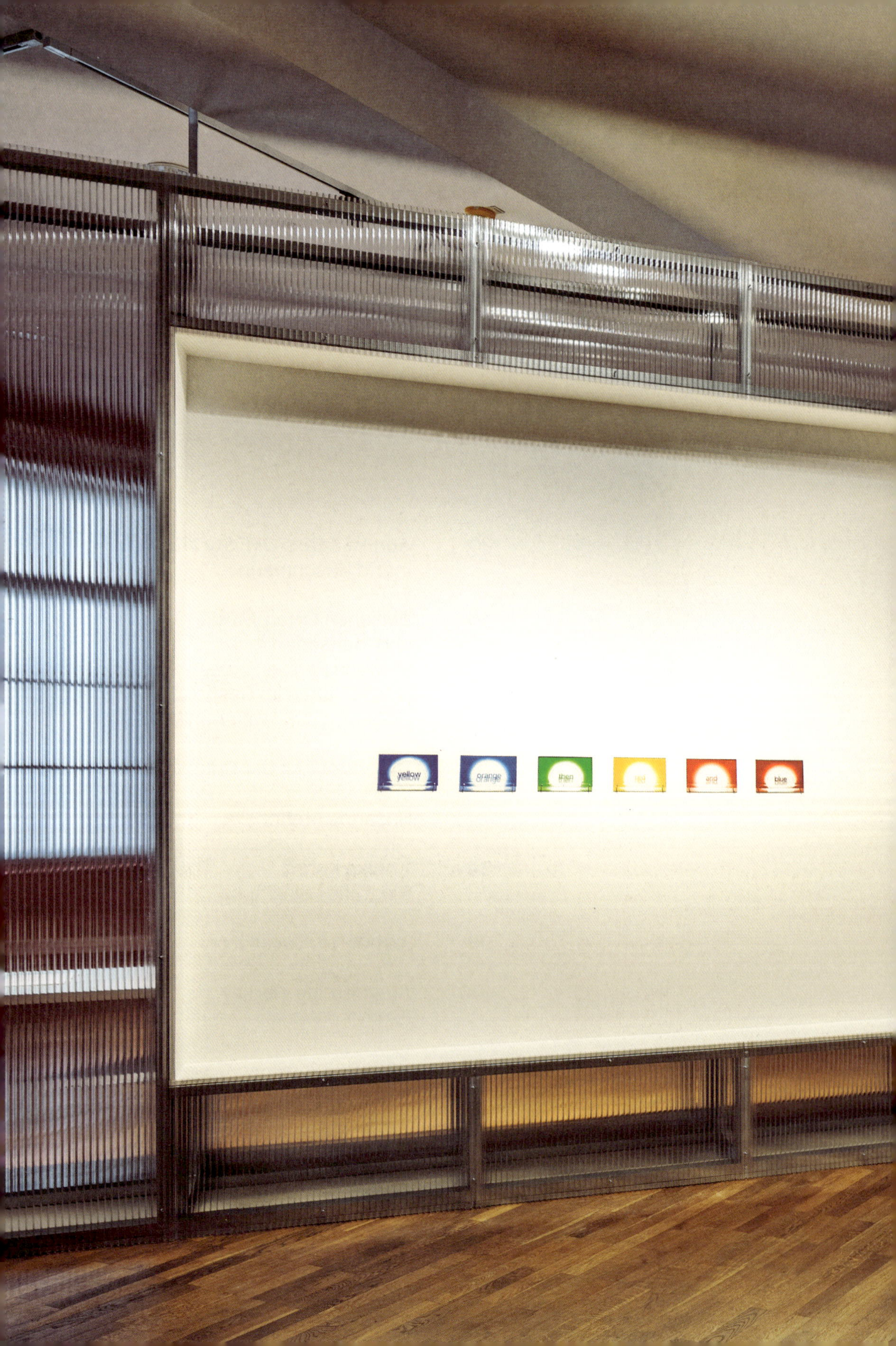
yellow
orange
then
red
and
blue

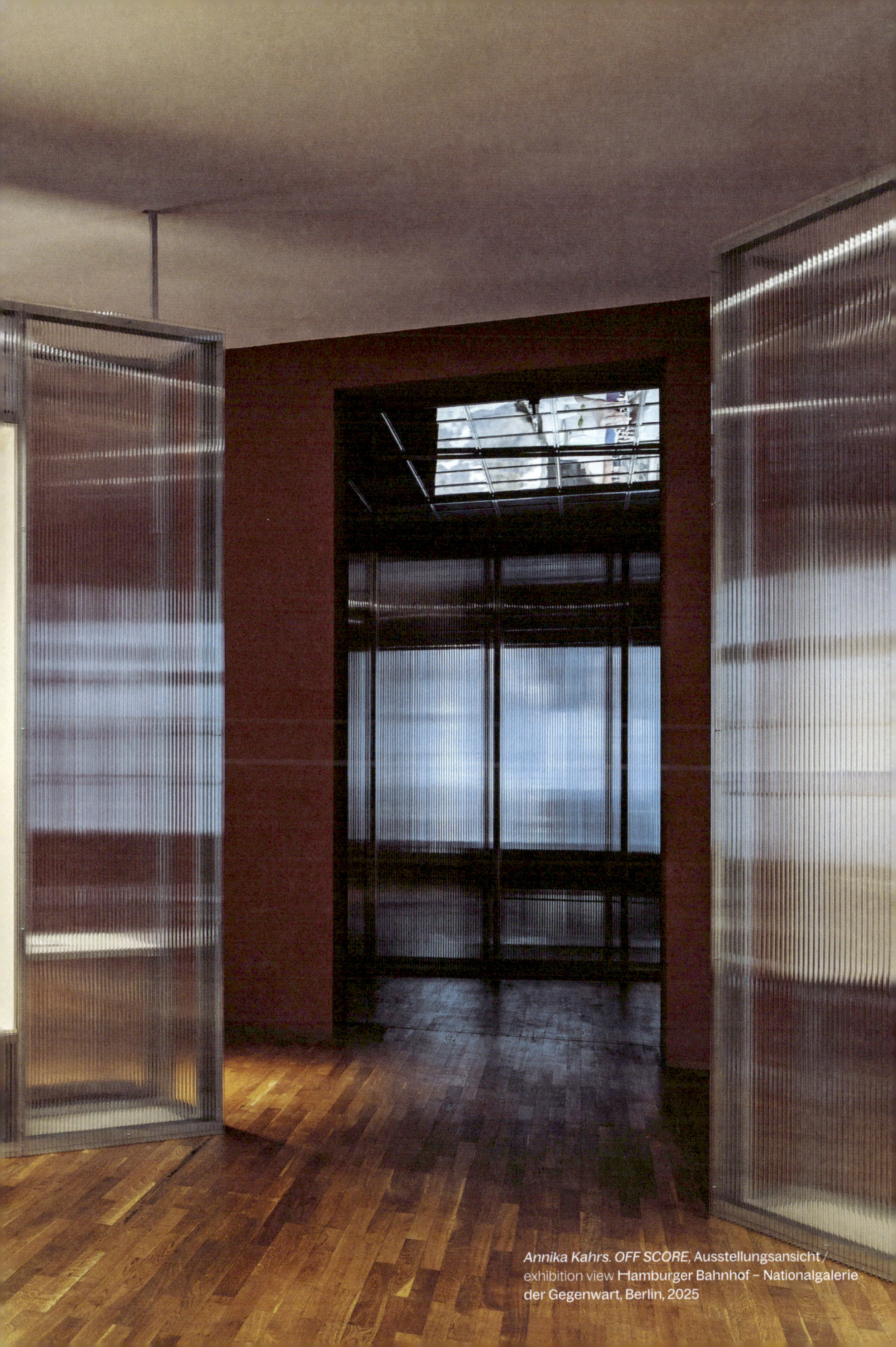

Annika Kahrs. OFF SCORE, Ausstellungsansicht / exhibition view Hamburger Bahnhof – Nationalgalerie der Gegenwart, Berlin, 2025

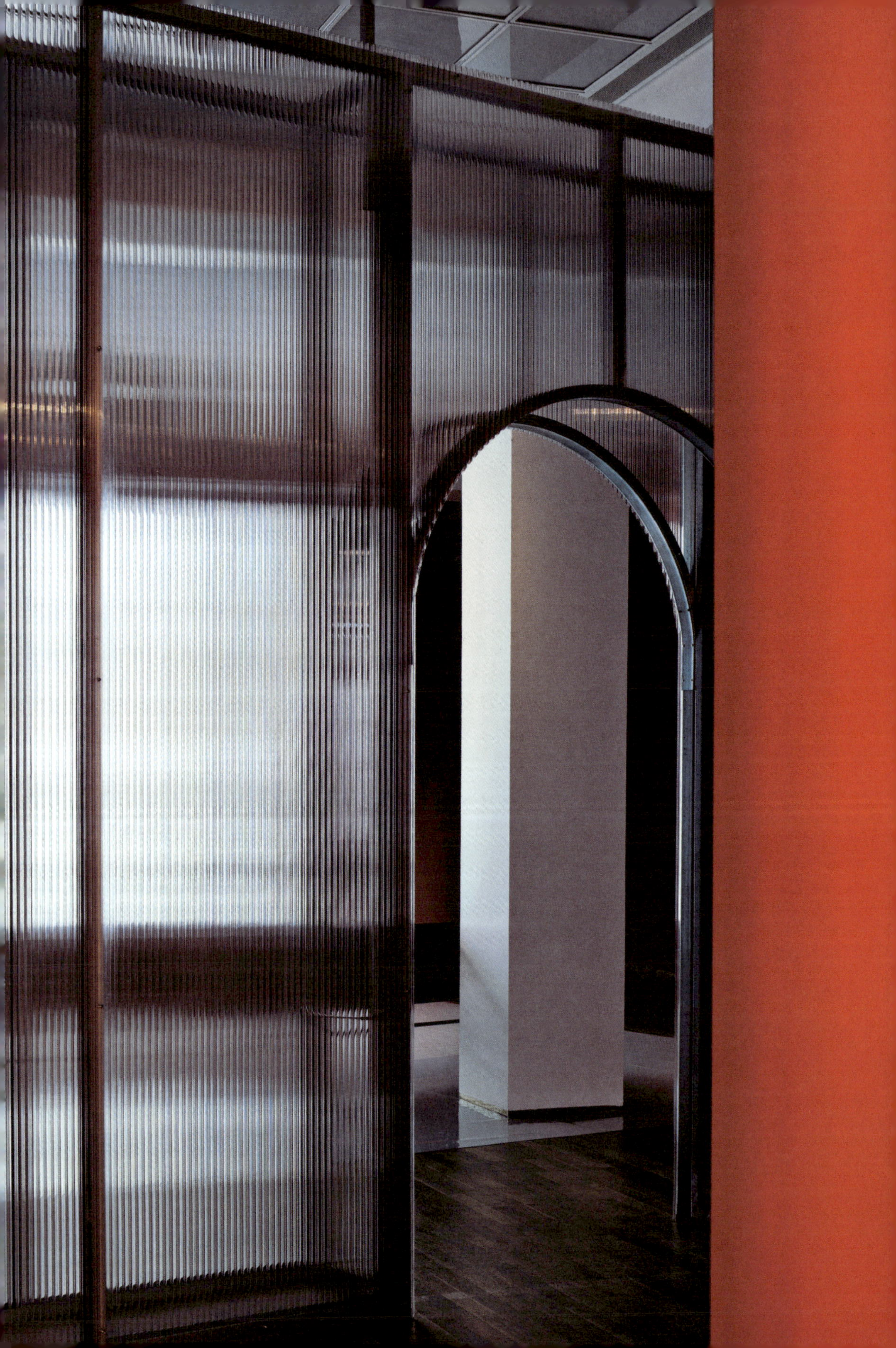

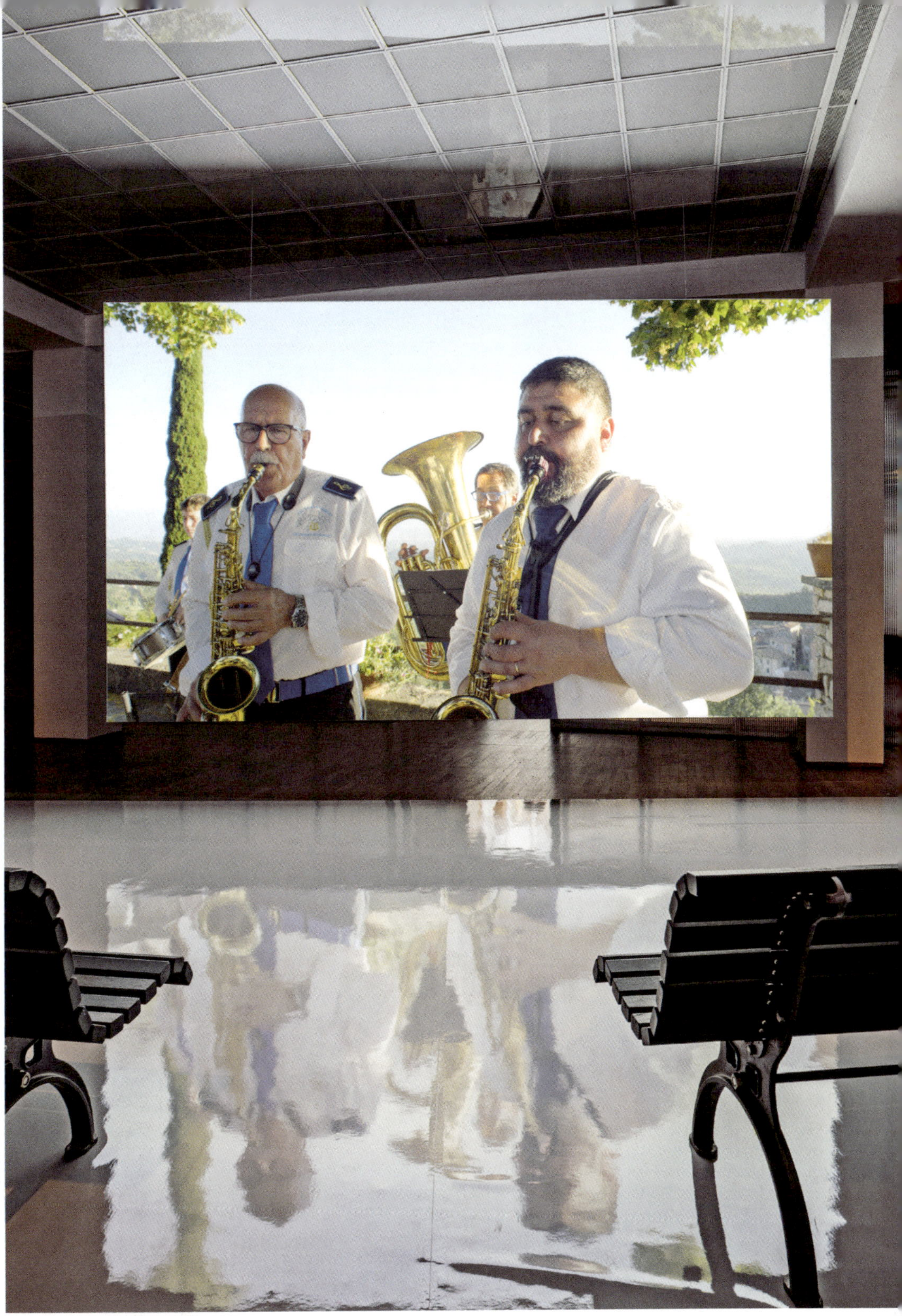

Annika Kahrs. OFF SCORE, Ausstellungsansicht / exhibition view Hamburger Bahnhof – Nationalgalerie der Gegenwart, Berlin, 2025

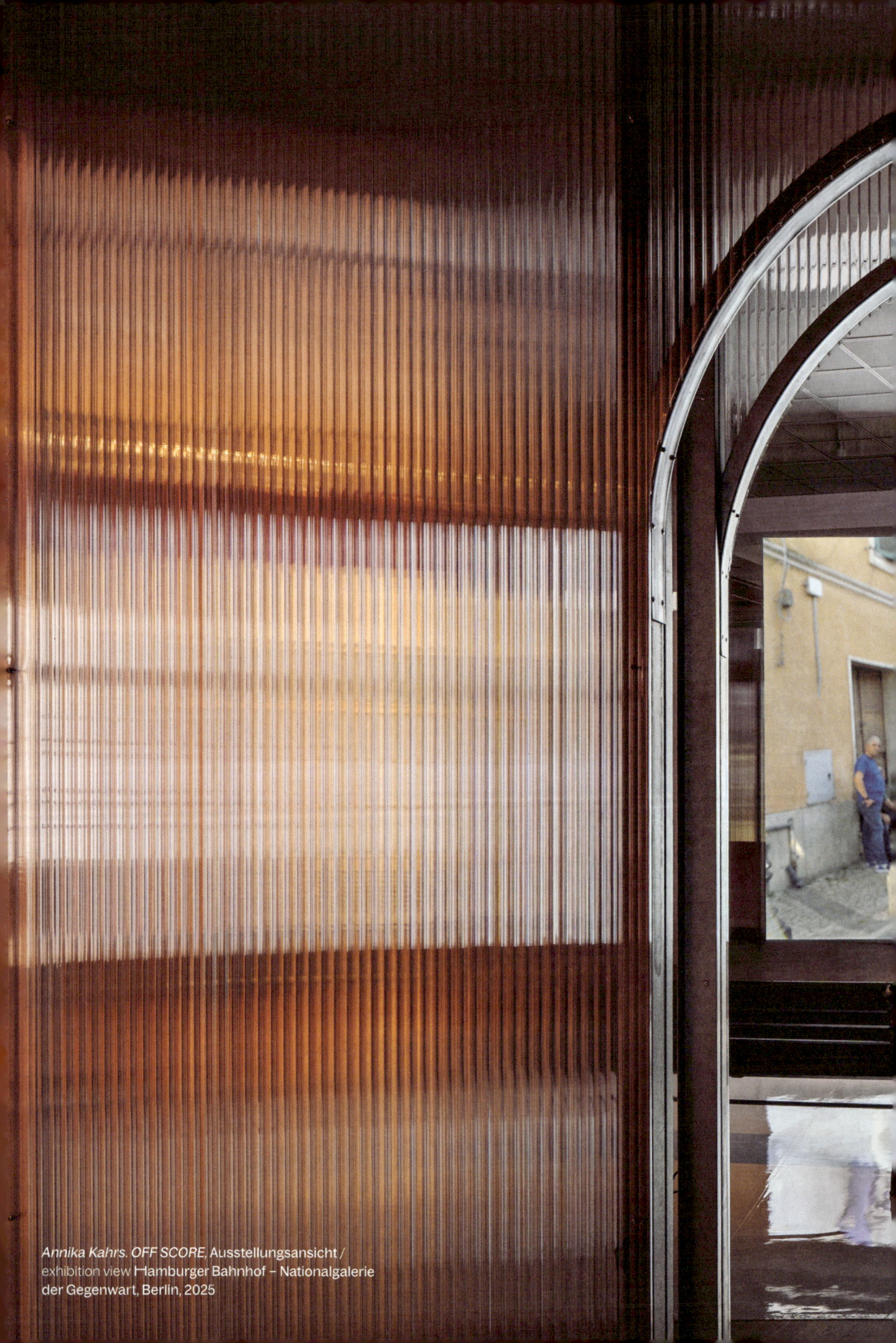

Annika Kahrs. OFF SCORE, Ausstellungsansicht / exhibition view Hamburger Bahnhof – Nationalgalerie der Gegenwart, Berlin, 2025

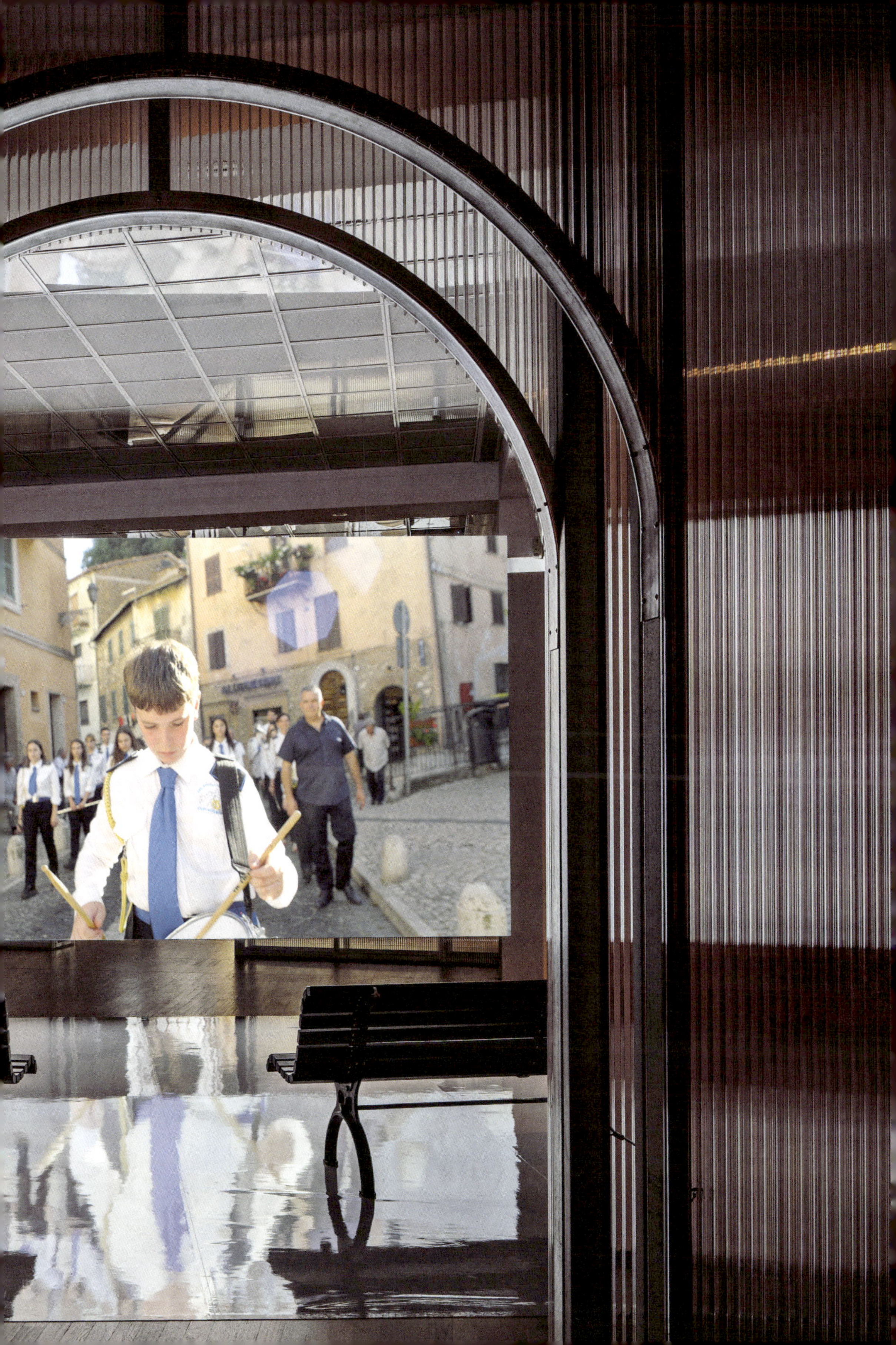

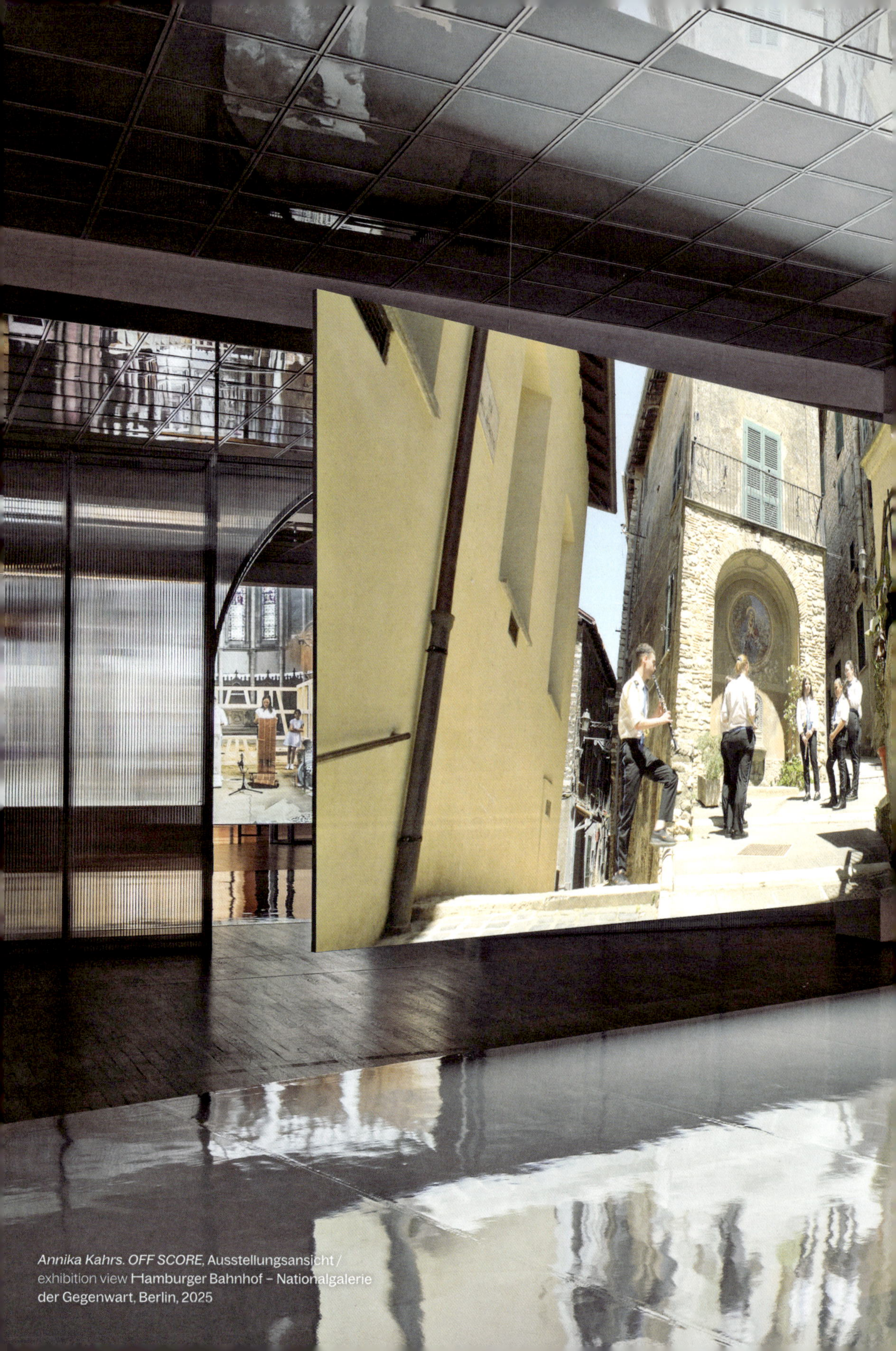

Annika Kahrs. OFF SCORE, Ausstellungsansicht / exhibition view Hamburger Bahnhof – Nationalgalerie der Gegenwart, Berlin, 2025

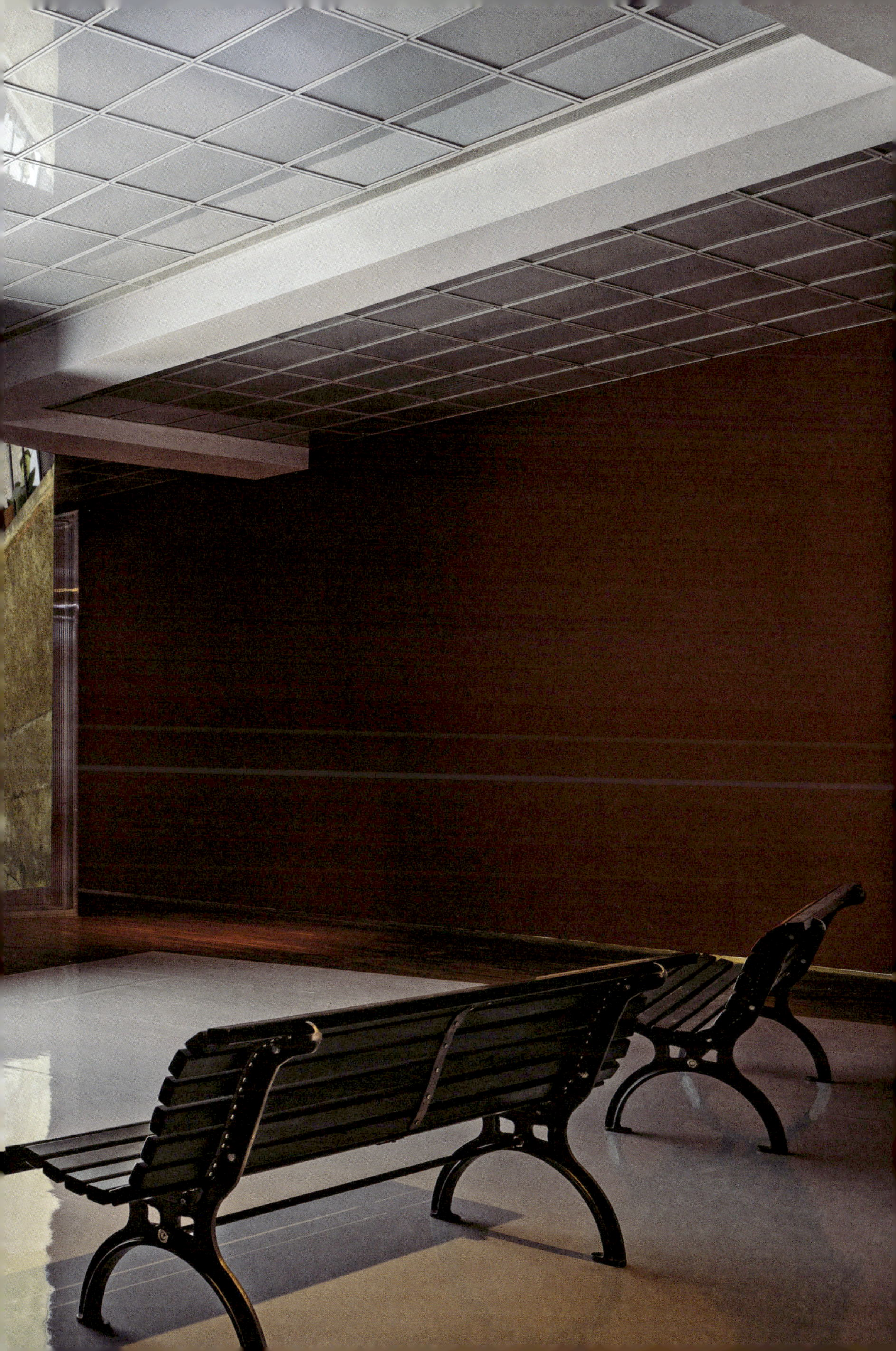

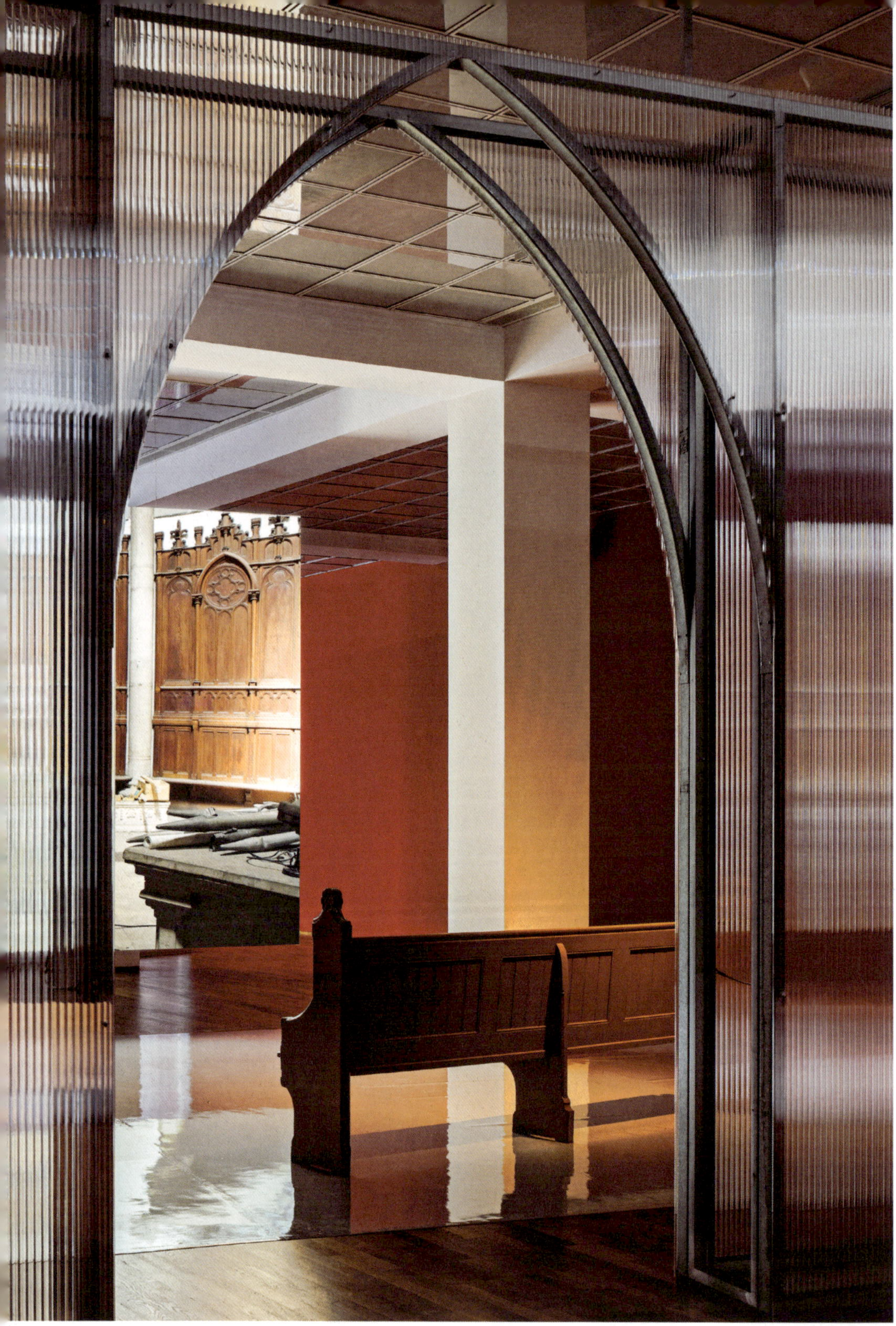

Annika Kahrs. OFF SCORE, Ausstellungsansicht / exhibition view Hamburger Bahnhof – Nationalgalerie der Gegenwart, Berlin, 2025

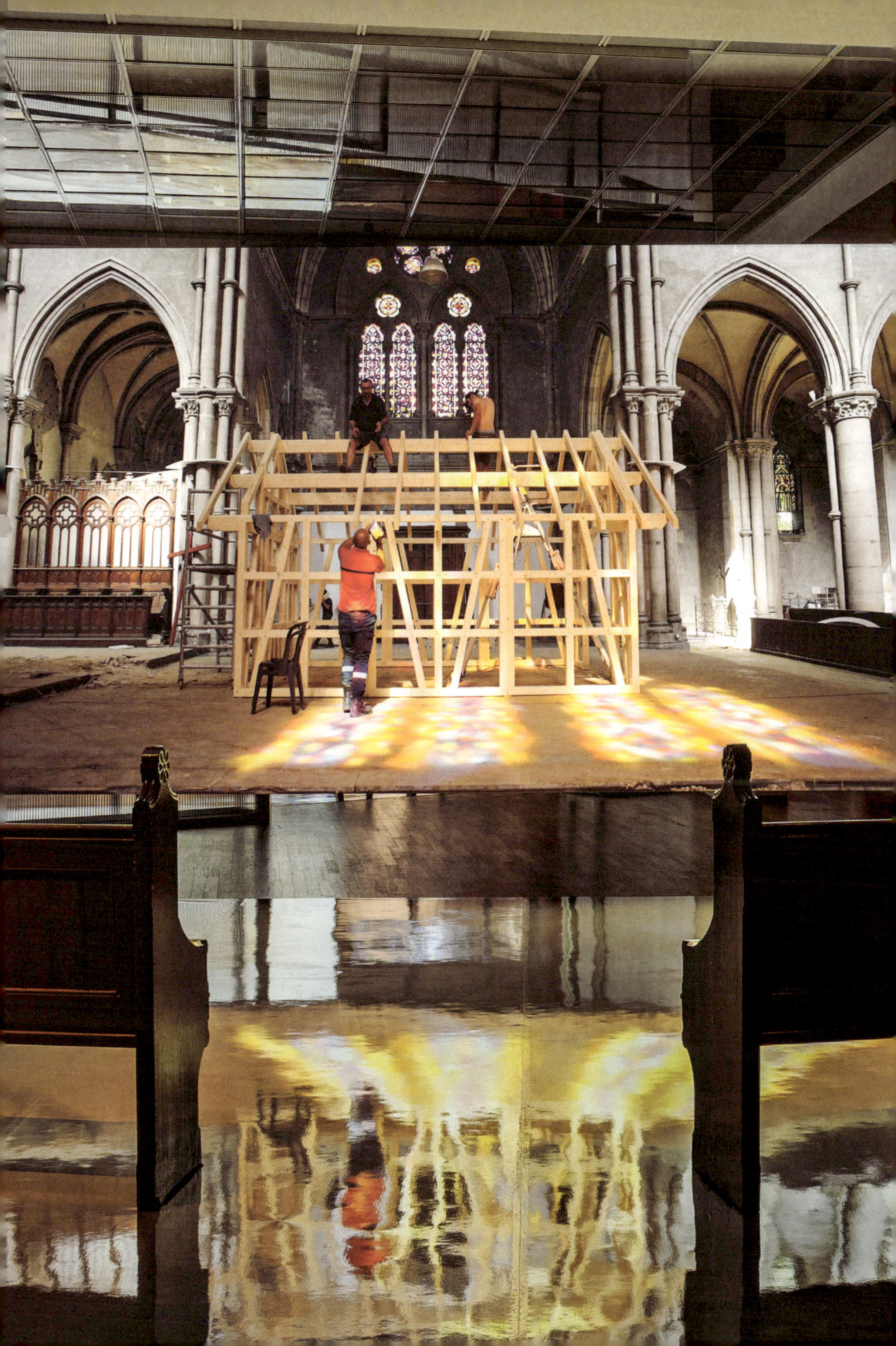

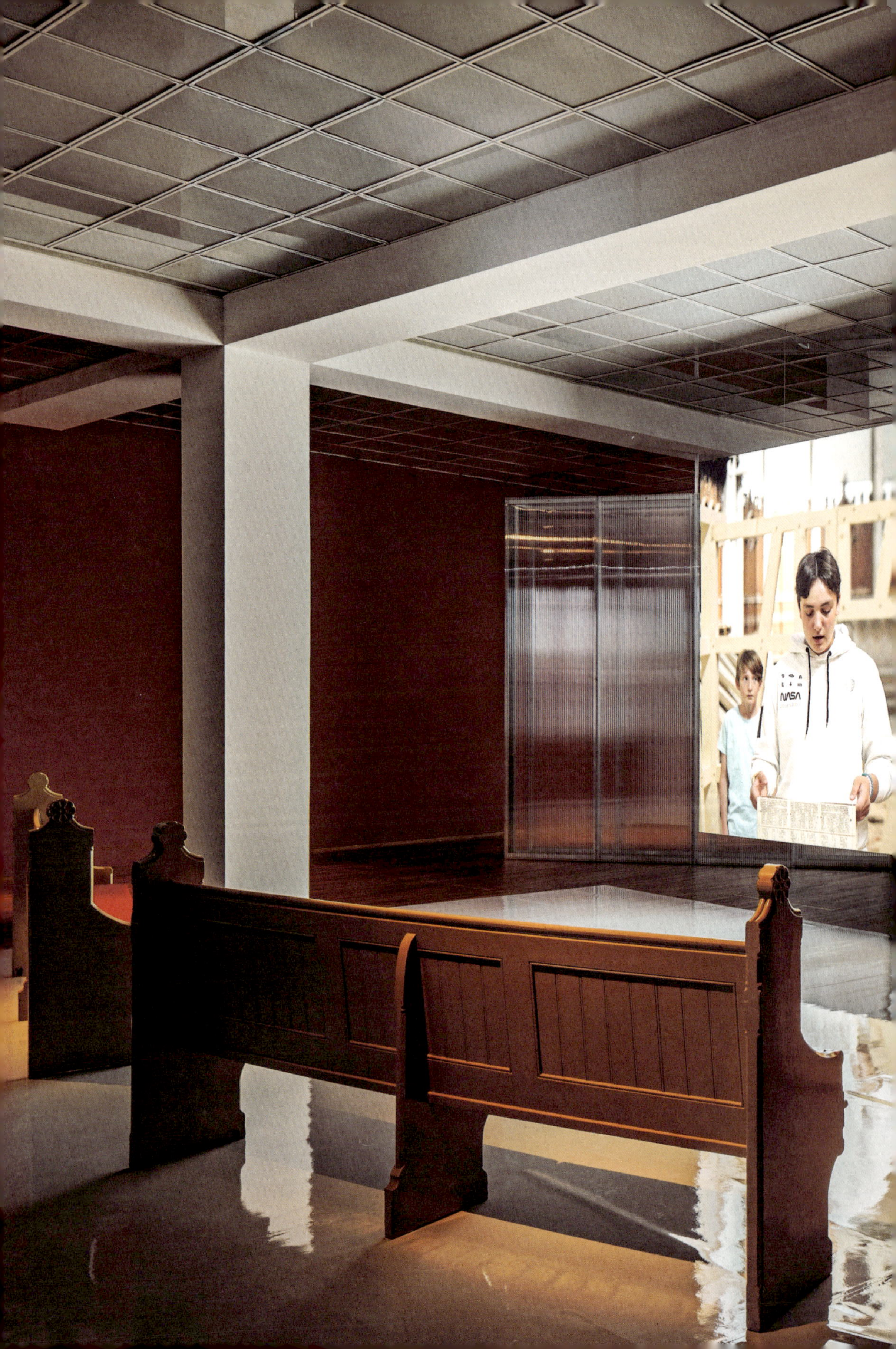
NASA

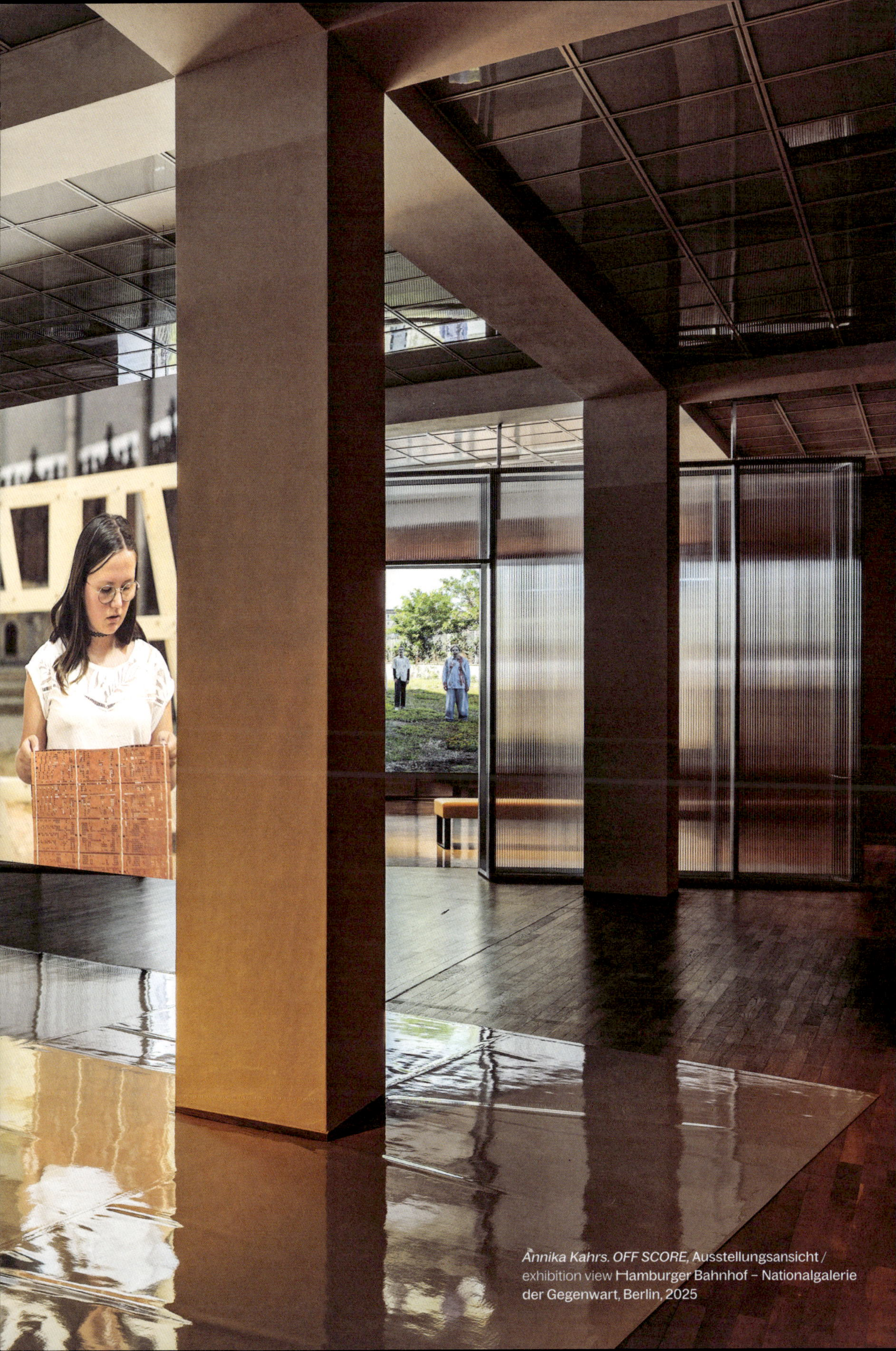

Annika Kahrs. OFF SCORE, Ausstellungsansicht / exhibition view Hamburger Bahnhof – Nationalgalerie der Gegenwart, Berlin, 2025

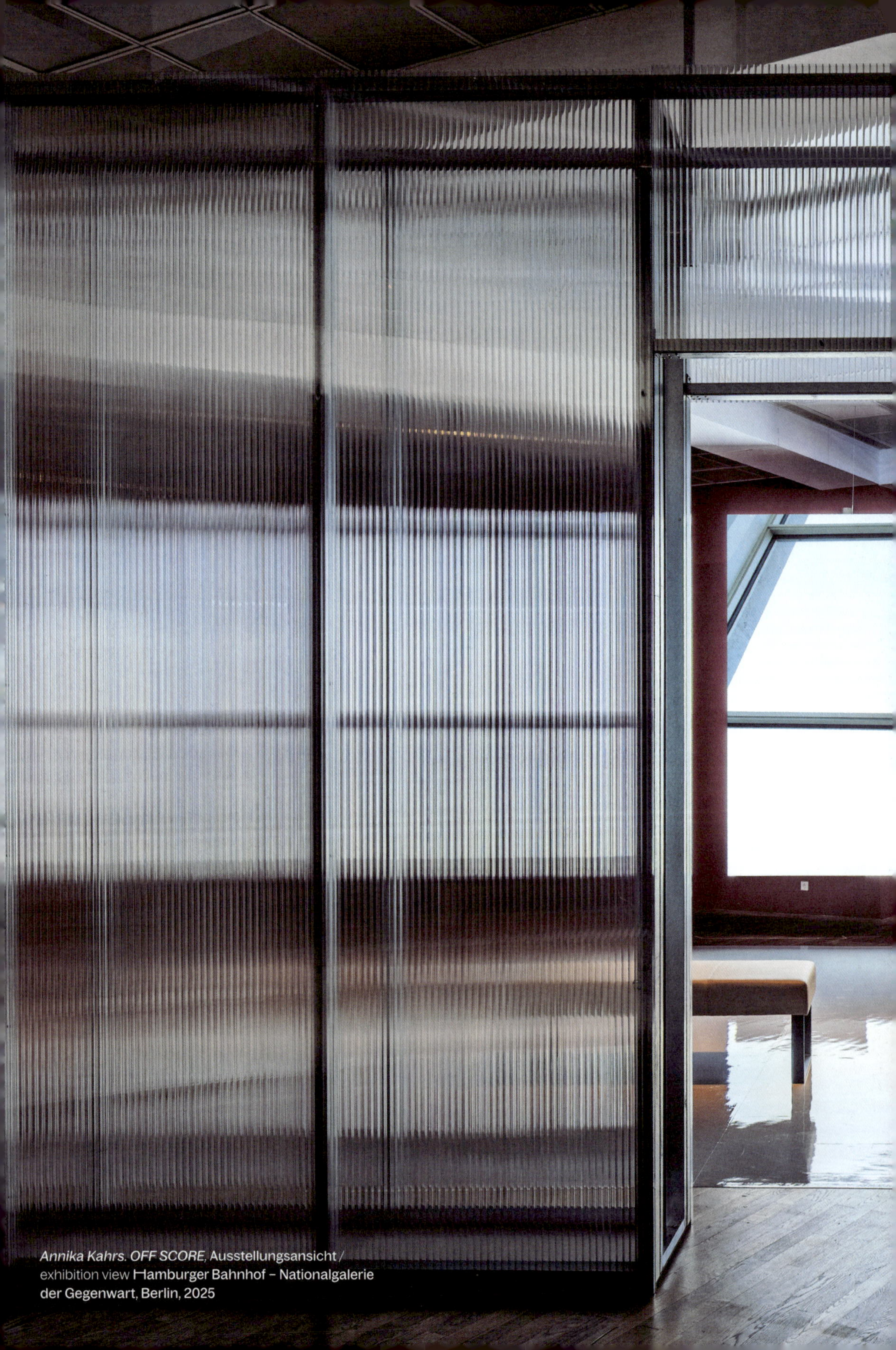

Annika Kahrs. OFF SCORE, Ausstellungsansicht / exhibition view Hamburger Bahnhof – Nationalgalerie der Gegenwart, Berlin, 2025

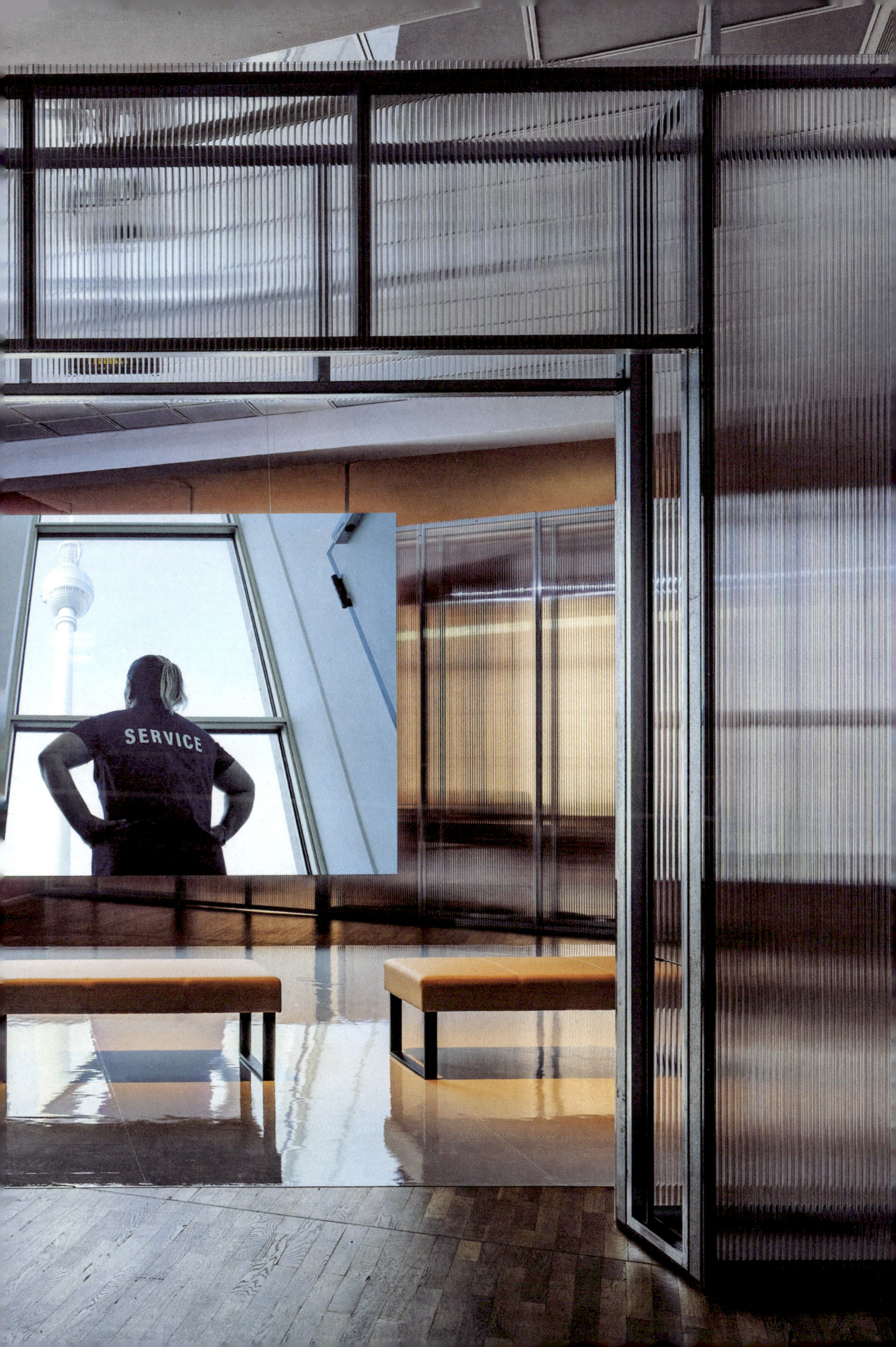
SERVICE

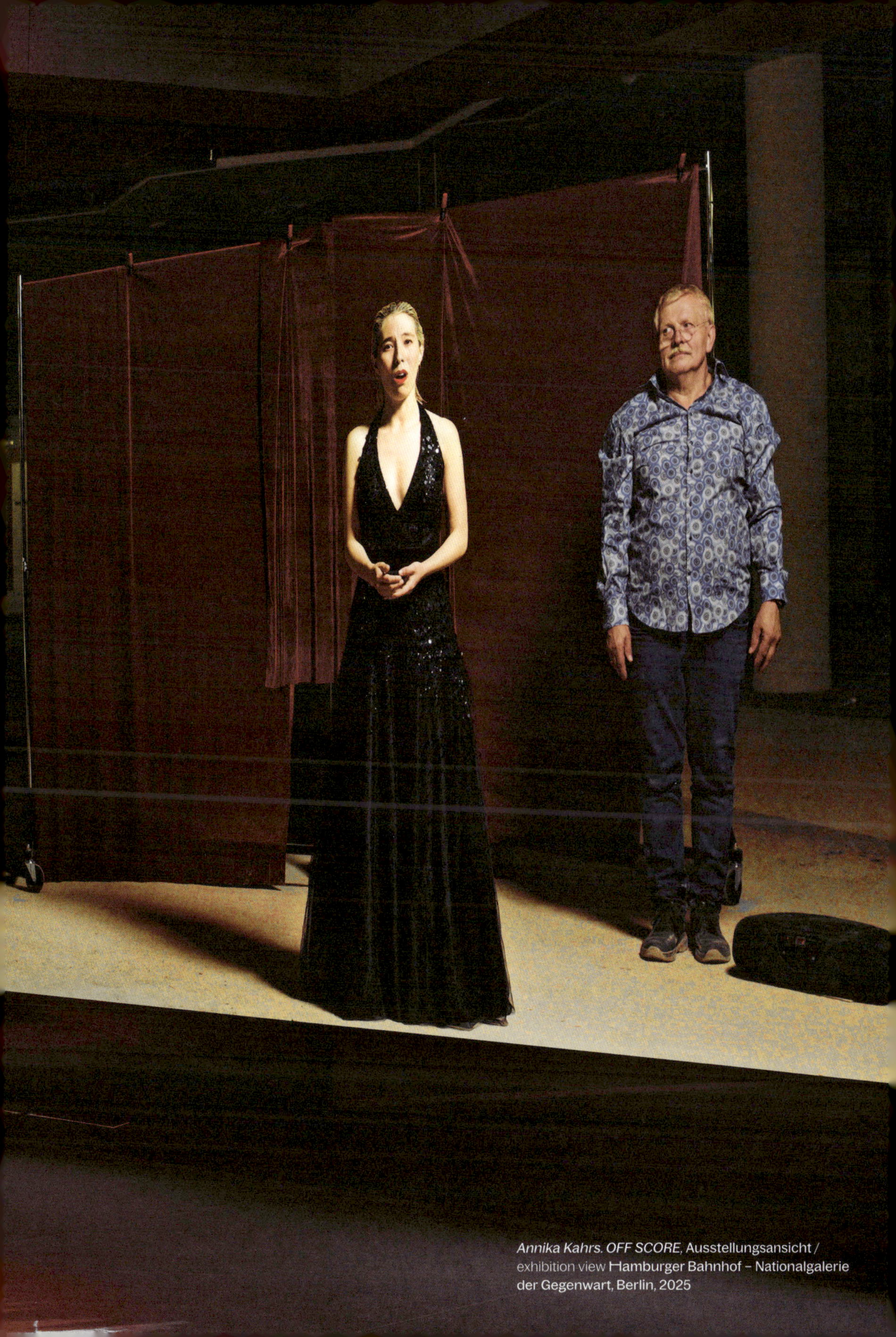

Annika Kahrs. OFF SCORE, Ausstellungsansicht / exhibition view Hamburger Bahnhof – Nationalgalerie der Gegenwart, Berlin, 2025

Annika Kahrs. OFF SCORE

Ingrid Buschmann

Annika Kahrs nutzt Musik und Klang als Material und Mittel zur Kommunikation. Ihre Filme, Soundinstallationen und Performances zeichnen sich durch ein konzeptuelles Vorgehen aus, das musikalisches Material nicht nur als Ausdrucksmittel, sondern als soziales und politisches Medium einsetzt. Kahrs hinterfragt tradierte Hörgewohnheiten, bricht mit Erwartungen und provoziert neue Perspektiven. Sie dekonstruiert traditionelle Mythen von Virtuosität, künstlerischer Perfektion und Genie und öffnet Raum für Spontaneität, Kollektivität und neue Formen des Hörens. Ihre Arbeiten erzeugen Gemeinschaft und entstehen oft in Kollaboration mit Profi- und Amateurmusiker*innen sowie Akteur*innen aus verschiedenen gesellschaftlichen Bereichen. So schafft sie kollektive Klangräume, in denen Stimme und

Annika Kahrs employs music and sound as artistic materials and as a means of communication. Her films, sound installations and performances are characterised by a conceptual approach that regards musical material not only as a means of expression, but also as a social and political medium. Kahrs challenges conventional listening habits, defies expectations and elicits new perspectives. By deconstructing traditional myths about virtuosity, artistic perfection and genius, she creates space for spontaneity, collectivity and new forms of hearing. Her works generate a sense of community and are often produced in collaboration with musicians (both professional and amateur) and other performers

Körper, Ort und Geschichte, Erinnerung und Utopie miteinander kommunizieren.

Stets stellt Kahrs grundlegende Fragen an die Musik selbst: Wann beginnt und wo endet sie? Was unterscheidet musikalischen Klang von Geräusch oder Lärm? Was sind die sozialen Aspekte von Musik? Welche Klänge verbinden wir mit bestimmten Erinnerungen? Diese Fragestellungen durchziehen ihr gesamtes Werk und sind eingebettet in ein tiefes Interesse an den sozialen und kommunikativen Aspekten des gemeinsamen Musizierens und Hörens. Dabei versteht sie Musik nie als abgeschlossenes Werk, sondern als soziale Praxis. Ihre künstlerischen Strategien – Irritation, Dekonstruktion, Verlangsamung, Übersetzung – durchbrechen Erwartungshaltungen, schaffen Dissonanzen und eröffnen neue Perspektiven.

Unter dem Titel *OFF SCORE* bietet die Ausstellung mit über zehn Videoarbeiten, Soundinstallationen und Performances erstmals einen umfangreichen Überblick über ihr Werk der letzten fünfzehn Jahre und rückt dabei die Verbindung zwischen Ort, Klang und Gemeinschaft in den Fokus. Die Arbeiten werden an jeweils ausgewählten Orten im Hamburger Bahnhof sowie im Musikinstrumenten-Museum, im Berliner Medizinhistorischen Museum der Charité, in der Heilige-Geist-Kirche und im öffentlichen Raum präsentiert.

Kahrs' Arbeiten entstehen häufig in architektonisch und historisch aufgeladenen Räumen – ehemalige Kirchen, Bahnhöfe, Kaufhäuser oder Lagerhallen –, die sie nicht als bloße Kulissen, sondern als aktive Akteure in ihren Werken versteht. Diese liminalen Orte – Orte des Übergangs – dienen ihr als Resonanzräume, in denen Geschichte, Erinnerung und Gegenwart aufeinandertreffen. Musik fungiert dabei als zentrales Medium, um diese transitorischen Prozesse hörbar und erfahrbar zu machen und soziale wie politische Schichten eines Raumes freizulegen.

Als Ausgangspunkt für die Ausstellung werden im Ostflügel des Museums drei Filmarbeiten gezeigt, die jeweils über Musik und Sound der Geschichte einer aufgegebenen

or participants from diverse social spheres. In this way, she creates collective sound spaces in which voice and body, place and history, memory and utopia enter into a dialogue.

Kahrs's practice raises fundamental questions about music itself. When does music begin and where does it end? What distinguishes the sound of music from other sounds, or from a discordant din? What are the social dimensions of music? What sounds do we associate with particular memories? Questions like these permeate Kahrs's oeuvre and reflect a profound interest in the social and communicative aspects of making or listening to music collectively. At the same time, she does not consider music to be a completed work, but regards it as a form of social practice. Her artistic strategies – disconcertion, deconstruction, deceleration, translation – are intended to thwart expectations, create dissonances and open up new perspectives.

Featuring more than 10 videos, sound installations and performances with a thematic focus on the interconnection of place, sound and community, *OFF SCORE* is the first major survey of Kahrs's work over the past 15 years. The selected works are presented in various spaces throughout Hamburger Bahnhof, as well as at the Musikinstrumenten-Museum [Museum of Musical Instruments], at Berliner Medizinhistorisches Museum der Charité [Berlin Medical History Museum of the Charité Hospital], at Heilige-Geist-Kirche [Church of the Holy Spirit] and in the public realm.

Kahrs's works are often created in architecturally and historically charged places – former churches, train stations, department stores or warehouses – which she regards not as mere backdrops but as active participants in her productions. These liminal spaces – places of transition – serve as resonance chambers in which history, memory and the present day converge. Music functions here as a key medium to make these transitory processes audible and experienceable, and to reveal the social and political layers of the space being explored.

Marking the starting point of the exhibition, three of Annika Kahrs's films are being screened in Hamburger Bahnhof's east wing; in these works, music and sound are used to trace the

Kirche in Lyon nachgehen, die Parade eines generationsübergreifenden Orchesters in einem italienischen Dorf zeigen oder, in ihrem neuen Video, in vier Berliner Kaufhäusern Orte an der Schwelle der Neuorientierung hörbar machen. Weitere Arbeiten der Ausstellung sind beim Gang durch das Museum zu erleben: In den beiden historischen Übergängen von den Ost- und Westflügeln zum Haupthaus des Museums ist die zweiteilige Soundinstallation *My Favorite Music* zu hören. Sie thematisiert die Beschallung des Hauptbahnhofs in Hamburg mit klassischer Musik, die dort zur Vertreibung von unerwünschten Menschen läuft. Aus einem separaten Raum im Forum des Museums erklingt das vierhändige Spiel eines klassischen Klavierstücks: *For Two To Play On One* ist eine fortlaufende Performance, die jeweils für nur eine*n Besucher*in zu erleben ist.

Die im Hauptausstellungsraum im Ostflügel des Museums gezeigten Filminstallationen stehen exemplarisch für Kahrs' künstlerische Praxis der letzten Jahre. Die drei Arbeiten werden in einer transluzenten Ausstellungsarchitektur in Szene gesetzt, die einen fließenden Übergang zwischen den verschiedenen Filmräumen, ihren jeweiligen Orten und Gemeinschaften, ermöglicht. Den Sound erlebt das Publikum über spezielle Kopfhörer und ein interaktives Audiosystem, das seinerseits eine Verräumlichung der Filmklänge und einen fluiden Übergang zwischen den einzelnen Arbeiten entstehen lässt.

Die Arbeit *La Banda* (2024) dokumentiert die von Kahrs inszenierte Parade eines generationsübergreifenden Orchesters durch das kleine italienische Dorf Olevano Romano. Die Arbeit ist weniger an der musikalischen Perfektion interessiert als am Moment des Zusammenseins, an der sozialen Interaktion im öffentlichen Raum. Musik wird hier zur Metapher für Gemeinschaft und den demografischen Wandel im ländlichen Raum.

Für ihre Arbeit *Le Chant des Maisons* (2022), entstanden im Rahmen der Biennale in Lyon, lud Kahrs Profi- und Amateurmusiker*innen sowie Handwerker*innen ein, gemeinsam in der entweihten Kirche Saint-Bernard

history of an abandoned church in Lyon; present an intergenerational orchestra parading through an Italian village; and – in a new video focusing on four department stores and shopping malls in Berlin – take places that are on the threshold of reorientation and render them audible. Further works by Kahrs can be experienced while moving through the museum: the two-part sound installation *My Favorite Music* can be heard in the two historical passageways that connect the east and west wings to the main building. This work addresses the use of classical music in Hamburg's main railway station to discourage "undesirable" people from hanging around there. And through the doors of a closed-off room in the Forum Hamburger Bahnhof, visitors can hear a classical piano piece for four hands being played: *For Two To Play On One* is an ongoing performance that can only be experienced by one visitor at a time.

The film installations in the main exhibition space in the east wing of Hamburger Bahnhof are representative of Kahrs's artistic practice in recent years. These three works are presented in a translucent architectural structure that enables smooth transitions between the different filmic realms, locations and featured communities. Visitors can listen to the accompanying soundtracks using specially adapted headphones and an interactive audio system, which in turn produces a spatialisation of the captured sounds and a fluid passage from one work to the next.

La Banda (2024) documents a performance staged by Kahrs that features an intergenerational orchestra parading through the small Italian village of Olevano Romano. The resulting film is less interested in presenting musical perfection than in exploring the theme of people coming together, of social interaction in the public realm. In this context, music becomes a metaphor for community and demographic changes in rural areas. For her work *Le Chant des Maisons* (2022), which was created as part of the 16th Biennale de Lyon, Kahrs invited professional and amateur musicians, as well as several carpenters, to take part in a musical performance in the deconsecrated Church of Saint Bernard in Lyon. While the musicians

zu musizieren. Während Musiker*innen unter anderem historische Orgellochkarten als Notationen nutzen, bauen Zimmerleute eine hölzerne Struktur – ein Haus – inmitten des sakralen Raumes. Die Klänge von Stimmen, Werkzeugen, Blasinstrumenten, Orgelpfeifen und die Raumresonanz verbinden sich zu einer dichten Klanglandschaft. Die Kirche selbst – mit ihrer Geschichte der sozialen Kämpfe der Seidenweber*innen von Lyon – wird zur Protagonistin der Arbeit. Kahrs betont den transitorischen Moment: Der Raum ist weder profan noch sakral, sondern etwas Drittes – ein Zwischenzustand, der neue Deutungen erlaubt.

In ihrer neuen, für die Ausstellung entstanden Arbeit *A Cashier's Opera* (2025) werden vier Berliner Kaufhäuser und Shopping Center – die Galeria am Alexanderplatz, die Mall of Berlin in Mitte und zwei im Ring Center in Lichtenberg – zur Bühne für musikalisch-performative Inszenierungen. Gemeinsam mit dem Solistenensemble Kaleidoskop, einem Jugendchor, einer Opernsängerin und einer DJ/Produzentin sowie Mitarbeitenden der Kaufhäuser entsteht ein Dialog über die Geschichte und den strukturellen Wandel dieser Orte. Das Kaufhaus, einst urbanes Zentrum und gesellschaftlicher Treffpunkt, erscheint hier als fragile Struktur zwischen Konsum und Gemeinschaft. Musik wird zum Mittel, diesen Wandel zu befragen und neue Denkräume zu schaffen.

Weitere Arbeiten führen die Besucher*innen aus dem Hauptausstellungsraum hinaus und überraschen an anderen Orten im Museum. Auf dem Weg zum Ostflügel hat man bereits eine Arbeit passiert, die ein besonders eindrückliches Beispiel für Kahrs' kritischen Umgang mit Klang im öffentlichen Raum ist. Die zweiteilige Soundinstallation *My Favorite Music* (2020) in den beiden historischen Übergängen des Museums beschäftigt sich mit der klassischen Musik, die seit 2001 im Hamburger Hauptbahnhof gespielt wird – nicht zur Unterhaltung, sondern zur Verdrängung von wohnungslosen und drogenabhängigen Menschen. Kahrs greift im ersten Teil in der Passage Ost die Musik am Hauptbahnhof

use, among other things, historical organ-playing cards with punched holes as notations, carpenters build a wooden structure – resembling a simple house – in the middle of the formerly sacred space. The sounds of voices, tools, wind instruments and organ pipes combine with the room acoustics to create a dense soundscape. The church itself – with its history linked to the social struggles of silk weavers in Lyon, leading to the Canut revolts – becomes a protagonist in Kahrs's work. The artist highlights a transitional moment: the space is neither secular nor sacred, but a third entity – an intermediate state that enables new interpretations.

In Kahrs's new work *A Cashier's Opera* (2025), which has been created especially for the current exhibition, four Berlin department stores and shopping centres – Galeria Berlin Alexanderplatz, the Mall of Berlin in Mitte, and two stores in the Ring Center in Lichtenberg – become stages for musical and performative productions. In collaboration with Solistenensemble Kaleidoskop, a youth choir, an opera singer and a DJ/producer, as well as employees from the respective department stores, Kahrs has created a dialogue on the history and structural transformation of such places. Once an urban centre and social hub, the department store appears here as a fragile structure situated between consumerism and community. Music becomes a means of examining this transformation and creating new worlds of thought.

Other works by Kahrs lead visitors out of the main exhibition space and take them by surprise in other locations throughout the museum. On their way to the east wing, visitors have already walked past a work that serves as a particularly striking example of Kahrs's critical approach to the use of sound in public spaces. Presented in the two historical passageways at Hamburger Bahnhof, the two-part sound installation *My Favorite Music* (2020) focuses on the classical music that has been played in Hamburg's main railway station – the Hauptbahnhof – since 2001; this is not intended to entertain travellers, but to deter homeless people and drug users from loitering. In the first part of Kahrs's piece, installed in the eastern passage, one hears recordings of the music played at the Hauptbahnhof along

samt ihren Umgebungsgeräuschen auf und kontrastiert sie in der gegenüberliegenden Passage West mit Interviews von Straßenzeitungsverkäufer*innen, die über ihre eigenen Musikvorlieben sprechen. Damit lädt sie nun wiederum zum aktiven Zuhören und Verweilen ein. Die Arbeit findet in den beiden Transiträumen des Museums, dem ehemaligen Bahnhof für die Zugverbindung zwischen Hamburg und Berlin, einen besonders passenden Ort.

Mit *For Two To Play On One* (2012) entwirft Kahrs eine intime Performance, in der das Publikum selbst Teil des Werks wird. Der separate Raum im Forum des Museums, aus dem verborgene Klavierklänge zu hören sind, ist nur für eine Person zugänglich. Sobald die Person den Raum mit den zwei Pianist*innen betritt, verstummt das Spiel. Die beiden Musiker*innen blicken sie schweigend an. Erst beim Verlassen des Raums wird das Stück fortgesetzt. Das Klavierzimmer wird hier zur Bühne, der*die Besucher*in zur handelnden Figur in einem offenen System ohne eigene Regieanweisung. Die Performance schafft einen ungewohnten, intimen Moment und unterläuft das traditionelle Verhältnis von Akteur*in und Zuschauer*in.

Mit der Ausstellung von Annika Kahrs geht der Hamburger Bahnhof über das Museum hinaus auch an andere Orte in der Stadt, die aufgrund ihres besonderen Charakters und der räumlichen Situation zur jeweiligen Konzeption der Arbeiten passen.

In Kooperation mit dem Musikinstrumenten-Museum wird dort die Filmarbeit *Ganz ungültig, nur ein Versuch* (2024) gezeigt. Die ‚Nullte', die ungültige Sinfonie (1869) des österreichischen Romantik-Komponisten Anton Bruckner wird zum Ausgangspunkt einer kollektiven Neuinterpretation. Fünf junge Protagonist*innen, aufgenommen an unterschiedlichen Orten der Musikrezeption und -produktion, überschreiben, löschen und verändern die ursprüngliche Partitur handschriftlich, die dann von fünf Musiker*innen allein in einem Konzertsaal aufgeführt wird. Einige Szenen dieser Videoarbeit wurden im Musikinstrumenten-Museum aufgenommen.

with ambient sounds; in the western passage, in the opposite wing of the museum, the classical music is contrasted with statements by street newspaper sellers who were interviewed about their personal musical preferences. With this juxtaposition, Kahrs is in turn inviting exhibition-goers to actively listen and pause for reflection. Given the history of the museum building, which was formerly the terminus for the railway line between Hamburg and Berlin, the location of this work in Hamburger Bahnhof's two transitional spaces seems highly appropriate.

With *For Two To Play On One* (2012), Kahrs has created an intimate performance in which the audience becomes an integral part of the work. From a closed-off room in Hamburger Bahnhof's Forum, visitors can hear the sound of piano playing. This room can only be accessed by one person at a time. As soon as they enter the room where the two pianists are playing, however, the music falls silent. The two musicians look the visitor in the eyes, without saying a word. Only once the visitor has left the room does the music continue. The piano room here becomes a stage; the visitor plays an active role in an open-ended system with no individual stage directions. Subverting the traditional relationship between actor and audience, the performance sets up an encounter that is unfamiliar but also intimate.

Annika Kahrs's exhibition also extends beyond Hamburger Bahnhof to include other locations in Berlin whose spatial situation or other characteristic features make them particularly well suited to the concept of the respective artworks.

In cooperation with the Musikinstrumenten-Museum, Kahrs's film *Ganz ungültig, nur ein Versuch* (2024) is being shown at that museum's location near Potsdamer Platz. In this work, the Austrian Romantic composer Anton Bruckner's symphony in D minor (1869), which became known as *Die Nullte* ["No. 0"] after being declared invalid by the composer, serves as the point of departure for a collective reinterpretation. Five young protagonists are filmed in different places of music reception and production as they erase, overwrite and make handwritten additions to the original score of Bruckner's

Die Filmarbeit *how to live in the echo of other places* (2022/25) wird stündlich nach Sonnenuntergang bis in den Abend hinein auf der großen LED-Wand am Kurfürstendamm zu sehen sein. Die für den Außenraum konzipierte Filmarbeit basiert auf kurzen Texten über die Erinnerung an besondere Orte während eines Sonnenuntergangs, die Kahrs für diese Arbeit von verschiedenen Personen angefragt hat. Das anonymisierte Material wird auf einen digital erstellten, ‚ortlosen' Sonnenuntergang Wort für Wort projiziert. Die etwa zwei- bis fünfminütigen Filme unterbrechen den Fluss der kurzen Werbeclips und laden zum Innehalten an diesem urbanen Ort ein.

Im Frühjahr 2026 findet als integraler Bestandteil der Ausstellung ein Performanceprogramm statt, das an drei Aufführungstagen im Musikinstrumenten-Museum, im Berliner Medizinhistorischen Museum der Charité und in der Heilige-Geist-Kirche einen jeweils spezifischen Ort gefunden hat. Das Programm *Hamburger Bahnhof On Tour* wurde anlässlich des 30. Jubiläums des Hamburger Bahnhof konzipiert, zu dem das Museum einen besonderen Schwerpunkt auf den Austausch und die Vernetzung mit anderen Berliner Museen und kulturellen Akteuren der Stadt legt.

Auch in ihren Performances untersucht die Künstlerin klassische musikalische Strukturen und hinterfragt die Codes und Parameter von Musikproduktion, Aufführungspraxis und Hörgewohnheiten. Musik wird dekonstruiert, Virtuosität hinterfragt und die Rolle des Publikums erweitert. Kahrs schafft Situationen, in denen musikalische Ereignisse zu gemeinschaftlichen Erlebnissen werden.

Mit *Strings* (2010) und *Alone Together* (2016) im Musikinstrumenten-Museum setzt sich Kahrs jeweils mit der Struktur des klassischen Quartetts auseinander. In *Strings* wird ein Streichquartett gezielt aus dem Takt gebracht, indem Musiker*innen nach jedem Satz Instrumente und Plätze tauschen. In *Alone Together* zerlegt ein Gesangsquartett einen dreiminütigen Jazz-Klassiker durch zeitliche Dehnung und räumliche Trennung in eine dreißigminütige Performance – eine

symphony. Five young musicians then perform the reworked piece in an empty concert hall. Some sequences of this video were filmed at the Musikinstrumenten-Museum.

For the duration of Kahrs's exhibition, her film *how to live in the echo of other places* (2022/25) is being shown hourly from sunset until late in the evening on a large LED wall on Kurfürstendamm. Conceived for an outdoor setting, this work is based on short texts about memories of particular places at sunset, which Kahrs requested from various people for this purpose. The anonymised texts are projected one word at a time onto a "placeless" sunset that has been digitally created. Lasting between two and five minutes, her films interrupt the constant flow of short advertisements and invite us to pause and reflect in this busy urban setting.

On three days in spring 2026, as part of Kahrs's exhibition, a performance programme will be presented in three chosen locations in Berlin: at Musikinstrumenten-Museum, Berliner Medizinhistorisches Museum der Charité and Heilige-Geist-Kirche. The programme *Hamburger Bahnhof On Tour* was conceived to mark the 30th anniversary of Hamburger Bahnhof and places particular emphasis on collaborating and networking with other museums and cultural agents in Berlin.

Annika Kahrs also uses her performance-based works to examine established musical structures and question the codes and parameters of music production, performance practice and listening habits. To this end, music is deconstructed, the notion of virtuosity is challenged, and the role of the audience is expanded. Kahrs creates situations in which music-related events become communal experiences.

With *Strings* (2010) and *Alone Together* (2016), which are being presented at the Musikinstrumenten-Museum, Kahrs explores the structure of the classical quartet. In *Strings*, a string quartet is deliberately thrown out of sync by making the musicians swap places – and hence instruments – after each movement in the piece they are performing. In *Alone Together*, a vocal quartet uses temporal extension (slowing down the tempo of a song after each rendition) and spatial separation (moving further

Studie über Synchronität, Autonomie und kollektives Scheitern, aus dem wiederum etwas Neues entsteht.

In ihrer neuen, für das Solistenensemble Kaleidoskop entworfenen, ortsspezifischen Performance *zum Sonnendeck* (2026) thematisiert Kahrs Krankheit und Veränderung als existenzielle Zustände. Der Aufführungsort – die beeindruckende Hörsaalruine im Berliner Medizinhistorischen Museum – wird zum Symbol für Verwundung und Transformation. Kahrs versteht Heilung nicht als Rückkehr zum alten Zustand, sondern als individuellen, transformatorischen Prozess, der sich hier performativ in Klang, Geste und Körperlichkeit ausdrückt.

In der Performance *the lord loves changes, it's one of his greatest delusions* (2018) in der Heilige-Geist-Kirche kombiniert Kahrs Orgelspiel mit einem Pfeifchor, der das musikalische Material bis zur Erschöpfung dekonstruiert. Basierend auf dem Werk *Gay Guerrilla* (1979) des experimentellen US-amerikanischen Komponisten Julius Eastman, das wiederum auf dem Choral *Ein feste Burg ist unser Gott* (vor 1529) von Martin Luther basiert, entfaltet sich ein vielschichtiger Kommentar über Wandel, Widerstand und die symbolische Kraft musikalischer Zitate. Die Performance, ursprünglich als Videoarbeit konzipiert, findet erstmals live in einer Kirche statt – einem Ort, der selbst durch sakrale und politische Geschichte aufgeladen ist.

Annika Kahrs' Arbeit zeichnet sich durch eine beständige Neukontextualisierung von Musik, Raum und Gemeinschaft aus. Die Ausstellung im Hamburger Bahnhof zeigt die ausgewählten Werke nicht in isolierten Einzelpräsentationen, sondern in einem Netzwerk, das verschiedene Museen, eine Kirche und den urbanen Raum miteinander verbindet. Ob im Konzertsaal, Kaufhaus, Bahnhof oder Kirchenraum – Kahrs schafft Situationen, in denen Klang zu einem Instrument wird, um Zusammensein, Erinnerung und Veränderung aktiv zu erfahren. Durch das Infragestellen von Aufführungspraxis, von Raum-Zeit-Strukturen und von Hierarchien in der Rezeption werden neue Möglichkeitsräume für Musiker*innen,

and further away from each other) to take a three-minute jazz standard apart and turn it into a thirty-minute performance; Kahrs's work becomes a study on synchronicity, autonomy and collective failure – from which something new emerges.

In *zum Sonnendeck* (2026), a new, site-specific performance created especially for Solistenensemble Kaleidoskop, Kahrs considers illness and change as existential states. The venue for this performance – the impressively restored ruin of the former Rudolf Virchow Lecture Hall at the Berliner Medizinhistorisches Museum – becomes a symbol of injury and transformation. Kahrs regards healing not as a return to a prior state, but as an individual, transformative process that is expressed here performatively through sound, gestures and physicality.

In the performance *the lord loves changes, it's one of his greatest delusions* (2018), which is being presented at the Heilige-Geist-Kirche in the Moabit district of Berlin, Kahrs combines organ music with a choir of whistlers who deconstruct the music being played to the point of complete exhaustion. Drawing upon the experimental American composer Julius Eastman's immersive work *Gay Guerrilla* (1979), which is in turn based on Martin Luther's chorale *Ein feste Burg ist unser Gott* [A Mighty Fortress Is Our God; probably written before 1529], Kahrs's piece offers a nuanced commentary on change, resistance and the symbolic power of musical quotation. This is the first time that Kahrs's work, which was originally conceived as a video, has been performed in a church – a place that is itself highly charged in terms of its religious and political history.

Annika Kahrs's artistic practice is characterised by a constant recontextualisation of music, space and community. Rather than being presented in isolation, the works selected for her exhibition at Hamburger Bahnhof form a network that incorporates various museums, a church and the urban environment. Whether it is in a concert hall, a department store, a railway station or a church – Kahrs creates situations in which sound becomes an instrument, enabling audiences to actively experience community,

Akteur*innen und das Publikum eröffnet. Musik wird zum Mittel, um Geschichte hörbar zu machen, soziale Codes zu befragen und neue Formen des Miteinanders zu erschaffen. Ihre Ausstellung *OFF SCORE* im Hamburger Bahnhof führt diese Ansätze exemplarisch zusammen und macht deutlich: Musik ist nicht nur das, was erklingt – sondern das, was zwischen uns entsteht.

memory and transformation. By questioning performance practice, space/time structures and hierarchies of reception, new realms of possibility are opened up for musicians, actors and audience members. Music becomes a means of rendering history audible, examining social codes and generating new forms of togetherness. Kahrs's exhibition *OFF SCORE* at Hamburger Bahnhof brings these approaches together in a representative manner, showing that music is much more than just the sounds we hear – it is what develops between us when we are listening to it.

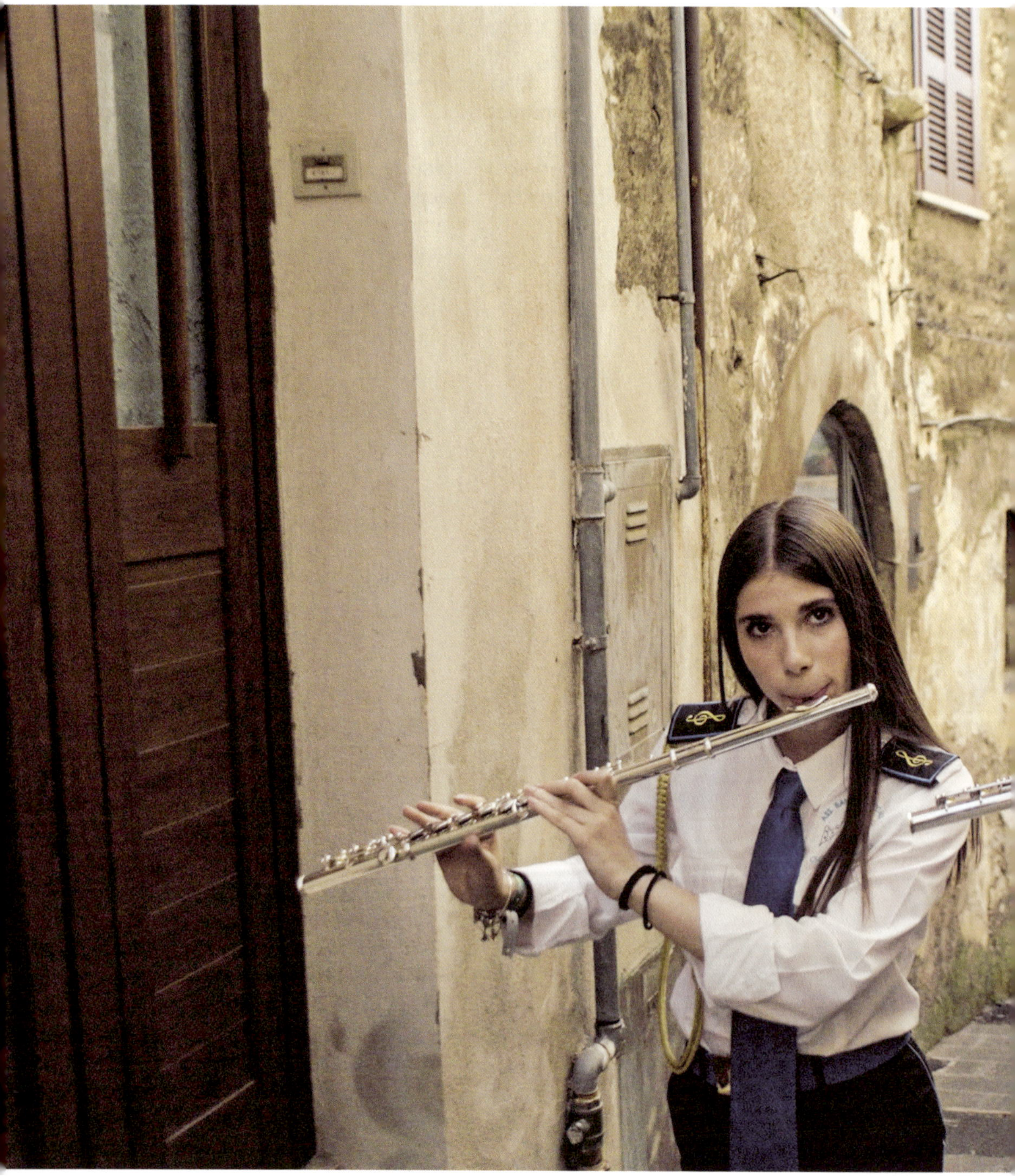

Annika Kahrs, *La Banda,* 2024, 4K Video, Farbe, Ton / colour, sound, **22 Min., Videostandbild** / video still

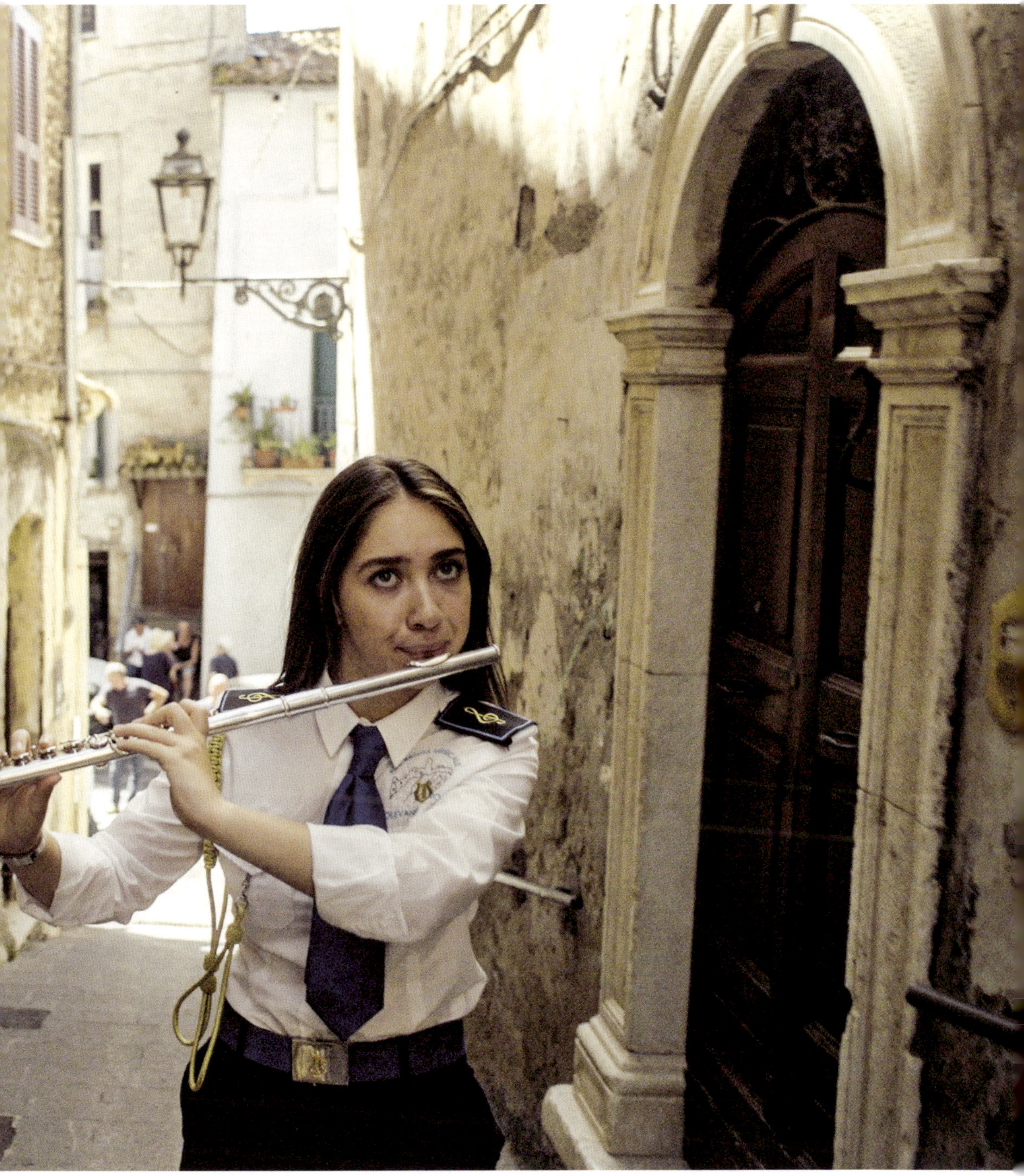

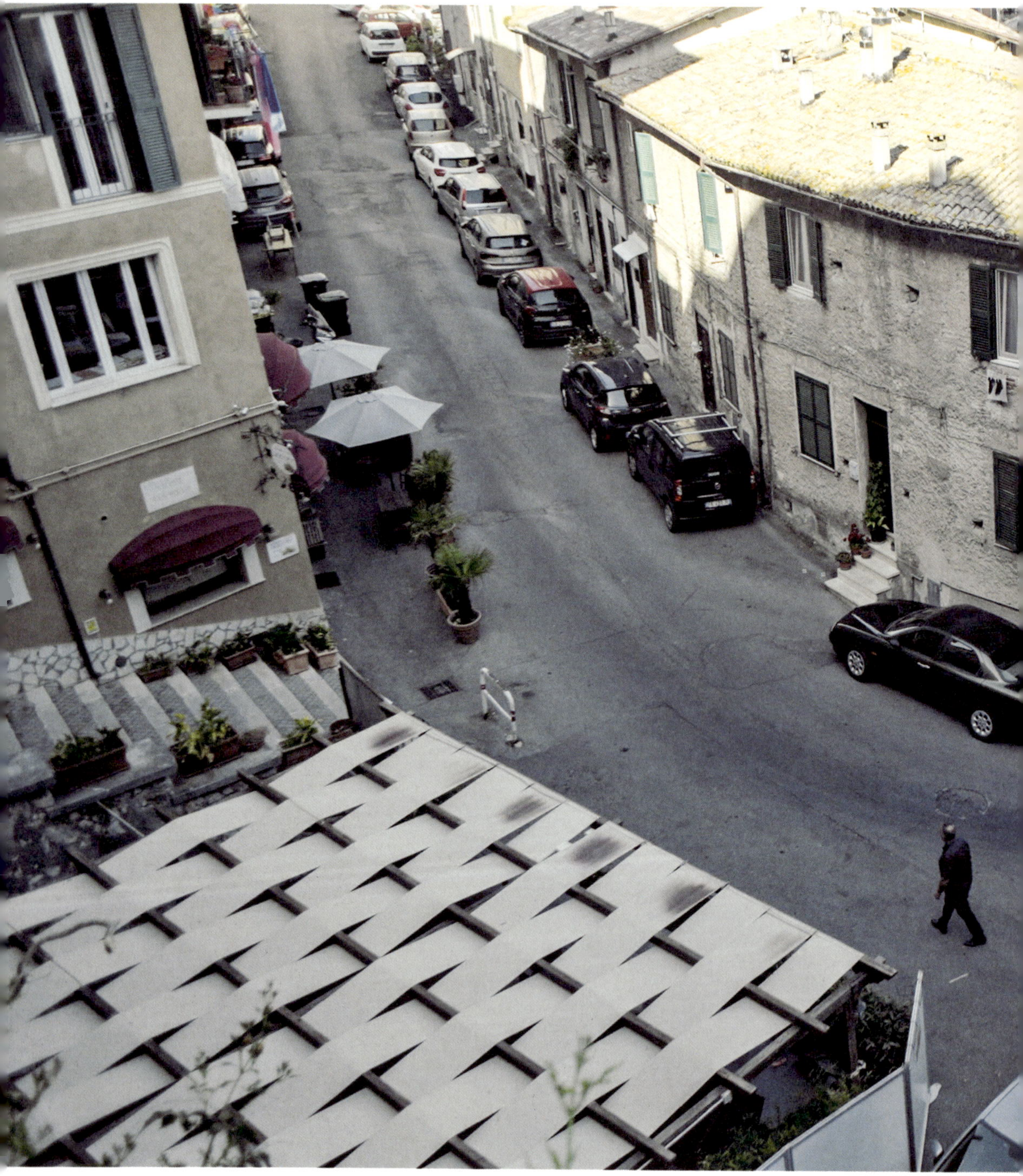

Annika Kahrs, *La Banda,* 2024, 4K Video, Farbe, Ton / colour, sound, 22 Min., Videostandbild / video still

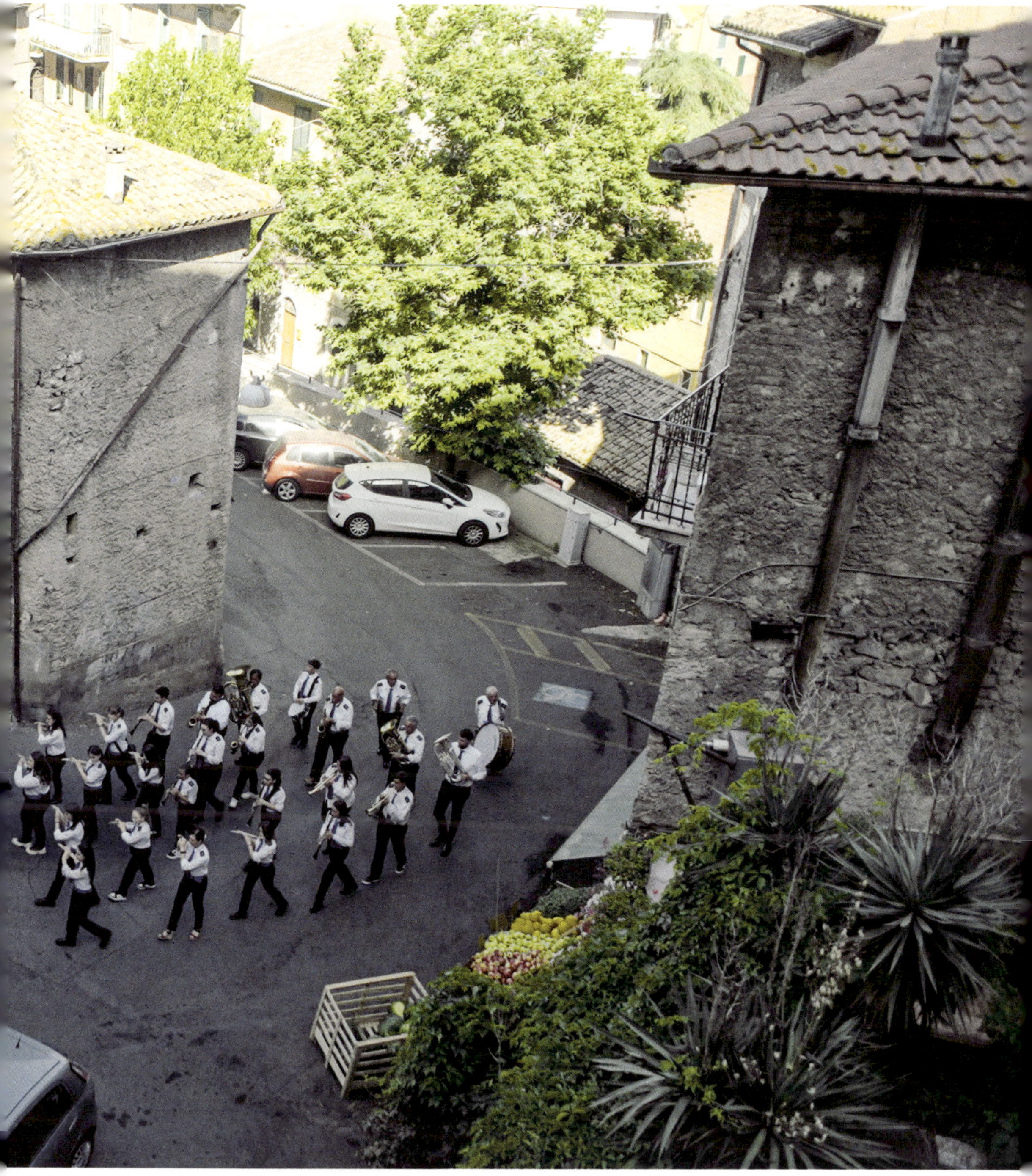

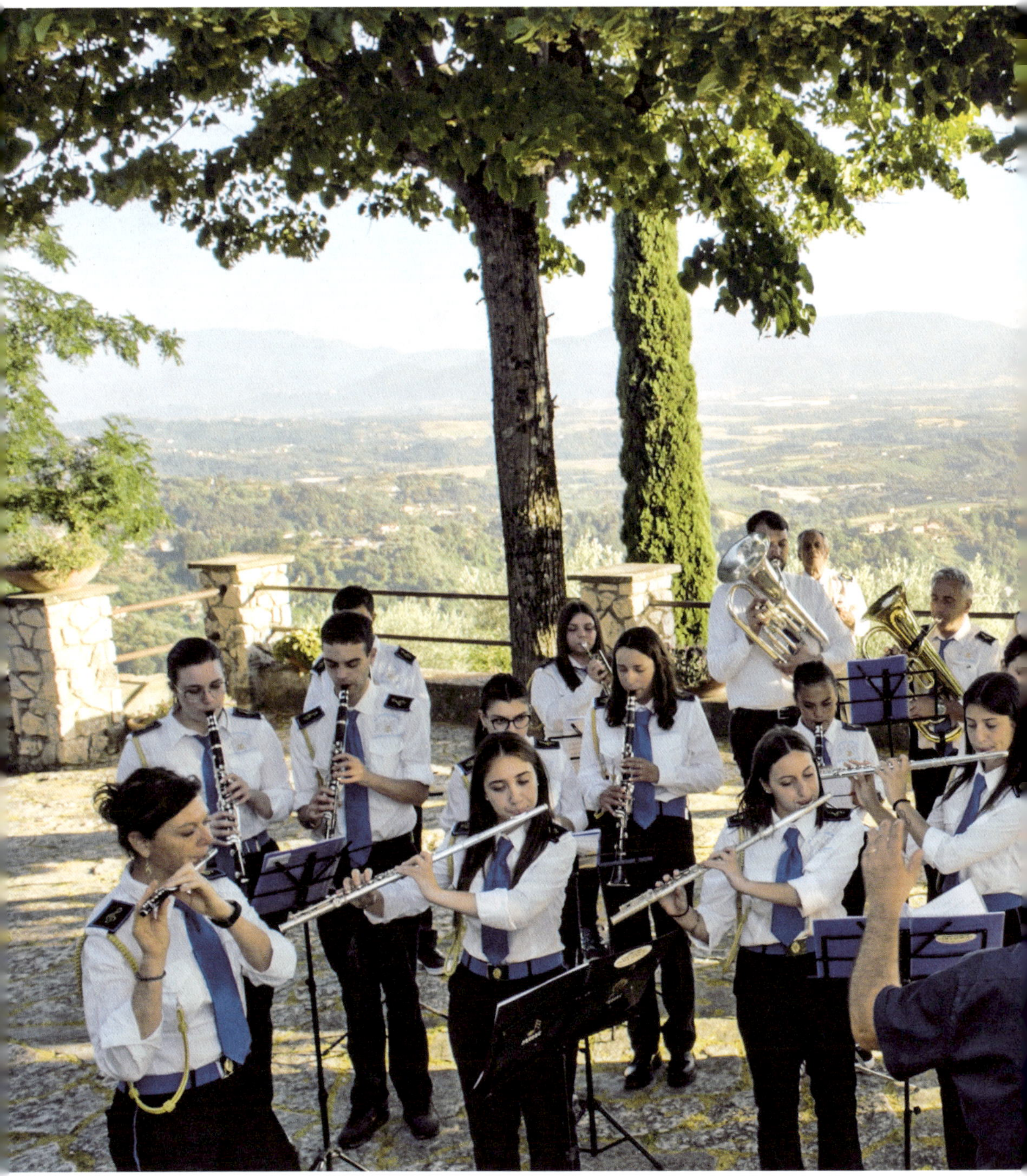

Annika Kahrs, ***La Banda,*** **2024, 4K Video, Farbe, Ton** / colour, sound, **22 Min., Videostandbild** / video still

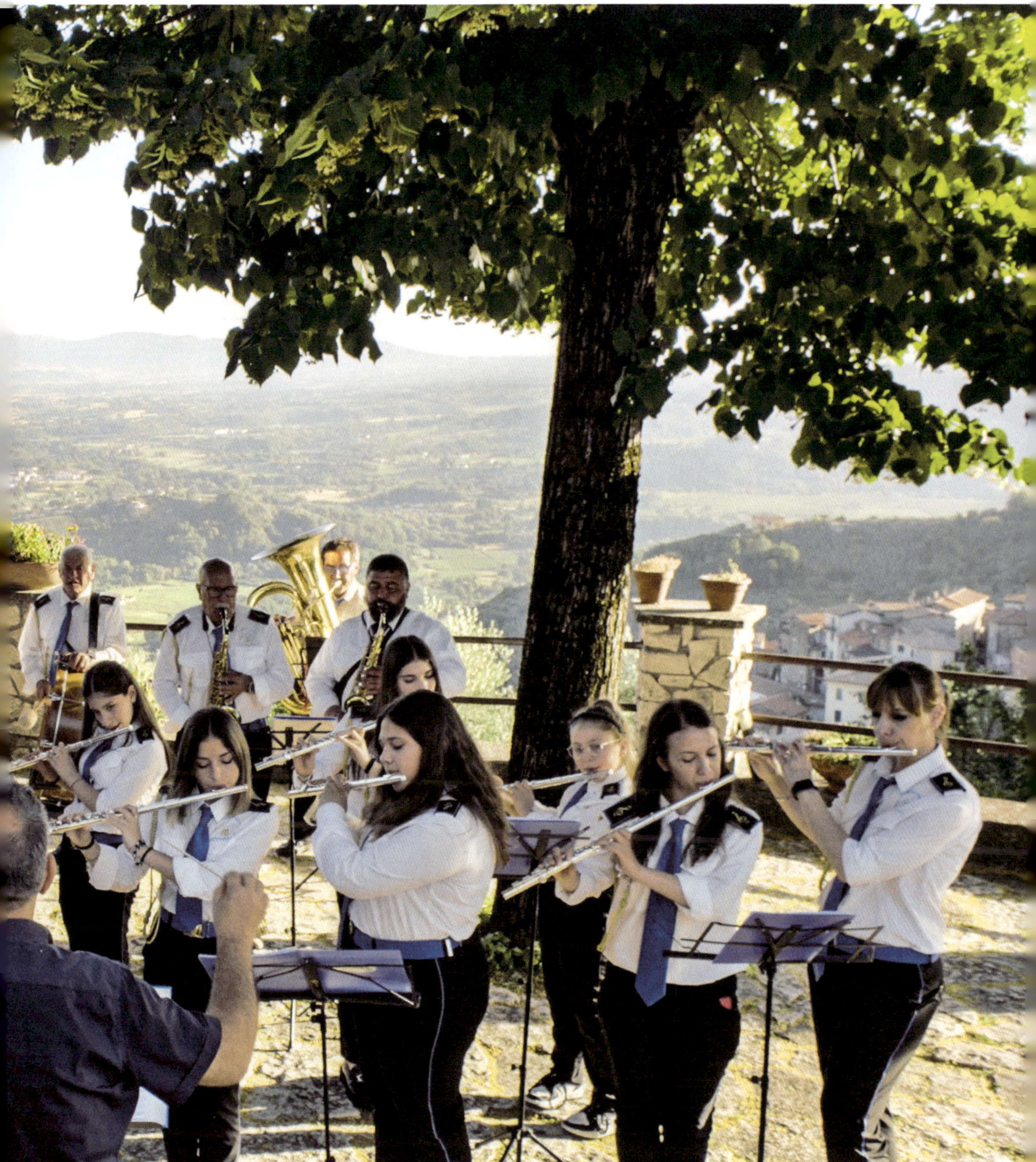

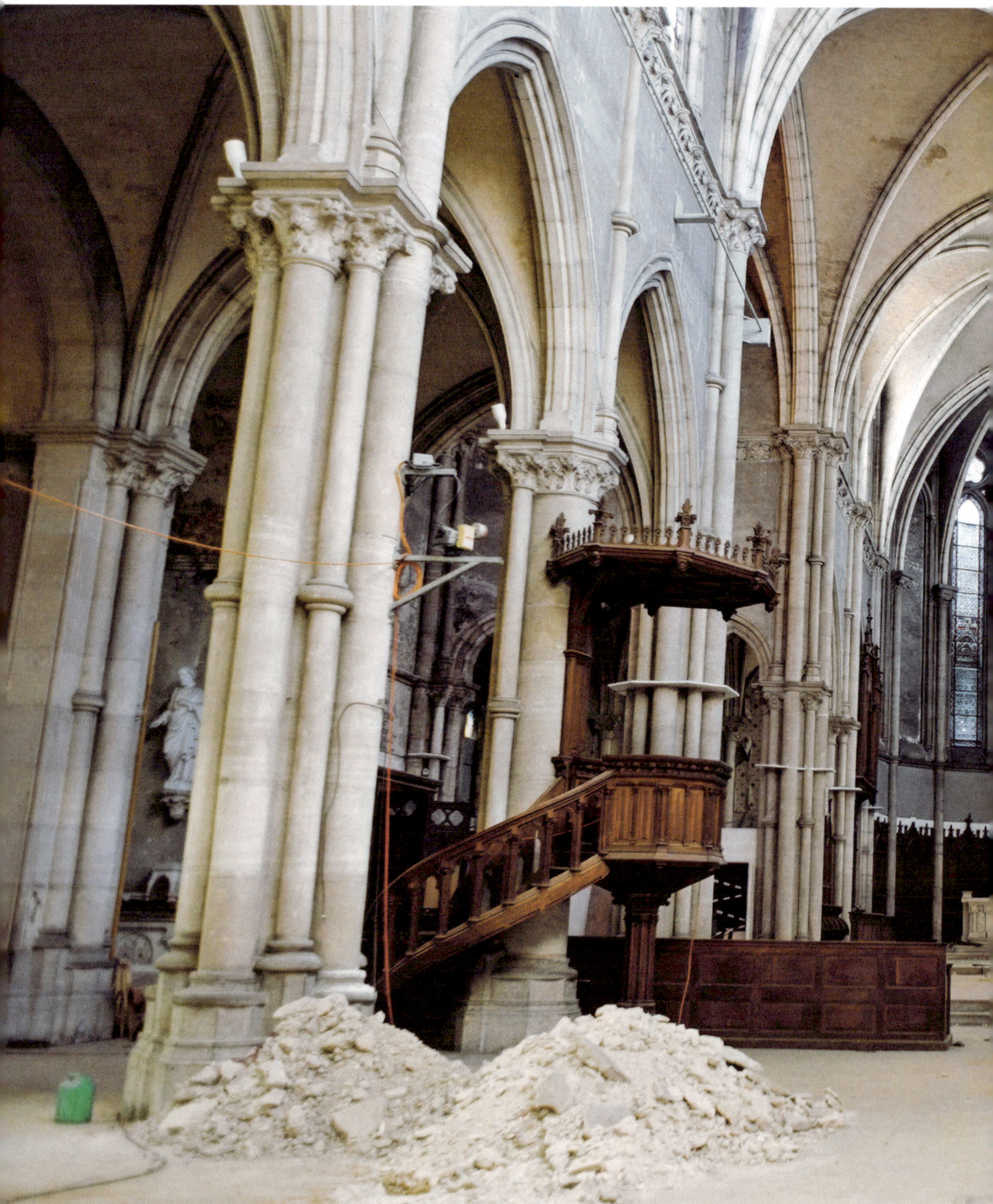

Annika Kahrs, *Le Chant des Maisons,* 2022,
4K Video, Farbe, Ton / colour, sound, 24:30 Min.,
Videostandbild / video still

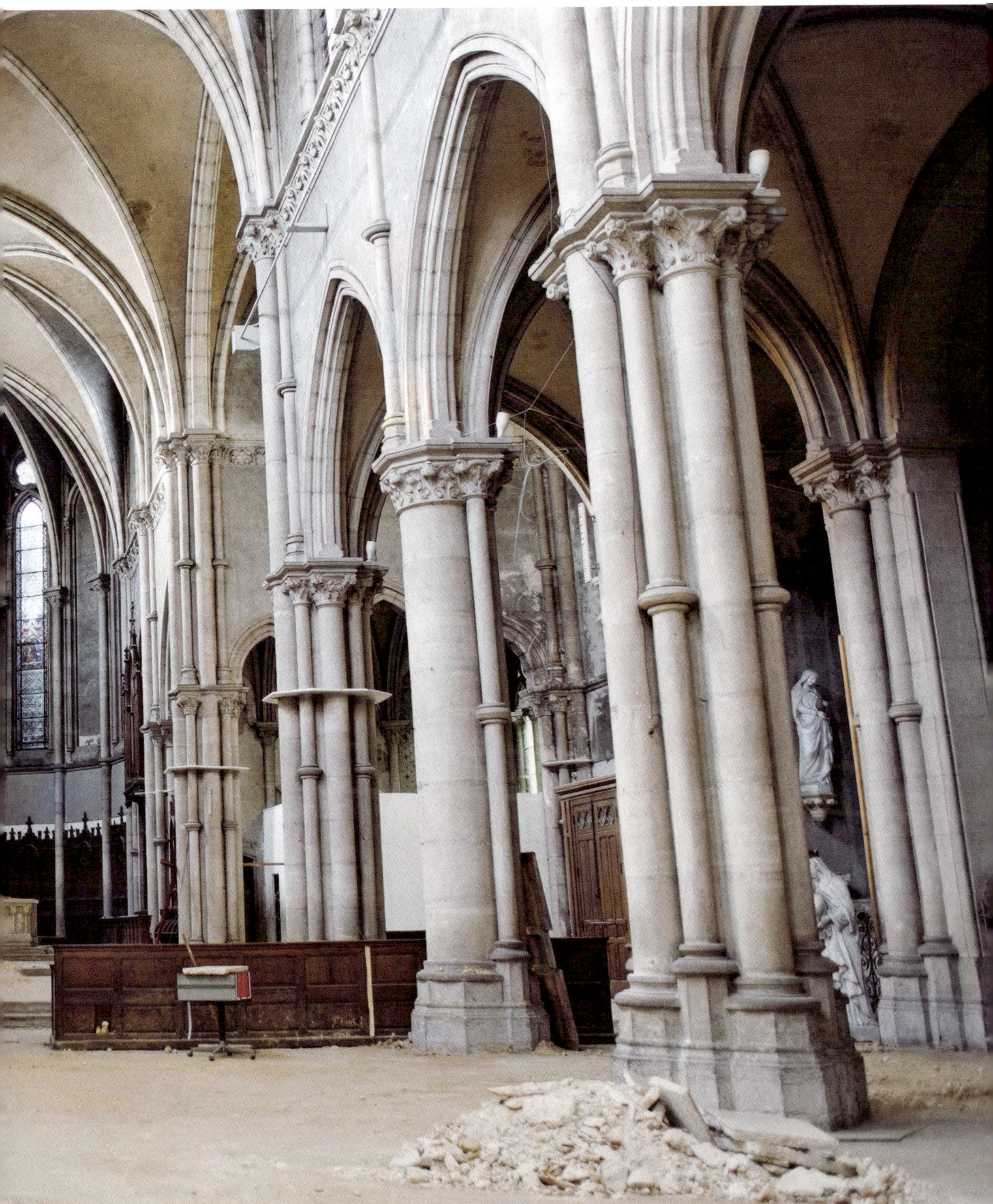

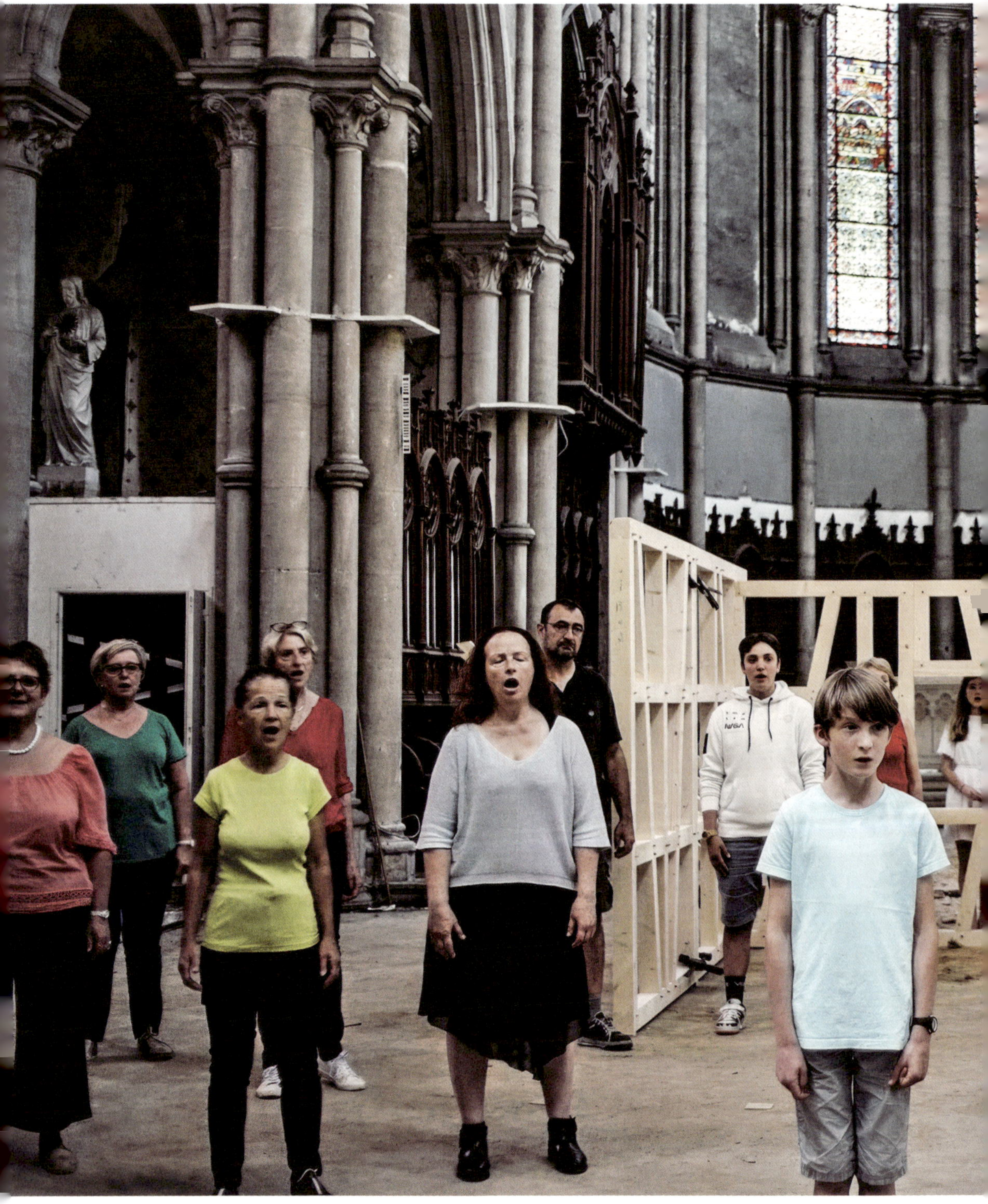

Annika Kahrs, *Le Chant des Maisons,* 2022,
4K Video, Farbe, Ton / colour, sound, **24:30 Min.,**
Videostandbild / video still

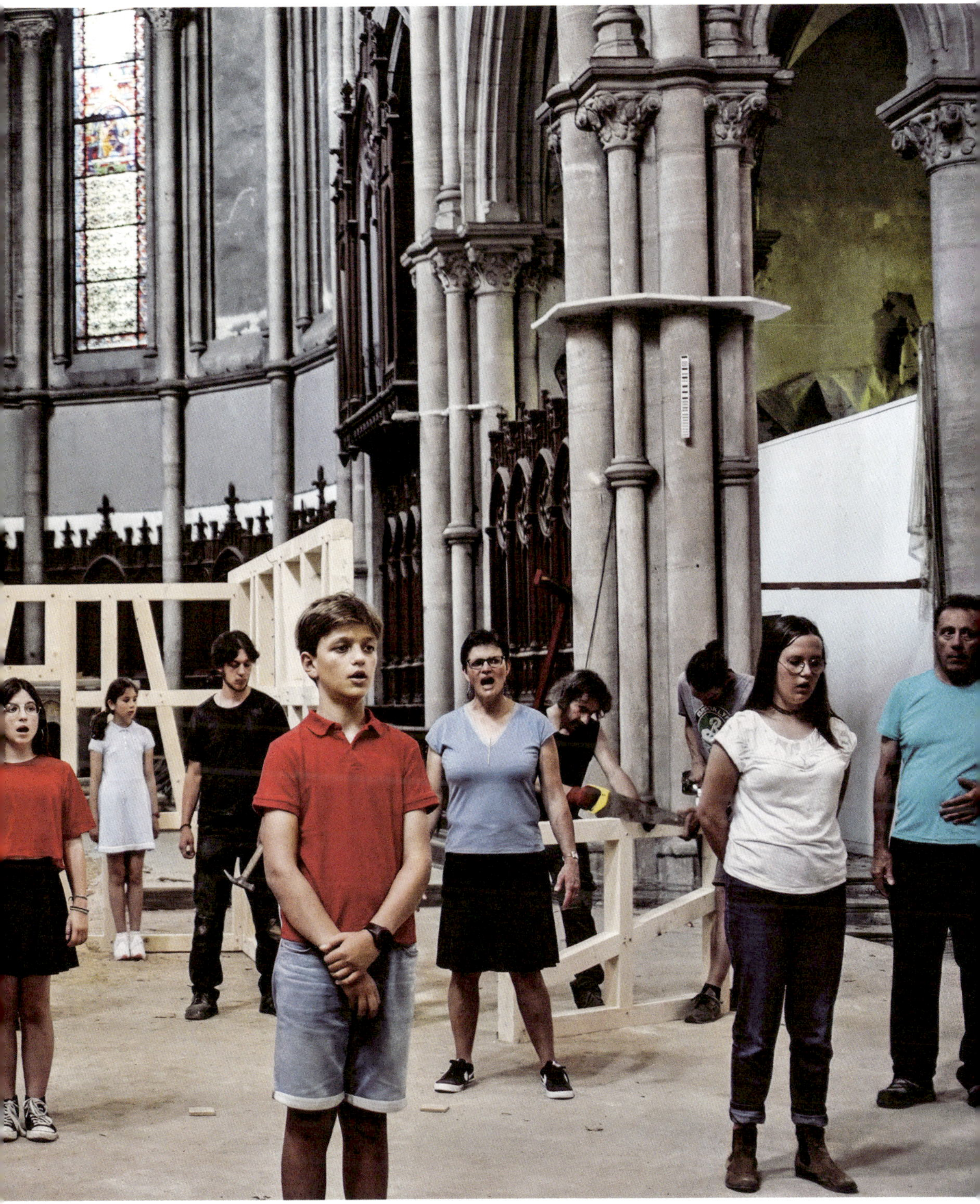

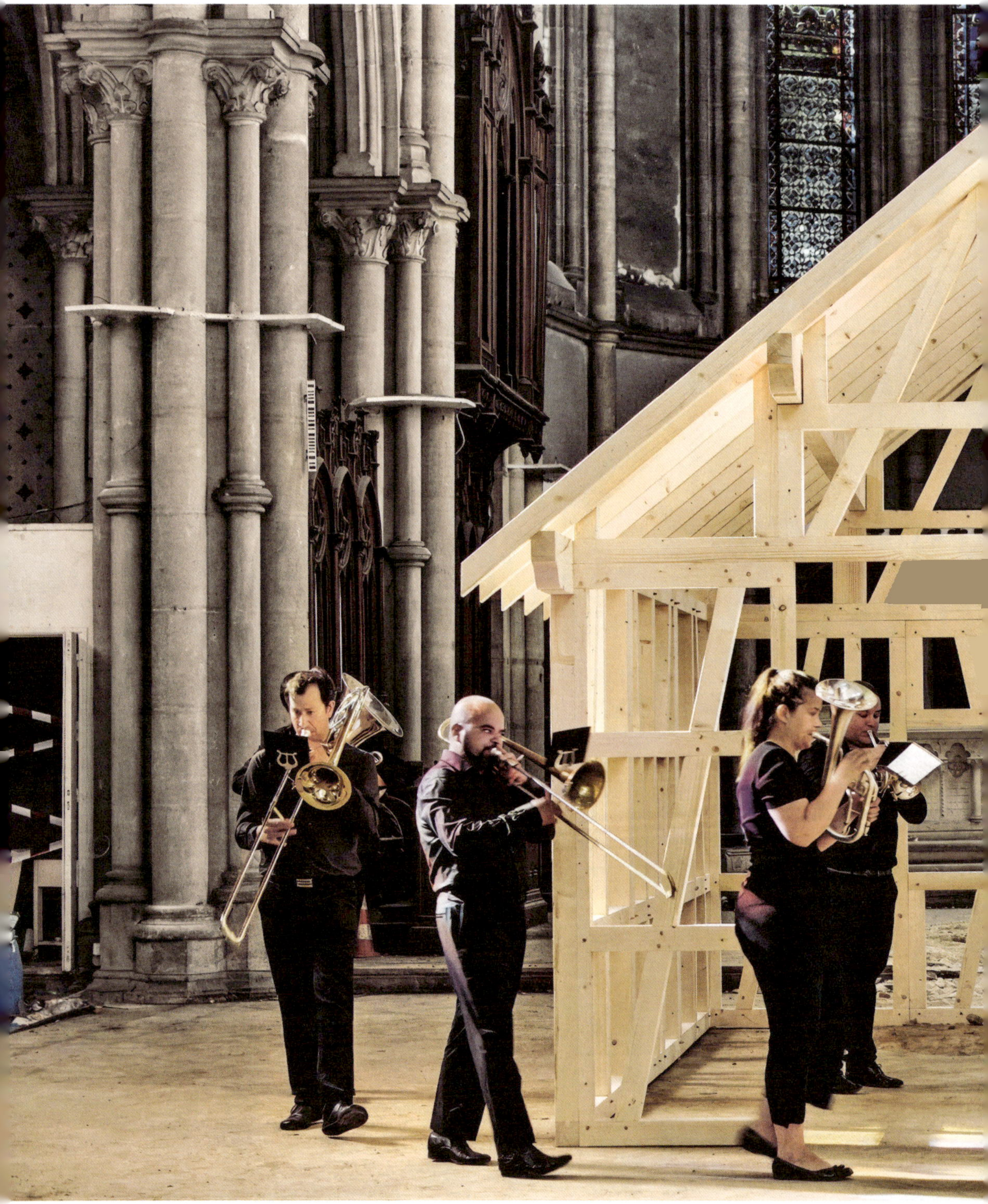

Annika Kahrs, *Le Chant des Maisons,* 2022,
4K Video, Farbe, Ton / colour, sound, **24:30 Min.,**
Videostandbild / video still

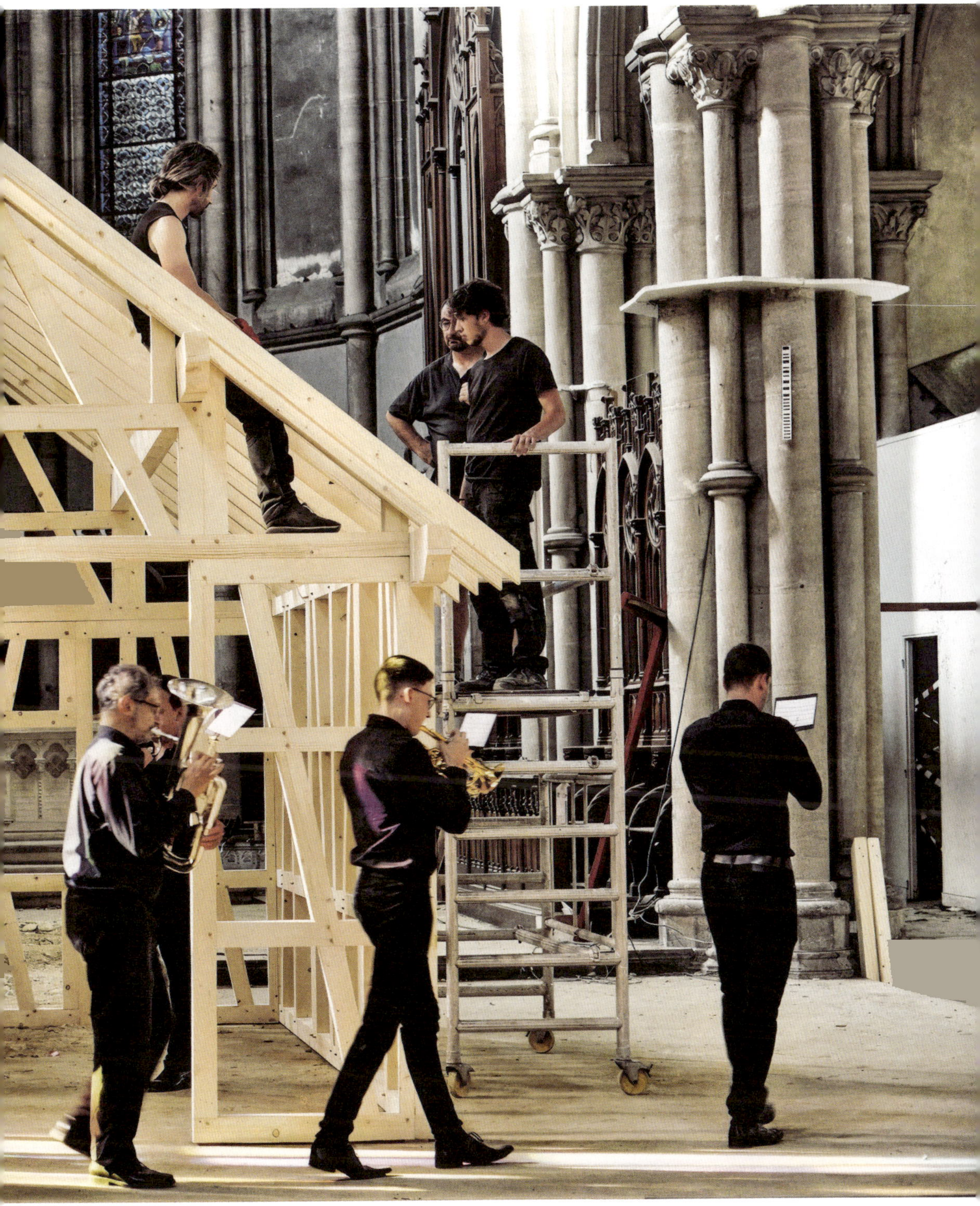

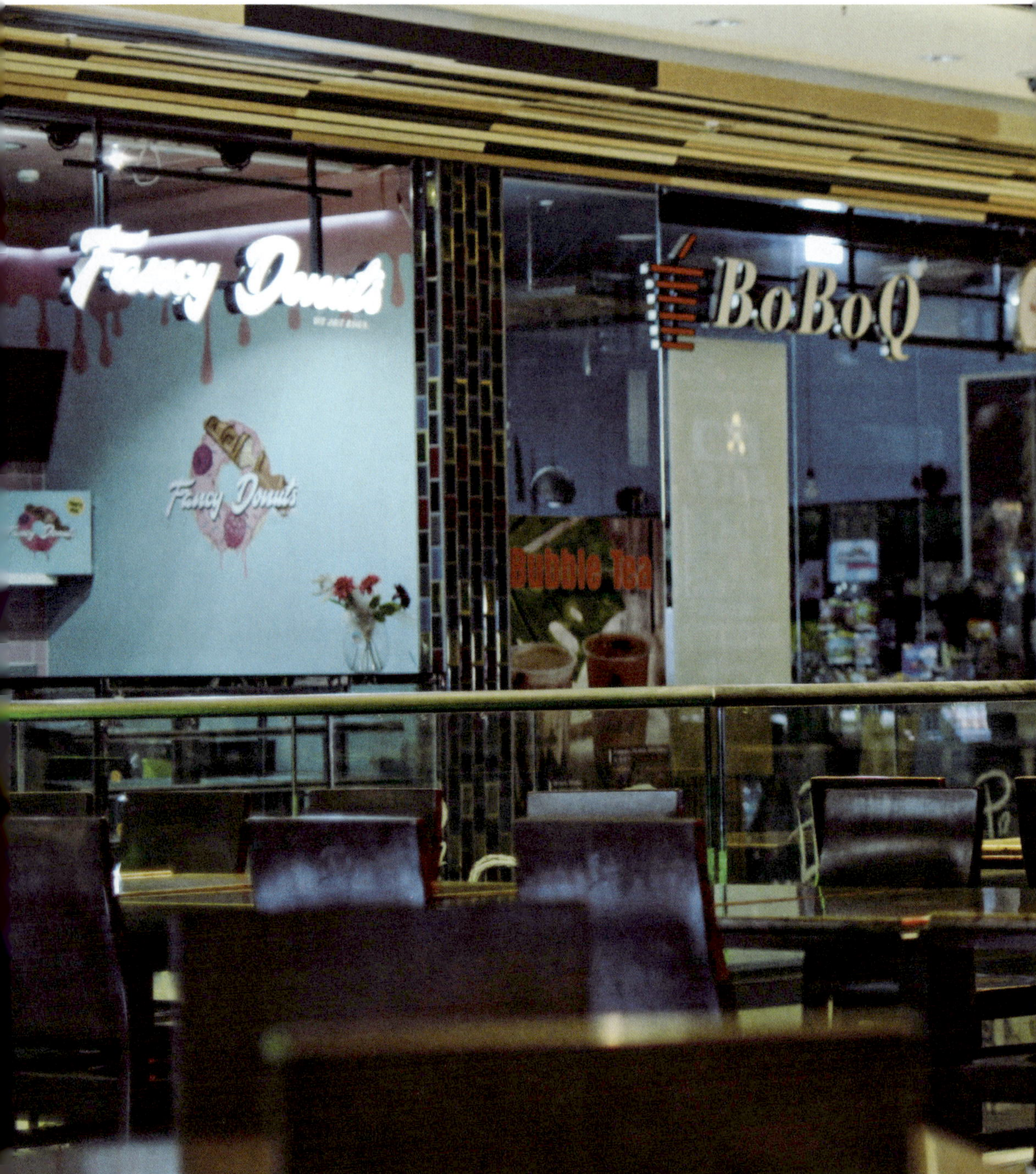

Annika Kahrs, *A Cashier's Opera,* 2025,
4K Video, Farbe, Ton / colour, sound, **36 Min.,**
Videostandbild / video still

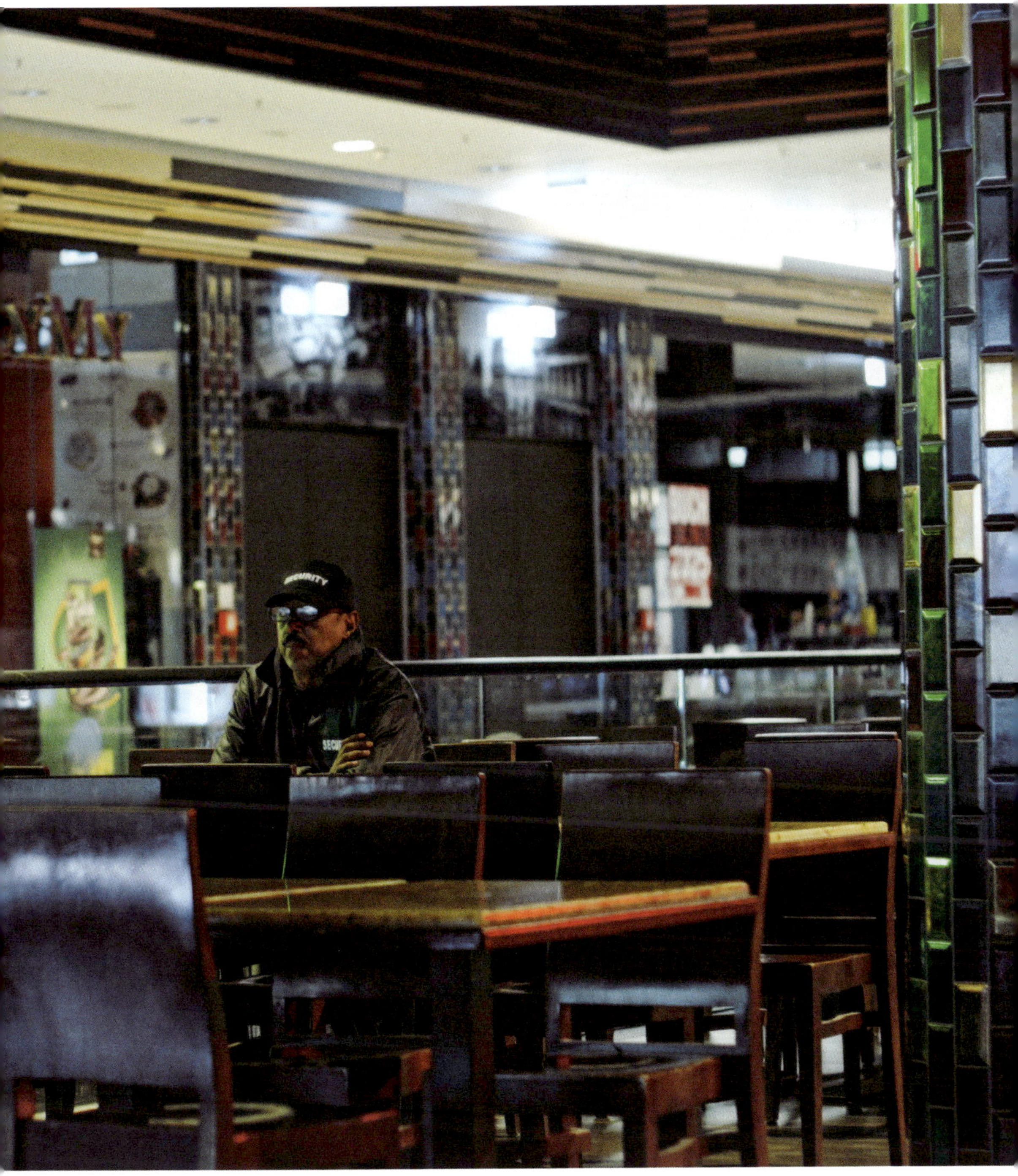
SECURITY

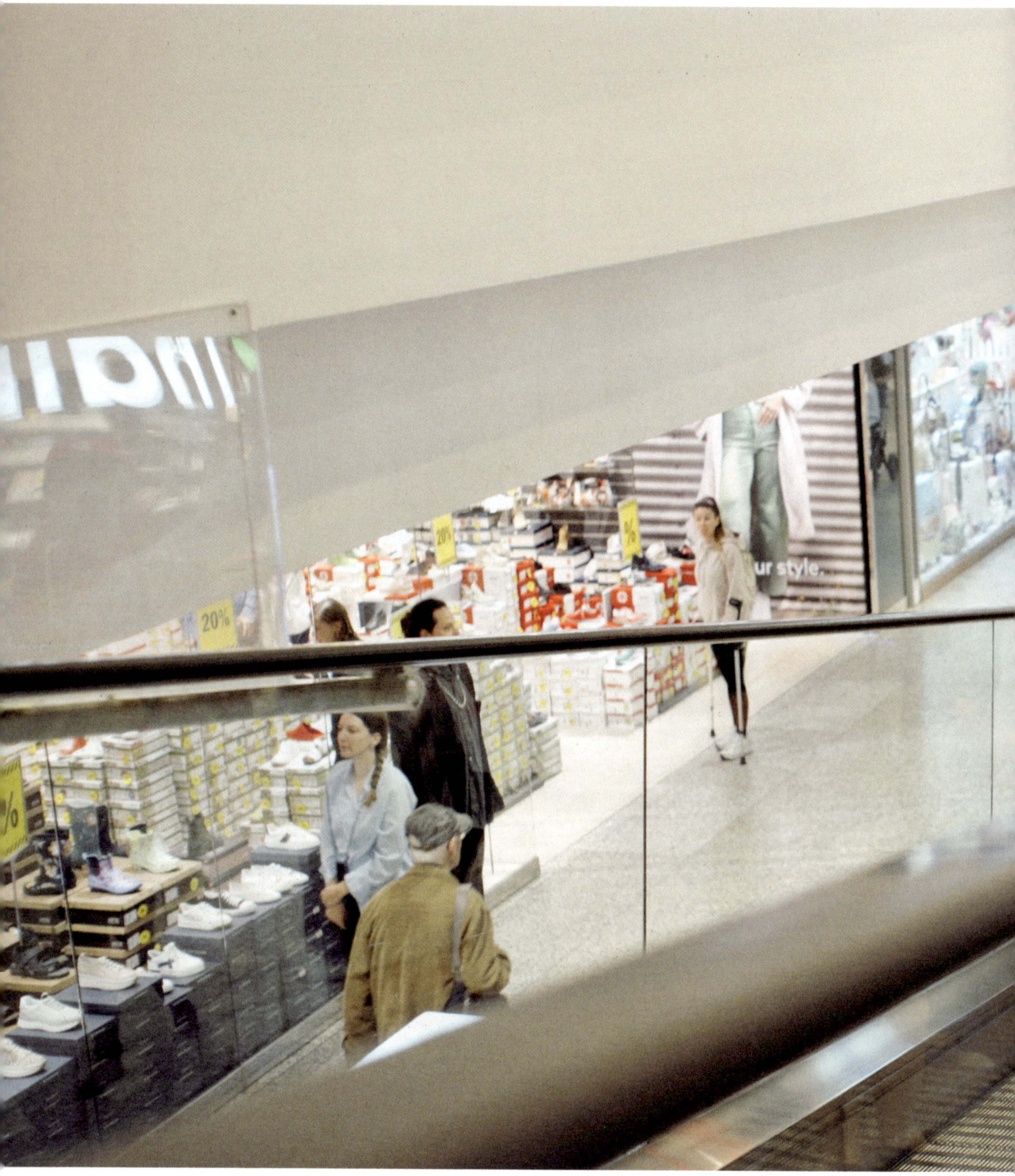

Annika Kahrs, *A Cashier's Opera*, 2025,
4K Video, Farbe, Ton / colour, sound, 36 Min.,
Videostandbild / video still

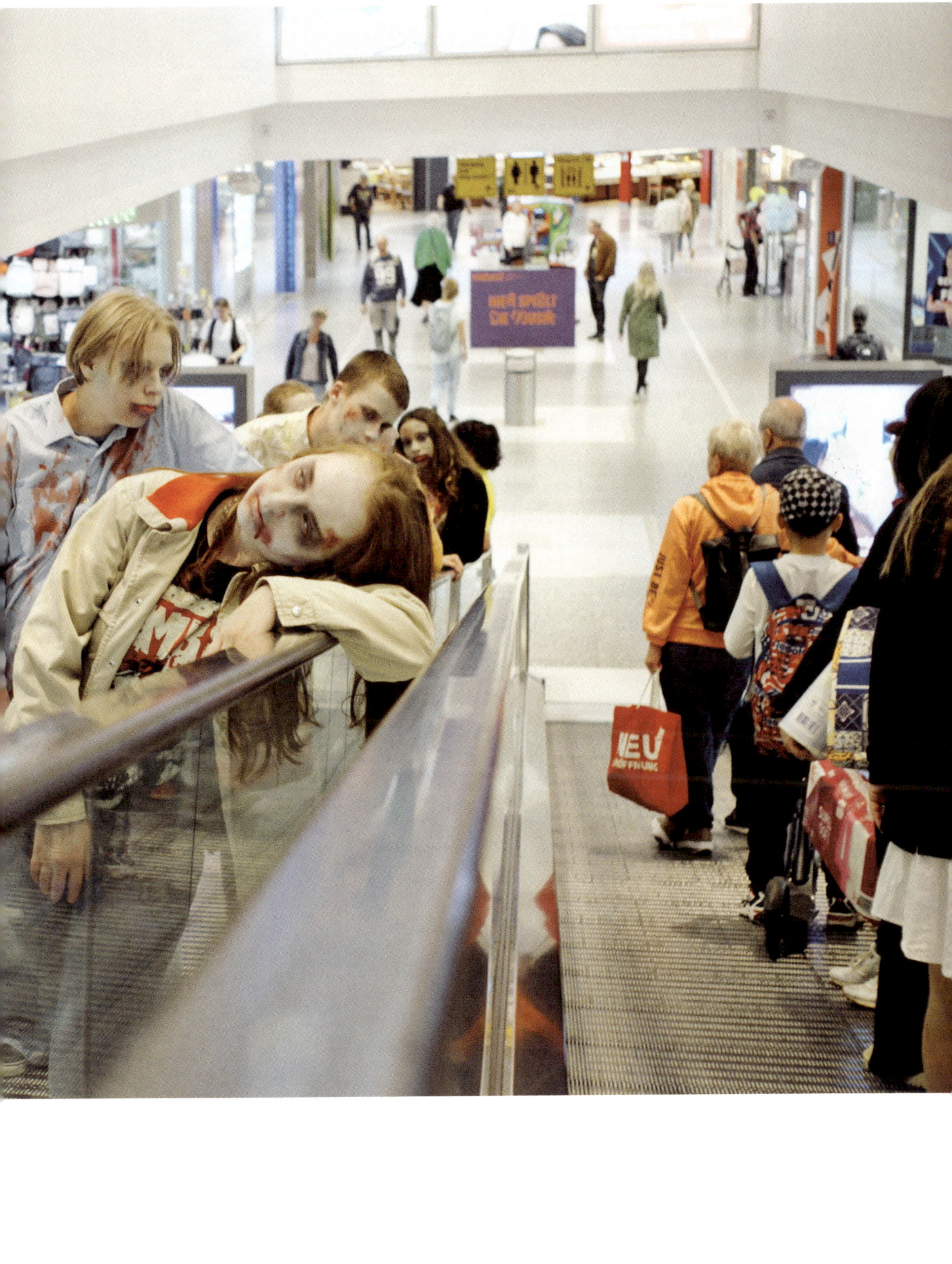
NEU

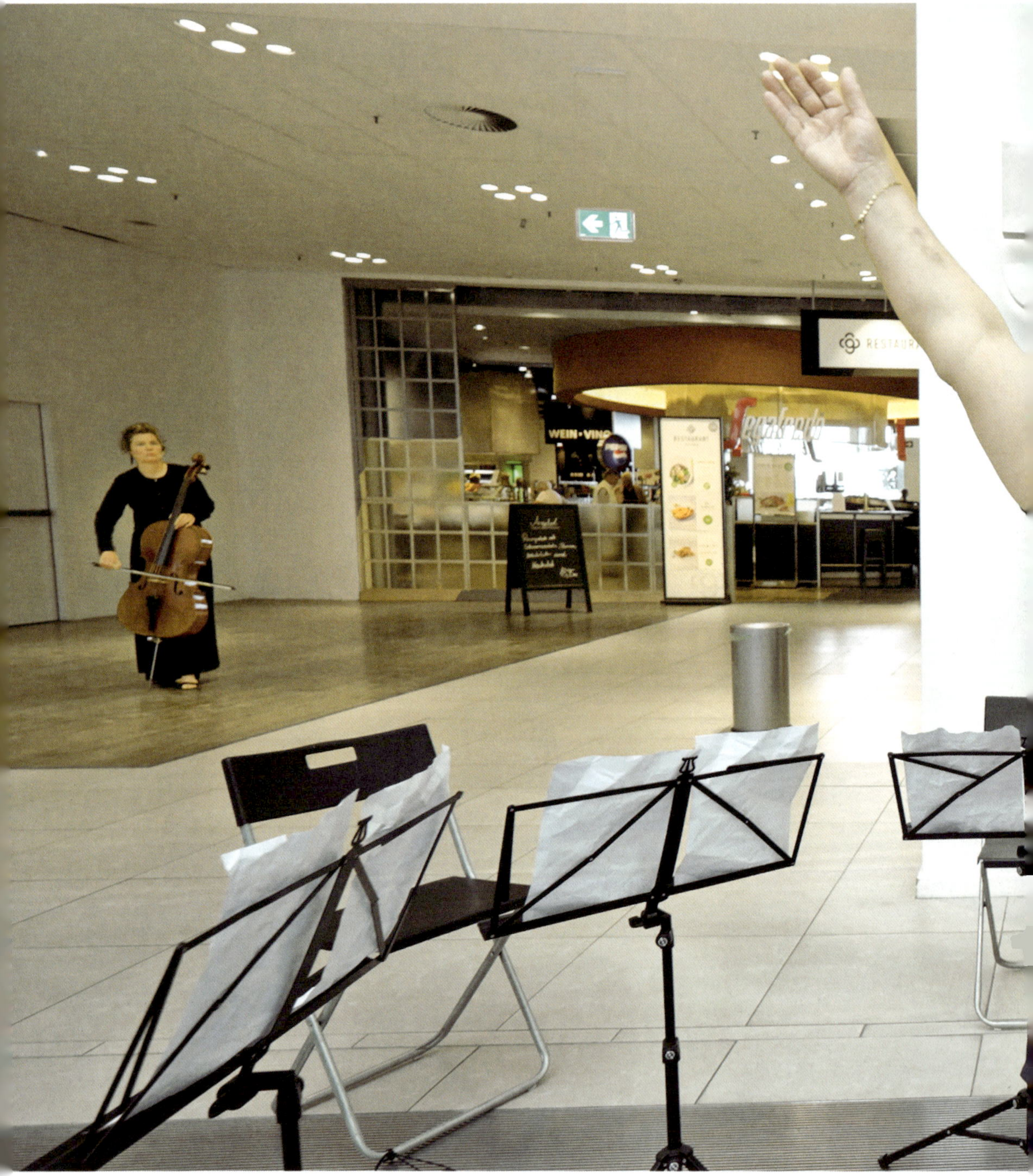

Annika Kahrs, *A Cashier's Opera,* 2025,
4K Video, Farbe, Ton / colour, sound, **36 Min.,**
Videostandbild / video still

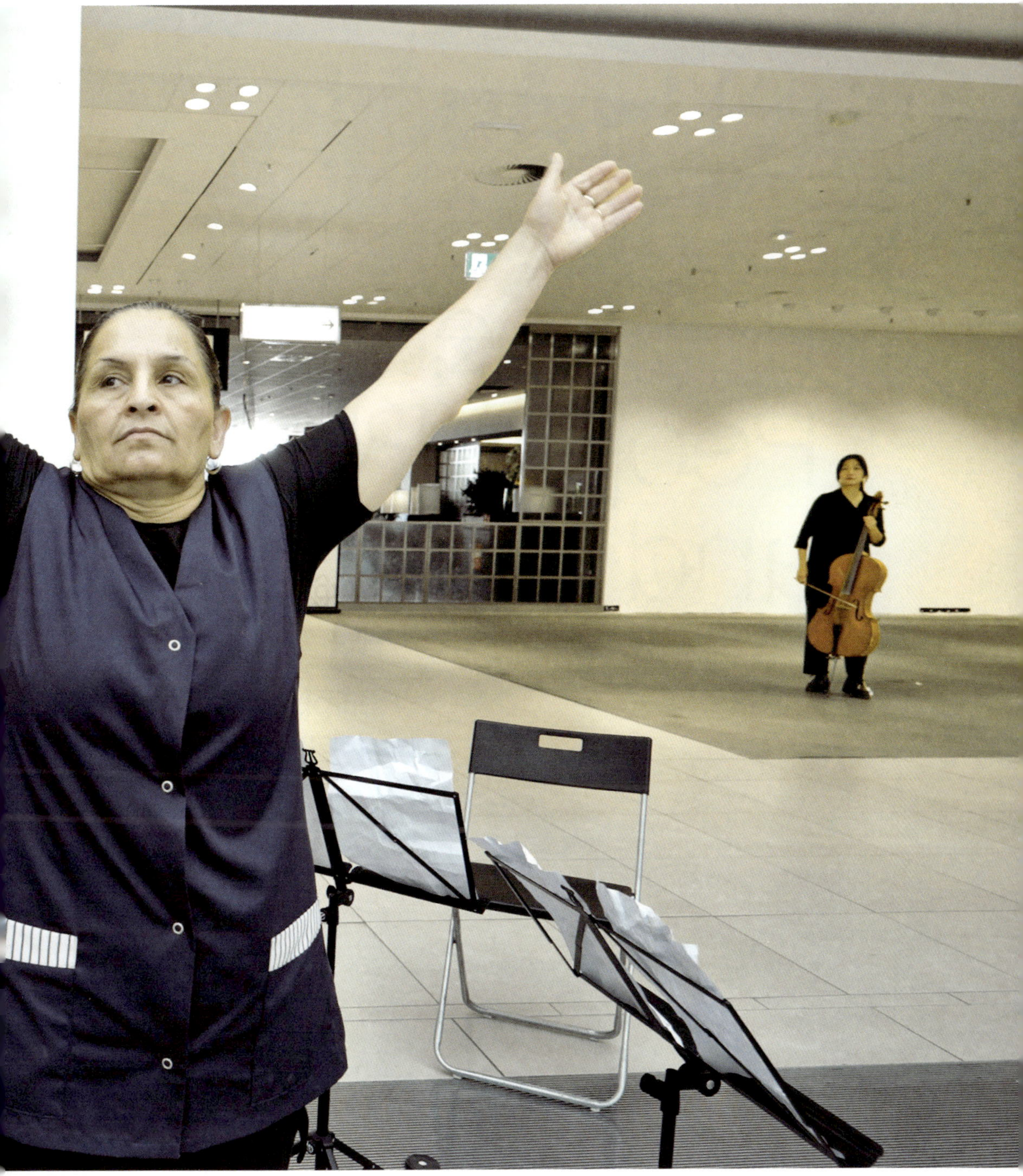

Zwischen Orten, Musik und Menschen

Between People, Places and Music

Philipp Lange im Gespräch mit / in Conversation with **Annika Kahrs**

Philipp Lange: Ein Merkmal deiner Ausstellung liegt darin, dass sie sich nicht auf einen einzigen Ausstellungsbereich im Hamburger Bahnhof konzentriert. Auch an anderen Orten begegnet das Publikum deinen Arbeiten, sowohl innerhalb des Museums, als auch stadtweit in Berlin. Wie kam es zur Idee dieser Expansion?

Annika Kahrs: Ursprünglich war nicht geplant, aus dem vorgesehenen Ausstellungsraum herauszugehen. In den ersten Gesprächen mit der Kuratorin Ingrid Buschmann hat sich diese Idee aber an einem gewissen Punkt entwickelt. Unsere Entscheidung war einerseits praktischer Natur, weil in meinen Arbeiten der Sound eine so zentrale Rolle spielt und es herausfordernd ist, sie gemeinsam in einem

Philipp Lange: A particular feature of your current exhibition is the fact that it's not confined to a single exhibition space at Hamburger Bahnhof. People will also find your works in other places, both inside the museum and at various locations across the city. What gave you the idea for this expansion?

Annika Kahrs: I didn't originally plan to extend the presentation beyond the designated space,

Raum zu zeigen, ohne dass sie sich akustisch überlagern – schließlich sollte eine größere Werkauswahl aus den letzten Jahren vertreten sein. Andererseits greift die Umgebung auch inhaltlich passend in die Arbeiten ein, seien es die historischen Übergänge zu den Seitenflügeln des Hamburger Bahnhof für *My Favorite Music* (2020) oder das Musikinstrumenten-Museum als externer Standort. Orte und ihre Bedeutungen spielen bei mir immer eine große Rolle. Ich hoffe, dass das Publikum wahrnimmt, welche Gedanken hinter den Positionierungen stecken, aber auch eigene Interpretationen entwickelt.

PL: In deinen Performances integrierst du die Besucher*innen oft in das Geschehen, vielleicht nirgendwo so stark wie in der Arbeit *For Two To Play On One*, die du 2012 für die Ausstellung *One on One* in den KW Institute for Contemporary Art produziert hast. Beim Betreten eines separierten Raums trifft man als alleinige*r Besucher*in auf ein Pianist*innen-Duo, das beim Öffnen der Tür abrupt mit dem zuvor hörbaren Klavierspiel abbricht. Erst bei Verlassen des Raums setzt es dieses fort. Kannst du anhand dieser Arbeit erörtern, welche Rolle das Publikum für dich spielt?

AK: In *For Two To Play On One* wird das Publikum unvorbereitet, vielleicht ungewollt aus der ausschließlichen Betrachter*innen-Rolle herausgebracht. Als ich die Arbeit 2012 konzipierte, wollte ich eine Situation schaffen, in der die Besucher*innen selbst zu Performer*innen werden, sich diesem Zustand aber auch wieder entziehen können und die Interaktion nicht für andere sichtbar ist. Die Pianist*innen habe ich angewiesen, die Arbeit nicht zu erklären, also nicht preiszugeben, dass sie weiterspielen werden, sobald man den Raum wieder verlässt. So kam es zu ungeahnten Reaktionen – auf beiden Seiten.

Ich traue sowohl dem Publikum als auch den Performer*innen sehr viel zu und gebe gerne ein Stück Kontrolle an beide Seiten ab. Das hat zur Folge, dass ich meine Arbeiten

but this idea emerged at some point during my first conversations with the curator, Ingrid Buschmann. On the one hand, the decision was made for practical reasons, because sound plays a pivotal role in my works and presenting them next to one another in an exhibition space without them overlapping acoustically is always a challenge; this display was, after all, going to feature a larger selection of my works from recent years. On the other hand, the settings I have chosen also echo the themes of the artworks – whether it is the two historical passageways to the east and west wings of Hamburger Bahnhof as an appropriate site for *My Favorite Music* (2020) or the Musikinstrumenten-Museum [Museum of Musical Instruments] as an external venue. Places and their various meanings are central to my practice. I hope visitors understand the ideas behind the choice of locations, but also develop their own interpretations.

PL: You often involve the audience in your performances – nowhere perhaps more intensely than in your work *For Two To Play On One* (2012), which you produced for the exhibition *One on One* at KW Institute for Contemporary Art in Berlin. In this piece, the audience can hear the sound of piano music coming from a closed-off room. Only one visitor at a time is allowed to enter. When they open the door, however, the two musicians at the piano immediately stop playing, and the performance doesn't continue until the visitor leaves the room. Taking this work as an example, can you tell me what role the audience plays for you?

AK: In *For Two To Play On One*, the viewer is unexpectedly, perhaps involuntarily, taken out of the role of being solely an observer. When I conceived this work in 2012, I wanted to create a situation where viewers become performers but can also remove themselves from this state, and where the interaction is not seen by anyone else. I instructed the pianists not to explain the work, in other words, not to share the information that they will continue playing as soon as the visitor leaves the room. This led to some unforeseen reactions – on both sides.

meistens erst richtig verstehen kann, wenn sie mit allen Beteiligten stattfinden. Dann muss ich sie neu kennenlernen. Eine so unmittelbare und situativ funktionierende Arbeit wie *For Two To Play On One* jetzt wieder aufzuführen, nachdem sie seit ihrer Erstpräsentation vor über zehn Jahren nicht mehr gezeigt wurde, ist zusätzlich aufregend. Heute – nach Pandemie, Social Media und politischen Umbrüchen – wird die Arbeit sicher anders rezipiert.

PL: Inwiefern hat *For Two To Play On One* als deine erste institutionelle Auftragsarbeit dazu beigetragen, deine künstlerischen Interessen zu formen? War sie ein Türöffner?

AK: Die Einladung zur Ausstellung von Susanne Pfeffer war kurz nach dem Abschluss meines Studiums eine Riesenchance. Ich bin froh, dass mir damals die Möglichkeit gegeben wurde, mich zu trauen, in größeren Dimensionen zu denken. Damals wusste ich noch nicht genau, was mich an Live-Performances interessiert. Umso wichtiger war es zu verstehen, welche Mechanismen dabei wirken. Interessanterweise weiß ich aber bis heute nicht, wie es sich anfühlt, diese Performance – meine eigene – wie das Publikum zu erleben. Wenn ich den Raum betrat, kam es mit den Pianist*innen immer zur Besprechung über die vielen unterschiedlichen sozialen Interaktionen, die sie erlebt hatten. Und noch heute erzählen mir Leute von ihren damaligen Erfahrungen und Emotionen. Ich finde es reizvoll, meine Konzepte in nur wenigen Sätzen erklären zu können, ohne vollends zu wissen, welche weiteren Ebenen sich noch entfalten werden. Wie Performance, Musik, Sound und Film dabei ineinandergreifen, finde ich bei jedem Projekt neu heraus, und ich glaube, dieser Prozess wird nie aufhören.

PL: Die Performance *Strings*, mit der du 2010 während deines Studiums erstmals größere Aufmerksamkeit erzielt hast, wird ebenfalls von präzisen Handlungsanweisungen bestimmt. Die Mitglieder

I have a lot of faith in both the audience and the performers, and I'm happy to relinquish some control to both sides. As a result, I can only fully understand my works when they are executed with everyone involved. I then have to get to know the works in a different way. It's particularly exciting for me to be restaging a work like *For Two To Play On One*, which operates in such a direct and situational manner, and hasn't been shown since it was first presented over a decade ago. Now – following the Covid pandemic, the rise of social media and major political upheavals – this work will no doubt be viewed and interpreted differently.

PL: To what extent did *For Two To Play On One* – your first institutional commission – shape your artistic interests? Did it open doors for you?

AK: Being invited by Susanne Pfeffer to take part in the exhibition *One on One*, not long after I'd completed my fine arts degree, was a huge opportunity for me. I'm so glad to have been given that chance to be bold and think on a larger scale. At the time, I didn't know exactly what it was about live performances that I found interesting, which made it all the more important to understand the mechanisms that underpin them. Interestingly, however, I still don't know how it feels to experience that performance – my own work – like the audience does. Whenever I went into the room, I always ended up talking to the pianists about the many different social interactions they were having. Even today, people still tell me about the experiences and emotions they had back then. I like the idea of being able to outline my concepts in just a few sentences, without knowing exactly what other layers may then unfold. With each new project, I find out how performance, music, sound and film are intertwined, and I don't think that process will ever end.

PL: The performance *Strings*, with which you first gained public attention in 2010, when you were still a student, is also defined by a set of precise instructions. The members of a string quartet are asked to swap places four times in a row during their

eines Streichquartetts wechseln ihre Sitzplätze viermal reihum, sodass sie wiederholt Instrumente spielen, die sie nicht beherrschen – das Konzert wird immer schiefer. Wie bereitest du deine Performer*innen auf ihren Auftritt vor und garantierst, dass sie sich in einer ungewohnten Situation wohlfühlen?

AK: In *Strings* laufen die ersten eineinhalb Minuten des Streichquartett Nr. 4 c-Moll (1801) von Ludwig van Beethoven perfekt, da die Musiker*innen zunächst ihre eigenen Streichinstrumente spielen. Mit dem Platzwechsel, den ungewohnten Instrumenten und neuen Notenblättern geraten sie jedoch außer Kontrolle. Ein wesentlicher Teil in der Vorbereitung liegt darin, zu besprechen, dass diese Aufführung möglich ist, weil sie als Kunst-Performance deklariert ist und nicht den Ansprüchen einer klassischen Bühne folgt. So wirkt sie mitunter sogar befreiend für die Musiker*innen.

In *For Two To Play On One* spielen die Pianist*innen verschiedene Klavierstücke zu vier Händen makellos – nur kommt es regelmäßig zu den Unterbrechungen. Sicherheitsvorkehrungen sind wichtig, beispielsweise durch eine Aufsicht vor dem Raum, in dem sich das vielleicht konfrontative Aufeinandertreffen unter Ausschluss anderer abspielt. Ich sehe es grundlegend als meine Aufgabe, darüber nachzudenken, wie sich alle Beteiligten sicher fühlen. Gleichzeitig möchte ich Raum lassen für überraschende und intime Momente.

PL: Im Hauptausstellungsraum, im Ostflügel des Museums, sind gleich drei deiner Filme zu sehen. Für die offene Struktur, in der sie parallel präsentiert werden, findet ein innovatives Kopfhörersystem Verwendung. Kannst du erklären, wie das funktioniert und welche Wirkung es auf die Wahrnehmung der Filme hat?

AK: Ich bin sehr froh, dass wir eine Lösung gefunden haben, die Filme gemeinsam in einem Raum zu zeigen, ohne dass sich der Sound überlagert. Das Besondere an den Kopfhörern ist, dass sie sich durch installierte Antennen

performance, so that they repeatedly have to play instruments they are not proficient in – as a result, the concert becomes increasingly discordant. How do you prepare the participants in your performances, and how do you make sure that they feel comfortable in such unfamiliar situations?

AK: In *Strings*, the first minute and a half of Ludwig van Beethoven's *String Quartet No. 4 in C minor* (1801) are performed impeccably, as the musicians are initially playing their own instruments. But when they have to swap places, play unfamiliar instruments and read from new sheet music, the players lose control over their performance. A crucial aspect of preparing the participants is discussing how this presentation is made possible by declaring it an art performance, which means it doesn't have to follow the conventions of a classical music concert. In this way, the performance can sometimes even be liberating for the musicians.

In *For Two To Play On One*, the pianists play various pieces for two hands flawlessly – except for the fact that they are regularly interrupted. Here, it's important to have security measures in place, such as a museum or gallery attendant outside the room where there may be a confrontational encounter between the pianists and one visitor to the exclusion of others. I see it as my fundamental responsibility to think about how I can ensure that all of those involved feel safe. At the same time, however, I want to leave room for surprising and intimate moments to occur.

PL: Three of your films are being screened jointly in the main exhibition space in the east wing of Hamburger Bahnhof. Here, an innovative headphone system is being used to facilitate the parallel presentation of the three works inside an open structure. Can you explain how this works, and what impact it has on how the films are perceived?

AK: I'm really happy that we've solved the problem of how to present the films all together inside one space, without the sound overlapping. What's special about these headphones is that

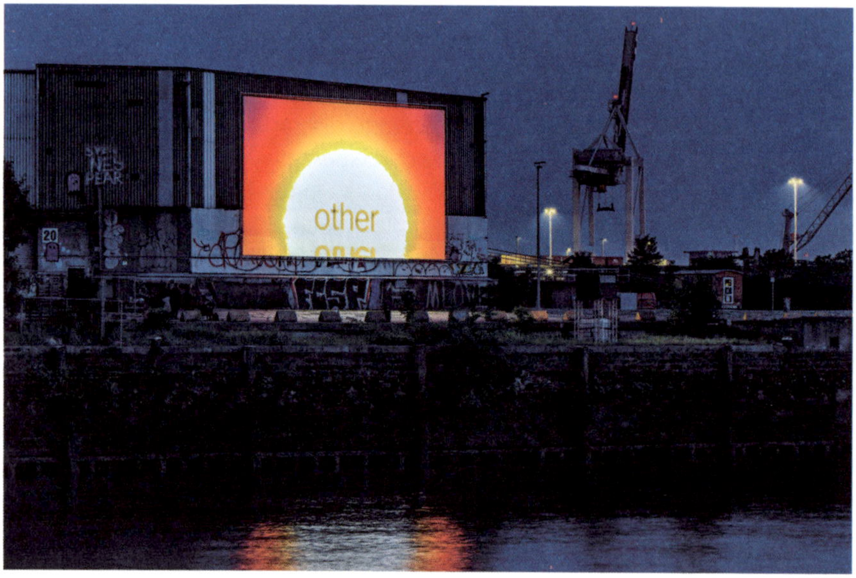

Annika Kahrs, *how to live in the echo of other places*, 2022, **11-Kanal Soundinstallation und Videoprojektion** / 11-channel sound installation and video projection, **Sound: ca. 80 Min., Video: Sonnenunter- bis -aufgang** / sunset to sunrise, **Installationsansicht** / installation view **HafenCity, Hamburg, 2022**

automatisch auf die jeweils vorliegende Arbeit einstellen. Der Sound wirkt dadurch offen, aber bleibt konzentriert und es gibt keine störenden Überschneidungen. Erst wenn du den Kopf drehst, ändert sich der Klang – und du wirst möglicherweise in eine andere Richtung gelockt. Wenn du zwischen den Arbeiten stehst, fließt alles auf choreografierte Art ineinander. Ich arbeite hierzu mit Ariel Schlichter am Sound-Design. Wir entwickeln zudem neue Soundscapes, die die Atmosphäre der Orte nachzeichnen und die auch zu hören sind, wenn man die Kopfhörer abnimmt. Diese komplexe Soundlandschaft wird räumlich gedacht und ersetzt die normalerweise durch Einbauten erzielte Raumakustik.

PL: Nicht nur deine Filme kommen hier auf besondere Weise miteinander in Berührung, sondern auch die darin auftretenden Menschen, die ganz unterschiedlichen Gemeinschaften und Gruppen zugehörig sind. Für mich spiegelt sich darin eine gewisse Fluidität wider, die dem gemeinschaftlichen Beisammensein innewohnt. Welche Aspekte sind für dich an diesem Raumkonzept am interessantesten?

they have built-in aerials which automatically adjust to the work the viewer is looking at. The sound seems open but remains focused and there are no distracting overlaps. Only when you turn your head does the sound change – and you might find yourself being drawn in a different direction. When you're standing between the works, everything merges in a choreographed way. I'm working with Ariel Schlichter on this sound design. We're also developing a new soundscape that reproduces the atmospheres of the spaces and can also be heard without the headphones. This complex soundscape is conceived spatially and replaces the room acoustics that are normally determined by furnishings and built-in elements.

PL: It's not just your films that are being brought together here in a special way, but also the people who appear in the films and belong to very different communities and groups. For me, this reflects a certain fluidity that is inherent in communal gatherings. Which aspects of this spatial concept do you find most interesting?

AK: I think it's exciting that the communities from these three films are coming together here.

AK: Es ist spannend, dass die Gemeinschaften aus den drei Filmen hier aufeinandertreffen. In meiner Arbeit geht es mir in erster Linie um die Menschen und deren Verhalten zueinander – mehr noch als um Musik und ihre Codes, auch wenn das Musikalische stets eine tragende Rolle spielt. In der Zusammenstellung lassen sich aber auch viele weitere Verbindungen zwischen den Arbeiten feststellen. Die Berliner Kaufhäuser, die in *A Cashier's Opera* (2025) als Schauplätze dienen, wirken mitunter kathedralenartig und erinnern somit an die Kirche Saint-Bernard in Lyon, in der sich *Le Chant des Maisons* (2022) abspielt. *La Banda* (2024) reflektiert die Vergänglichkeit und die aktuelle Transformation des uralten, geschichtsträchtigen Dorfes Olevano Romano in Italien. So betrachtet berührt es ähnliche Aspekte wie ein leerstehendes, von der Krise betroffenes Kaufhaus oder die seit Jahren ungenutzte, entweihte Kirche. Ein gemeinsamer roter Faden der drei Arbeiten liegt darin, dass sie von einem konkreten Ort ausgehen und von dessen Wandel und Bedeutung erzählen.

> PL: Begreifst du deine filmischen Arbeiten als Dokumentationen, als Porträts von Orten und den Menschen, die sie beherbergen?

AK: Meine Arbeiten sind keine Dokumentationen im klassischen Sinn. Sie bestehen aus performativen Annäherungen und halten Momente fest, in denen Menschen, Orte und Situationen offen aufeinandertreffen. Im Grunde kann man sagen, dass ich mit meinem Team Performances inszeniere, die wir dann filmisch komprimieren. Trotzdem folgen meine Arbeiten nicht nur bestimmten Skripten. Ich lasse viel Raum für Spontaneität und das Prozesshafte, um zu beobachten, wie die Menschen, Klänge und Orte sich gegenseitig beeinflussen. So filmen wir beispielsweise auch in den Drehpausen und integrieren diese Szenen. Auch die Vor- und Nachrecherche hat einen maßgeblichen Einfluss, indem wir etwa Interviews mit den Beteiligten führen. Dieses Material taucht in den Filmen zwar nicht direkt auf, ist aber wichtig für mein Verständnis

My work is primarily about people and how they behave towards each other – more than about music and its codes, even if the musical aspect always plays a key role. When the various pieces are presented in juxtaposition, however, it's possible to identify many other connections between them. The cathedral-like ambience of the Berlin department stores and shopping centres that provide the settings for *A Cashier's Opera* (2025), for example, recalls the Church of Saint Bernard in Lyon where *Le Chant des Maisons* (2022) was staged. *La Banda* (2024) reflects upon transience and the current transformation of Olevano Romano, an ancient Italian village that is steeped in history. Viewed in this light, the work touches on similar aspects to those addressed by a vacant, crisis-hit department store or a deconsecrated church that has not been used for years. A common thread running through all three works is the fact that they take a specific place as their starting point and tell us something about its significance and transformation.

> PL: Do you regard your films as documentaries – as portraits of places and the people they accommodate?

AK: My works aren't documentaries in a conventional sense. They consist of performative approaches and capture moments when people, places and situations come together in an open-ended encounter. Basically, you could say that my team and I stage performances that we then condense into films. Nevertheless, my works don't just follow a set script. I leave a lot of room for spontaneity and processual development in these interactions, in order to see how the people, sounds and places influence each other. For example, we continue filming during the breaks between shoots, and these impromptu scenes are also integrated into the finished work. Prior and follow-up research also has a significant influence; this includes, for example, conducting interviews with the participants. While this material doesn't appear directly in the films, it's important for my understanding of what happens and to avoid any false interpretations being projected onto the events. For me, these interstices –

über das Geschehen, um keine falschen Interpretationen hineinzuprojizieren. Solche Zwischenräume – also alles, was außerhalb des geplanten Geschehens stattfindet – finde ich fast am schönsten. Das Zusammensein der Personen, ihre Reaktionen und der Ort legen ganz viel offen.

PL: Wer sind die Personen, mit denen du deine Filmarbeiten umsetzt? Wie geht ihr gemeinsam vor?

AK: An einem Projekt arbeite ich normalerweise mehrere Monate mit meinem Team zusammen. Seit über zehn Jahren gehört der Komponist Louis d'Heudières dazu. Mit ihm bespreche ich meine Konzeptideen, für die er musikalische Vorschläge einbringt, die wiederum in Handlung umgebaut werden, vice versa. Wir arbeiten in einem intensiven Tandem, aber die musikalischen Kompositionen und Arrangements stammen letztlich immer aus seiner Feder. Es ist wichtig, dass jemand aus dem Musik- und Soundbereich beteiligt ist. Ich bin keine Musikerin, was auch ein Vorteil sein kann, weil ich einen anderen, unbefangenen Blick auf Musik habe.

Das Filmteam besteht im Kern aus Karsten Krause, Levente Pavelka, Patrick Dadaczyński. In der Sound-Postproduktion arbeite ich mit Ariel Schlichter zusammen. Während die Vorbereitungszeit immer sehr lange andauert, drehen wir meistens nur ein bis zwei Tage. Anfangs aus finanziellen Gründen hat sich das längst als Prinzip durchgesetzt, da die kurze Zeit eine fokussierte Energie mit sich bringt – insbesondere wenn die Menschen zum ersten Mal in ihrem Leben vor der Kamera stehen. Dass dabei alles reibungslos abläuft, verdanke ich der Produktionsleiterin Rosanna Graf und der Hilfe von Kenna Capalbo. Aber es sind auch noch viel mehr Menschen involviert. Bei genauerem Hinsehen wird deutlich, dass immer eine große Gruppe beteiligt ist.

PL: Lass uns die einzelnen Filme näher anschauen. *A Cashier's Opera* ist eine Auftragsarbeit für die Ausstellung und geht

i.e. everything that occurs outside what was originally planned – are almost the best part. A great deal is revealed by the people coming together and how they react to what happens, as well as by the place itself.

PL: Who do you collaborate with on the production of your films? What does the collective process look like?

AK: I usually spend several months working on each project with my team. The composer Louis d'Heudières has been part of this team for over 10 years now. I talk to him about my conceptual ideas, on the basis of which he makes suggestions regarding the music; these are in turn transformed into narrative scenarios, and vice versa. Although our collaboration is an intensive tandem process, ultimately the musical compositions and arrangements always come from him. It's important for someone from the field of music and sound to be involved. I'm not a musician, which can also be an advantage because I have a different, impartial perspective on music.

The core film team consists of Karsten Krause, Levente Pavelka and Patrick Dadaczyński. I collaborate with Ariel Schlichter on audio post-production. While we always have a very long period of preparation, we usually only shoot for one or two days. Initially this was for financial reasons, but it has long since become a guiding principle for us because the short amount of time focuses everyone's energies – especially when people are performing in front of a camera for the first time in their lives. Our production manager, Rosanna Graf, makes sure that everything runs smoothly, and Kenna Capalbo provides valuable assistance. But many others – friends and colleagues – also contribute to the creation of my works. When you look closely, you can see that there's always a large group of people involved.

PL: Let's now take a closer look at the individual films. *A Cashier's Opera* was commissioned for the current exhibition and will subsequently enter the collection of the Nationalgalerie. *Le Chant des Maisons* was commissioned for the 16th edition of

über in die Sammlung der Nationalgalerie. *Le Chant des Maisons* ist 2022 im Auftrag der Lyon Biennale für ihre 16. Ausgabe entstanden. *La Banda* wiederum resultierte relativ spontan aus deinem Residency-Aufenthalt 2024 in Olevano Romano in der Nähe von Rom. Was war der Antrieb zur Umsetzung dieser Arbeit – ohne institutionellen Rückenwind?

AK: Tatsächlich war nicht geplant, eine neue Arbeit während meiner Residency in der Casa Baldi zu machen, weil der Zeitraum von drei Monaten viel zu kurz ist. Die Villa liegt auf einem Berg mit Blick auf eine wunderschöne Landschaft, die über Jahrhunderte vielfach künstlerisch festgehalten wurde. Eines Abends habe ich beim Spaziergang durch das eigentlich ruhige Dorf ein eigenartiges, aber charmantes Konzert aus Blechblasinstrumenten gehört. Es kam von einem generationsübergreifenden Orchester, das wöchentlich probt und bei lokalen Veranstaltungen auftritt. Während sich die ländliche Gegend immer weiter ausdünnt, wirkte das Orchester auf mich wie ein sozialer Kleber, der das Dorf zusammenhält. Mich hat fasziniert, dass Musik ein so verbindendes Element darstellt. Das jüngste Mitglied war acht Jahre alt, das älteste über achtzig – und sie haben auf meine Anfrage hin Interesse an einer Zusammenarbeit geäußert, sodass ich mich schnell an die Konzeptentwicklung gemacht habe. Louis d'Heudières verstand sofort, welche Bilder und Emotionen mir vorschwebten und hat ein Stück für das Orchester komponiert.

Kurz vor meiner Abreise haben wir gedreht. Der Film folgt den Musiker*innen, während sie als allmählich anwachsende Parade durch die Straßen marschieren, und endet auf der Terrasse der Casa Baldi, wo sie sich der weiten Landschaft und dem zu Füßen liegenden Dorf zuwenden. Trotz der einfachen Handlung ist die Arbeit sehr aufgeladen. Sie spürt diese Gruppe. Und sie reflektiert die Geschichte und den demographischen Wandel. Das hoffnungsvolle Bild zum Abschluss war mir wichtig. Erst kürzlich hat sich durch zwei Ausstellungseinladungen ergeben, dass ich

the Biennale de Lyon in 2022. *La Banda*, on the other hand, developed relatively spontaneously from your residency in Olevano Romano, near Rome, in 2024. What inspired you to create that work – without a commission from an institution?

AK: I really hadn't planned to create a new work during my residency at Casa Baldi, because three months is much too short for that. Casa Baldi is located in a villa on a mountain, overlooking a stunning landscape that has been captured in countless artworks over the past centuries. One evening, as I was walking through the otherwise quiet village, I heard a curious but very charming concert of brass music. It was being played by an intergenerational orchestra that rehearses once a week and performs at local events. While the population in the rural area is steadily declining, the orchestra seemed to me like a kind of social glue holding the village together. I found it fascinating that music can be such a unifying element. The youngest member of the orchestra was eight years old and the oldest was over 80. When I asked if they would be interested in collaborating with me, they said yes, so I quickly began developing a concept. Louis d'Heudières immediately understood the images and emotions I had in mind; based on these ideas, he composed a piece for the orchestra to play. We shot the film shortly before I left. It follows the musicians as they march through the streets in a gradually increasing group; the parade ends on the terrace of Casa Baldi, where the players turn to face the vast landscape and the village below. Despite the simple narrative, the work is highly charged. It conveys a sense of this group and reflects not only the history of the place, but also the demographic changes it is undergoing. The hope-filled image at the end of the film was important to me. Two recent exhibition invitations have motivated me to create a trilogy by adding two further parts to this film.

PL: In *Le Chant des Maisons* you allude to the first major workers' protests in France, which had a significant impact on the flourishing silk weaving industry in Lyon in the mid-19th century. I had the chance to see

den Film um zwei weitere Teile zu einer Trilogie erweitern werde.

PL: In *Le Chant des Maisons* beziehst du dich auf die ersten großen Arbeiter*innen-Proteste in Frankreich, die in der Mitte des 19. Jahrhunderts die in Lyon florierende Seidenweberei bestimmten. Ich durfte die Arbeit auf der Lyon Biennale sehen und sie für einen Ausstellungskatalog der Kunsthalle Bremen näher besprechen. In dem Zusammenhang habe ich mich intensiver mit der visuellen Gestaltung beschäftigt, darunter auch mit dem Aspekt Kleidung. Welche Rolle spielt für dich – auch mit Blick auf andere Arbeiten – das Kostümbild? Wie entscheidest du, was die Beteiligten tragen sollen?

AK: Ich versuche, Kostümbilder zu vermeiden, in denen sich die Beteiligten verkleidet fühlen, genauso wie ich auch nicht möchte, dass sie sich zum Schauspielern gezwungen fühlen. Deine Beobachtung in dem Text, dass der auftretende Chor keine liturgische Kleidung mehr trägt wie damals, fand ich sehr interessant. Tatsächlich hatte das aber keine symbolische Bedeutung, sondern war vielmehr der Tatsache geschuldet, dass ich die Sänger*innen gebeten hatte, das zu tragen, womit sie sich beim Auftritt wohlfühlen. Dass die Handwerker in dem Film wiederum ihre Berufskleidung tragen, war wichtig, um ihre Rolle visuell zu repräsentieren – so wie auch die Orchestermitglieder in *La Banda* ihre Uniform wie bei jedem Konzert anhaben.

Für die neue Arbeit *A Cashier's Opera* mache ich mir aktuell etwas mehr Gedanken über die Outfits, weil wir uns in Kaufhäusern befinden, die natürlich stark mit Mode in Verbindung stehen. Die darin auftretenden Menschen sollen aber auch diesmal tragen, was in dem Setting am natürlichsten für das ist, worum es mir geht.

PL: Wieso hast du dich für Kaufhäuser als Dreh- und Angelpunkt deiner Neuproduktion für die Ausstellung entschieden?

this work at the Lyon Biennale and to discuss it in greater depth for the catalogue of a group exhibition you took part in at Kunsthalle Bremen. In that context, I looked more closely at the visual design, including the aspect of clothing. What role does costume design play for you – also with regard to your other works? How do you decide what the participants will wear?

AK: I try to avoid clothing designs that make the participants feel as if they are wearing an unnatural costume, in the same way that I don't want them to feel that they have to give some kind of acting performance. I found the observation you made in your text – that the choir in this work is not wearing liturgical clothing, as choirs did in the past – very interesting. But that actually had no symbolic significance; it was simply due to the fact that I had asked the singers to wear whatever they felt comfortable performing in. It was, however, important for the craftsmen in the film to be wearing their work clothing, so as to visually represent their role – just as the members of the orchestra in *La Banda* are wearing the uniforms they usually have on when they perform a concert.

I'm currently giving a bit more consideration to the outfits for my new work, *A Cashier's Opera*, as it deals with department stores and these are, of course, closely associated with fashion. But the people who appear in this film should also wear what seems most natural in the setting I'm interested in exploring.

PL: What made you choose department stores as the main focus of the new work you are producing for this exhibition?

AK: For me, it was important to create a work that has a connection to Berlin, although this is not an easy time for the city, be it due to the political swing to the right or

AK: **Es war mir wichtig, eine Arbeit mit Berlin-Bezug zu machen, wenngleich es keine einfache Zeit für die Stadt ist, sei es durch den Rechtsruck oder die drastischen Budget-Kürzungen im Kulturbereich, die dieses Jahr in Kraft traten. Vor den vielen historisch aufgeladenen Orten habe ich mich etwas gescheut, da sie oftmals schon stark durchexerziert wurden – auch künstlerisch. Das Kaufhaus habe ich gewählt, weil es selbst vom Umbruch betroffen ist, etwa durch den Online-Handel. Viele Kaufhäuser stehen heute leer, es wird über Umnutzungen diskutiert. Dabei waren Kaufhäuser ursprünglich als soziale Orte gedacht, mit Grünflächen, kulturellen Angeboten, Arztpraxen und Raum für Begegnung.**

the drastic budget cuts in the cultural sector that came into effect this year. I was slightly wary of the numerous historically charged sites in Berlin, as these have already been investigated many times and from many different angles – also by artists. I chose department stores because they are directly affected by current upheavals such as the surge in online shopping. Many stores are now standing empty and plans for converting or repurposing these buildings are being discussed. Yet department stores were originally conceived as social hubs with green spaces, cultural events, doctor's surgeries and places for people to meet. The architect Victor Gruen, a pioneer in the creation of shopping malls in the United States, conceived them in the mid-20th

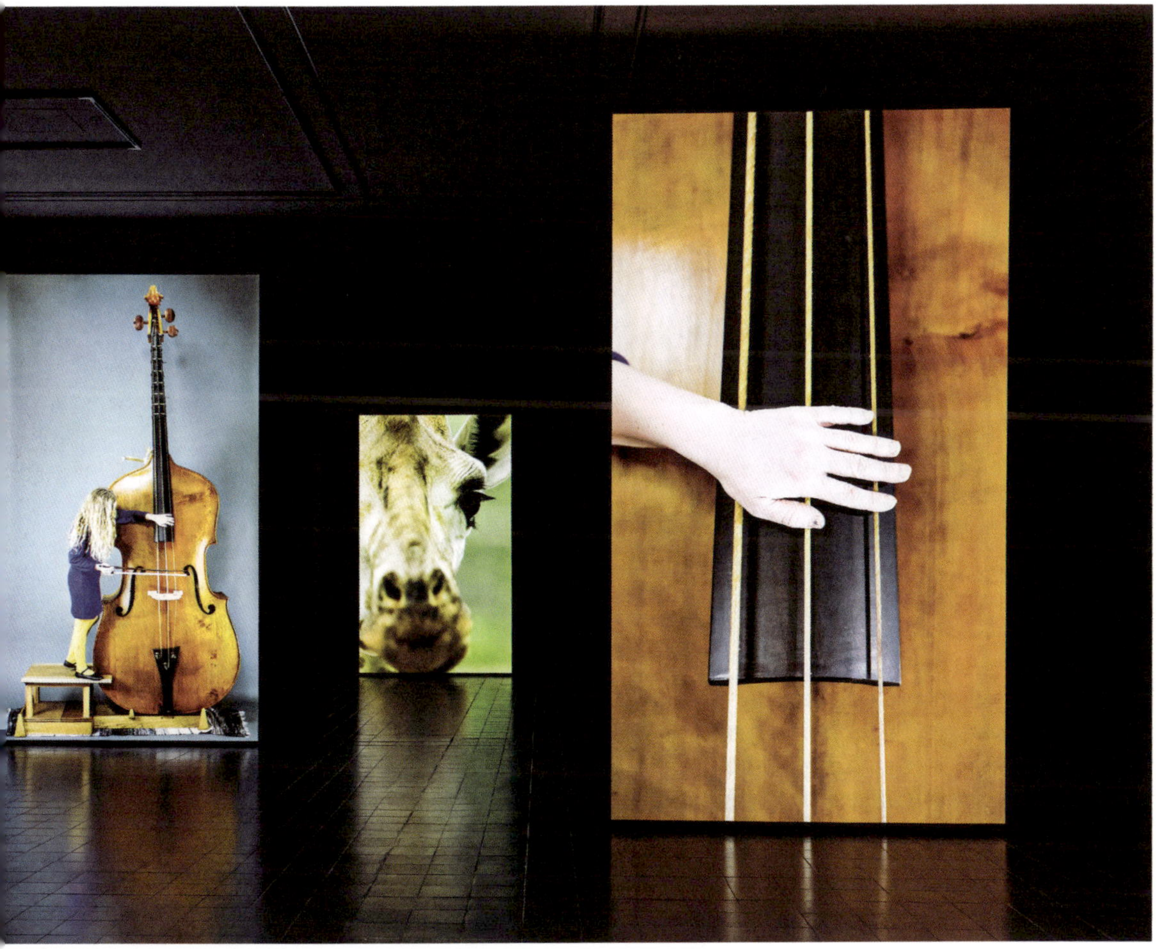

Annika Kahrs, *Infra Voice*, 2018, 3-Kanal Video- und Soundinstallation / 3-channel video and sound installation, **10:35 Min., Ausstellungsansicht** / exhibition view **Hamburger Kunsthalle, Hamburg, 2022**

Victor Gruen, einer der Vordenker der amerikanischen Shopping Malls, entwarf sie in der Mitte des 20. Jahrhunderts als multifunktionale Zentren, die nicht nur dem Konsum, sondern auch dem sozialen und kulturellen Leben dienen sollten – aber dieses Konzept ging auf Dauer nicht auf.

Im Vergleich zu einer verlassenen Kirche oder einer großen Lagerhalle – wie in *how to live in the echo of other places* (2022) – sind mir Kaufhäuser außerdem viel vertrauter. Dennoch war es eher Liebe auf den zweiten Blick. Kaufhäuser changieren zwischen Schönheit, Hässlichkeit und Alltäglichkeit, aber jedes einzelne hat auch eine individuelle Geschichte und Architektur, wie etwa die Galeria Berlin Alexanderplatz, als Centrum Warenhaus einst das größte Kaufhaus der DDR.

Die Diskussionen um den Leerstand werden stark geführt, vor allem wenn sich die Immobilie in Bestlage befindet. Über die Menschen, die von der Kaufhauskrise direkt betroffen sind, wird öffentlich jedoch weniger gesprochen. Das ist eine sehr diverse Gruppe, bestehend aus der Kund*innenschaft, Jugendlichen, für die es wichtige Aufenthaltsräume sind, und allen, die dort arbeiten: die Center und Store Manager*innen, Verkaufs- und Reinigungskräfte, Sicherheitsdienste usw. Sie alle interessieren mich.

PL: Die Arbeit berührt einige Themen, die in Berlin kontrovers diskutiert werden: Stadtplanung, soziale Ungleichheit, der Umgang mit Leerstand. Verfolgst du das Ziel, einen kritischen Diskursbeitrag zu leisten?

AK: Kurz nach der Ankündigung der drastischen Kultureinsparungen durch den Berliner Senat fiel ein Satz des Bürgermeisters, der mich bis heute beschäftigt. Er fragte sinngemäß, warum man Opernhäuser mit Steuergeldern finanzieren solle, wenn die „steuerzahlende Verkäuferin im Supermarkt" doch gar nicht in die Oper ginge. Das ist eine bezeichnende Perspektive von der Politik, sowohl auf Kultur als auch auf eine ganz spezifische Gruppe von Menschen, denen pauschal

century as multifunctional centres that would not only serve consumer needs, but also enhance social and cultural life; in the long term, however, this plan did not come to fruition.

Compared with an abandoned church or a large warehouse – like the one in *how to live in the echo of other places* (2022) – department stores are also much more familiar to me. Nevertheless, it was more of a case of love at second sight. Department stores oscillate between beauty, ugliness and mundanity, but each one also has its specific history and architectural identity – such as the Galeria Berlin Alexanderplatz, which – as Centrum Warenhaus – was once the largest department store in East Germany.

There are heated debates around the issue of properties standing empty, especially when these are in prime locations. But there is much less public discussion about the people who are directly affected by the department store crisis. This is a very diverse group that includes customers, young people for whom retail outlets are important places to hang out, and everyone who works there: the centre and store managers, sales and cleaning staff, security personnel, etc. All of these people interest me.

PL: *A Cashier's Opera* touches on some themes that are the subject of controversial debate in Berlin: urban planning, social inequality, approaches to vacant properties. Are you aiming to make a critical contribution to these debates?

AK: Shortly after the Berlin Senate announced that drastic cuts were going to be made in the cultural sector, the city's mayor said something that has stuck in my mind. He was essentially asking why opera houses should be funded with tax revenue when "the tax-paying supermarket cashier" doesn't even go to the opera. That's a telling political perspective – not only on culture, but also on a very specific group of people, who across the board are denied any interest in culture. Behind this statement also lies the assumption that culture must be financially self-sustaining – as if that were reason enough to cut public funding. Quite apart from the fact that

abgesprochen wird, sich für Kultur zu interessieren. Dahinter steht auch die Annahme, Kultur müsse sich selbst tragen – als wäre dies ein ausreichender Grund, öffentliche Mittel zu kürzen. Ganz abgesehen von der Ausgrenzung einer bestimmten Gruppe von der Kulturteilhabe und den offensichtlichen Existenzbedrohungen zahlreicher Kulturstätten, müsste man erstmal prüfen: Gehen Kassierer*innen tatsächlich nicht in die Oper? Interessieren sie sich wirklich nicht dafür? Und wäre allgemein die Hemmschwelle für einen Besuch nicht noch größer, wenn die Tickets teurer würden? Die Idee zu *A Cashier's Opera* war zunächst eine direkte Reaktion auf diese Aussage. Im Laufe der Konzeptentwicklung hat sich die Arbeit jedoch zu etwas Vielschichtigerem entwickelt, um vor allem die Bedeutung, Geschichte und den Wandel von Kaufhäusern in Berlin zu beleuchten. In dem Film werden unterschiedliche Kaufhäuser durch Performances aktiviert: Ein jugendlicher ‚Zombie-Chor' übernimmt eine Mall und performt ein A-cappella-Stück – eine Szene über Vergänglichkeit mit vielen kulturgeschichtlichen Anspielungen. Ein Sicherheitsmitarbeiter trifft während seiner nächtlichen Runden auf eine musikalische Darbietung, die dazu einlädt, über Kaufhäuser als Möglichkeitsräume nachzudenken. In vier Akten wird das Kaufhaus zur Bühne – nicht für die Warenpräsentation, sondern für eine akustische Auseinandersetzung mit seinen gesellschaftlichen, architektonischen und politischen Strukturen, um diese Orte genauer zu betrachten und anders zu sehen. Gleichzeitig wird deutlich, dass es auch um multiple Krisen geht, die vom Kaufhaus bis zur Kulturszene reichen.

PL: In deinen Filmen bleibt die Kamera gerne auf Umgebungsdetails ruhen, beiläufige Gesten fängst du ebenfalls sehr feinfühlig ein. Worin liegt hier dein Interesse?

AK: Zu Beginn des Drehs gibt es einen Plan, der aber währenddessen oft verworfen wird, weil wir immer wieder Neues entdecken. Mir ist wichtig, das gefilmte Material selbst zu

this approach excludes a particular group from cultural participation and poses an existential threat to numerous cultural venues, one ought to first of all find out if it's even true that cashiers don't go to the opera. Do they really have no interest in it? And would the barrier to attending the opera not be even higher for people in general if tickets cost more?

The idea behind *A Cashier's Opera* was initially a direct response to the mayor's statement. During the elaboration of the concept, however, the work became something more complex that aimed above all to highlight the significance, history and transformation of department stores and shopping centres in Berlin. In the film, a number of these are "activated" by performances: a choir of young "zombies" takes over a mall and performs an a cappella piece in a scene that addresses the theme of transience and contains many historical and cultural references; a security guard on his nightly rounds encounters a musical performance that invites listeners to consider department stores as realms of possibility. In four acts, these venues become stages – not for the presentation of goods for sale, but for an acoustic exploration of their social, political and architectural structures, encouraging us to examine these places more closely and view them in a different way. At the same time, it becomes evident that *A Cashier's Opera* addresses multiple crises in areas that range from department stores and shopping malls to the cultural scene.

PL: In your films, the camera often lingers on details of the surroundings, and incidental gestures are also captured with great subtlety. Why have you chosen to include such elements in your films? What interests you about them?

AK: We have a plan when we start filming, but this often gets overturned because we're always discovering new things. It's important for me to personally view the filmed footage and also to edit it myself. It's a meditative process that involves a lot of observation and decision-making. I love watching scenes over and over again, discovering details that I didn't notice during the shoot.

sichten und auch selbst zu schneiden. Das ist ein meditativer Prozess, in dem ich viel beobachte und entscheide. Ich liebe es, Szenen immer wieder anzuschauen und auf Details zu stoßen, die mir beim Dreh entgangen sind. Mir würde es schon ein wenig im Herzen wehtun, wenn jemand anderes schneiden würde, weil ich dann nicht wüsste, was ich alles abgebe. Wichtig ist wiederum, dass andere aus dem Team nochmal draufschauen und mir beim Fine-Tuning helfen, denn oft verliere ich den Blick in bestimmten Details. Den Betrachter*innen möchte ich schließlich die Möglichkeit geben, in Ruhe zu entdecken und zu beobachten.

PL: Wenn sich im Schnitt nochmal so viel ändert, weicht das Resultat dann sehr von dem ab, was du dir zuvor ausgemalt hast?

AK: Ich schätze, dass spontane Änderungen beim Schnitt ungefähr ein Drittel einer Filmarbeit einnehmen – und das können sogar grundlegende Entscheidungen zur Präsentationsform sein. Die Videoinstallation *Infra Voice* (2018), in der Giraffen auf den Klang des historischen Streichinstruments Oktobass treffen, war ursprünglich nicht als Dreikanal-Installation gedacht. *Le Chant des Maisons* sollte nie in Kapitel unterteilt sein. Und bei *Gravity's Tune* (2023) war anfangs nicht geplant, dass zwei wissenschaftliche Vorträge über Gravitationswellen in den Film integriert werden. Es war ein absoluter Zufall, dass der Physiker Keith Thorne seine Vorträge fast wortgleich an den beiden Drehorten hielt, in Los Angeles und Livingston, Louisiana. Durch den Schnitt wirkt er im Film wie eine Art Vermittler zwischen den Welten: dem Teleskop, dem LIGO-Institut zur Erforschung von Gravitationswellen (Laser Interferometer Gravitational-Wave Observatory) und der Konzertbühne, auf der die wissenschaftlichen Erkenntnisse als Musikstück interpretiert werden.

PL: Elemente aus deinen Filmen treten mitunter auch als Objekte installativ im Raum auf. Erweiterst du den Film damit ins Dreidimensionale?

I would find it a bit painful if someone else did the editing, because then I wouldn't know what I had given up. But it's also important that other members of the team engage in the fine-tuning process. Since I tend to dive deeply into details, they really help me to keep the big picture in mind. Ultimately, I want to give viewers the chance to discover and interpret things for themselves.

PL: If so much changes during the editing process, is the result very different to what you had previously imagined?

AK: I would estimate that spontaneous changes during the editing process make up around a third of each film – and these can even be fundamental decisions on the form of presentation. For example, the video installation *Infra Voice* (2018) – in which giraffes are confronted with the sound of an octobass, a historical string instrument – was not originally conceived as a three-channel installation. *Le Chant des Maisons* was never intended to be divided into chapters. And when I started working on *Gravity's Tune* (2023), I hadn't planned to incorporate two scientific lectures on gravitational waves into the film. It was pure coincidence that the lectures given by physicist Keith Thorne in the two filming locations – Los Angeles and Livingston, Louisiana – were almost identical. The edited footage makes him appear like a kind of a mediator between the worlds: between the telescope, the science lab LIGO (Laser Interferometer Gravitational-Wave Observatory) and the concert hall stage where the scientific findings are interpreted as a musical composition.

PL: Elements from your films sometimes appear as objects installed in the exhibition space. Are you thereby extending the film into the third dimension?

AK: The first time I ventured into the realm of installation was in the presentation of *Le Chant des Maisons*. I had of course created spatial stagings prior to that, but at the Lyon Biennale in 2022 I presented objects in the exhibition space that clearly related to the film. In the huge factory hall where I was able to mount a large-scale

AK: Zum ersten Mal ins Installative gegangen bin ich mit *Le Chant des Maisons*. Natürlich gab es davor immer räumliche Inszenierungen, aber ich hatte bis zur Lyon Biennale 2022 noch keine klar zugehörigen Objekte im Raum präsentiert. In der riesigen Fabrikhalle, in der ich meinen Biennale-Beitrag großformatig zeigen durfte, waren auch historische Lochkarten ausgestellt, die einst bei der Seidenweberei verwendet wurden und den im Film genutzten perforierten Orgelspiel-Karten stark ähneln. Außerdem waren die hölzernen Bauteile jenes Hauses zu sehen, das im Film von den Handwerkern inmitten der Kirche aufgebaut wird.

Für *La Banda* habe ich mit speziellen Sitzkissen erstmals neue, funktionale und spielerische Objekte für den Raum entworfen. In Anlehnung an die zahlreichen Verkaufsschilder an den Häusern in Olevano Romano, die ich als Marker für die Transformation des Dorfes begreife, entstand zudem eine Serie neu konzipierter Schilder. Mit diesen Wandobjekten kann die Erzählung aus dem Film noch weitergehen, da sie neue Denkräume öffnen. Ein Film ist für mich mehr als nur das bewegte Bild und eine Ausstellung gibt die Möglichkeit, das weiterzudenken.

> PL: À propos Ausstellung: Lass uns zu den historischen Übergangen des Hamburger Bahnhof gehen, in denen du *My Favorite Music* zeigst. Warum wird die Arbeit ausgerechnet in diesen Zwischenräumen gezeigt, die die Ost- und Westflügel mit dem Hauptgebäude verbinden?

AK: *My Favorite Music* ist eine Soundinstallation von 2020, die sich mit dem Hauptbahnhof in Hamburg beschäftigt. Schon während meines Studiums lief in den Unterführungen klassische Musik, wo sonst Durchsagen heraustönen. Eigentlich etwas Schönes, allerdings ursprünglich gedacht, um Menschen fernzuhalten, die dort schlafen, herumlungern oder Drogen konsumieren würden. Es ist eine bemerkenswerte Annahme, dass eine bestimmte Kunstform – in diesem Fall klassische Musik – so unerträglich sei, dass sie

presentation of my Biennale contribution, I displayed some historical punch cards that were once used in silk weaving and look very similar to the perforated organ-playing cards used in the film. The installation in Lyon also included the wooden components of the house-like structure that can be seen in the film, being built by the carpenters in the middle of the church.

The special floor cushions I designed for *La Banda* were the first new functional and playful objects I had made for a spatial installation. In allusion to the numerous 'For Sale' signs on the houses in Olevano Romano, which for me symbolise the transformation of the village, I also created a series of new signs. The film narrative can thus be extended via these wall objects, as they open up new worlds of thought. In my view, a film is more than just the moving image, and an exhibition provides a good opportunity to elaborate on this idea.

> PL: Apropos exhibition – let's talk about the historical passageways in Hamburger Bahnhof where you are showing *My Favorite Music*. What made you decide to present the work in these intermediate spaces which connect the east and west wings to the main building?

AK: *My Favorite Music* is a sound installation from 2020 that relates to Hamburg's main railway station – the Hauptbahnhof. Back when I was a student, the station operators had already started playing classical music over loudspeakers in the underpasses. Although this sounds like a nice idea, the music was actually intended to discourage people from loitering, sleeping or using drugs there. It's a remarkable assumption that a particular art form – in this case classical music – is so unbearable that it will drive certain groups of people away. What significance is attributed to music here? Music is meant to be something people consciously listen to, are touched by and willingly spend time with, but here it has been turned into the complete opposite.

For my work, I recorded a lot of sounds in situ. In these field recordings you can hear the surroundings, including the voices of passers-by and occasionally some rude remarks. I also

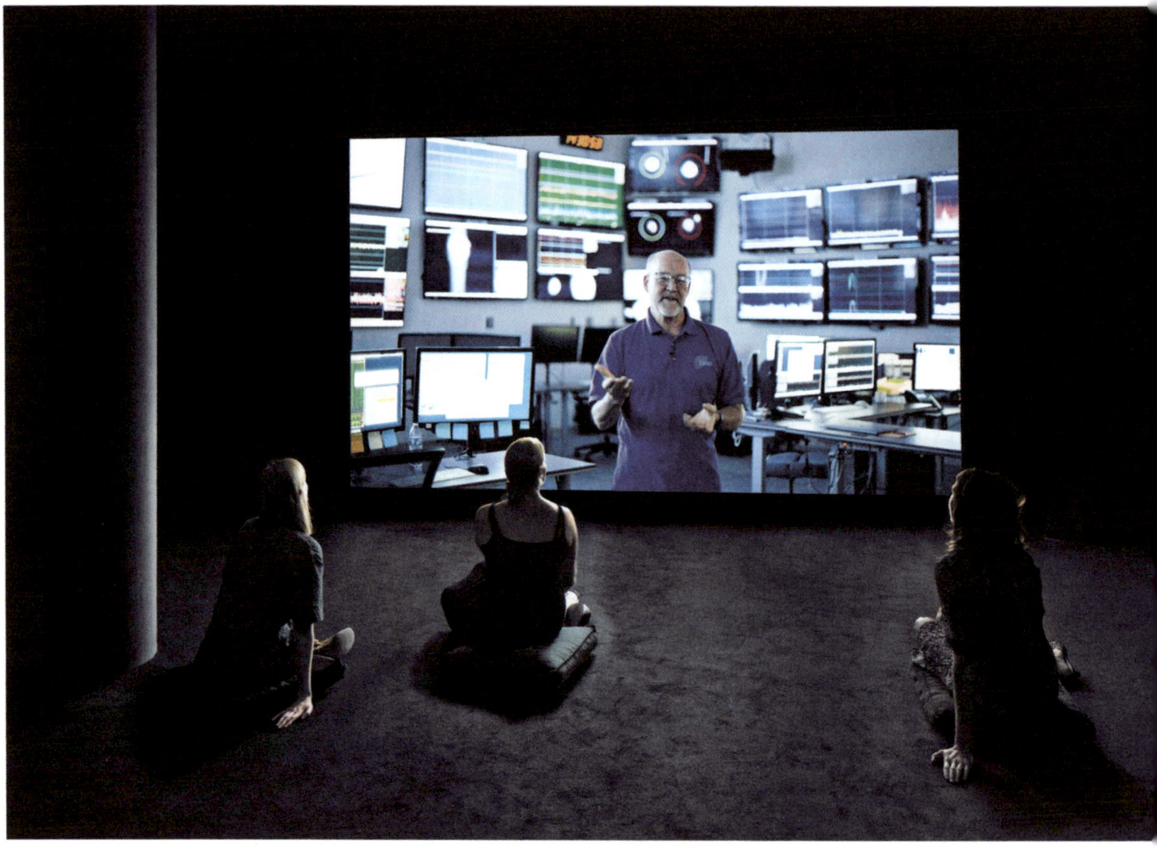

Annika Kahrs, *Gravity's Tune*, 2023, 4K Video, Farbe, Ton / colour, sound, 25:35 Min., Ausstellungsansicht / exhibition view Schering Stiftung, Berlin, 2023

bestimmte Personengruppen vertreibt. Welche Bedeutung wird der Musik hier zugesprochen? Musik, die eigentlich dazu da ist, bewusst gehört zu werden, zu berühren und mit ihr zu verweilen, wird hier ins komplette Gegenteil verkehrt.

Für meine Arbeit habe ich Tonaufnahmen in situ gemacht. Bei diesen Field Recordings hört man die Umgebungsgeräusche, darunter Passant*innen und Pöbeleien. Zusätzlich habe ich Verkäufer*innen der Straßenzeitung *Hinz&Kunzt* interviewt und sie nach ihren Bezügen zu Musik und nach ihren Lieblingssongs befragt. Einfache Fragen, auf die viel erzählt werden kann und die viel auslösen. Mir ging es darum, jene Menschen einzubeziehen, die diese Musiksituation tagtäglich erleben.

Diese Arbeit nun im ehemaligen Bahnhof zu zeigen, der für die Zugverbindung Berlin–Hamburg diente, ist natürlich sehr passend. Wie in Hamburg nimmt man den Sound in

interviewed people who sell the street newspaper *Hinz&Kunzt* about their relationship to music and their favourite songs. Simple questions that can be elaborated upon easily and reveal a lot. My aim was to involve the people who experience this music-related situation on a daily basis.

It is of course very fitting to be showing this work here, in the building that once served as a terminus of the Berlin-Hamburg railway line. As in Hamburg's main station, the sounds being played in the passageways of Hamburger Bahnhof during my exhibition might be perceived only incidentally by visitors. But they also have the opportunity to sit down and listen to the original voices of the interviewees over headphones; their responses, in German and Romanian, have been transcribed and translated into different languages for visitors to read.

PL: Underpasses, department stores, a church or a whole village – your artworks

den Zwischengängen des Museums vielleicht auch erst nur beiläufig wahr. Man kann sich aber auch hinsetzen und sich die originalen Stimmen aus den Interviews, auf Deutsch und Rumänisch, mit Kopfhörern anhören und sie transkribiert und in verschiedene Sprachen übersetzt lesen.

PL: Unterführungen, Kaufhäuser, eine Kirche oder ein ganzes Dorf – deine Arbeiten setzen sich mit den unterschiedlichsten Räumen auseinander. Was definiert für dich einen Raum? Was macht einen Ort für dich besonders?

AK: Ein Raum besteht für mich nicht nur aus Wänden, sondern aus einer Stimmung, seiner (akustischen) Geschichte und den Menschen, die sich in ihm aufhalten. Er weckt mein Interesse, wenn in ihm mehr Fragen aufkommen als Antworten gefunden werden und wenn er sich im Wandel befindet – in welche Richtung auch immer. Für mich ist es spannend, in Momenten des Potenziellen einzugreifen. In der verlassenen Kirche in Lyon, die einer von vielen besichtigten Orten während der Vorbereitung der Biennale war, zeigte sich mein Bedürfnis, etwas mit dem Ort zu machen, sehr eindeutig. Es gab Impulse, die sofort inhaltliche Gedanken hervorgerufen haben. Ähnlich ging es mir mit *how to live in the echo of other places* (2022). Mit dem letzten unsanierten Speichergebäude in der Hamburger HafenCity lag ein riesiger Imaginationsraum, ein großes Fragezeichen vor mir. Niemand wusste, was mit dem Gebäude passiert. Die Stadt hatte Pläne für das teure Grundstück und die Bürger*innen hatten Ideen, weil sie sich dort gerne aufhielten. Es war noch alles möglich und vieles vorstellbar. Dieses Noch-nicht-Festgelegte, das Liminale ist zentral für meine Arbeitsweise. Ich suche solche Orte, aber sie finden mich auch.

Was über sie in der Politik, der Presse oder innerhalb bestimmter Communities diskutiert wird, fließt in meine Konzeptentwicklungen mit ein, wie aktuell bei den Shopping Malls. Ich finde, dass Kunst ein gutes Mittel sein kann, gemeinsam über Orte nachzudenken und neue Perspektiven zu eröffnen.

address a wide range of places and spaces. What defines a space for you? What makes a place special in the context of your work?

AK: For me, a space consists not only of its walls but also of its specific atmosphere, its (acoustic) history and the people who spend time there. A place will spark my interest if it provides more questions than answers, and if it is undergoing a process of transformation –no matter what direction this will take it in. I find it exciting to intervene in precisely such moments of potentiality. In the abandoned church in Lyon, which was one of many places I visited during my preparations for the Biennale, I had a very strong sense that I wanted to do something with that space. Certain impulses there immediately sparked ideas for the content of the work. It was a similar situation with *how to live in the echo of other places* (2022). The last unrenovated warehouse building in Hamburg's HafenCity presented itself to me as a huge realm of the imagination, a big question mark. Nobody knew what was going to happen with this building. The City of Hamburg had plans for the valuable piece of real estate, and Hamburg citizens had their own ideas, because it was a popular place to hang out. Everything was still possible, and many different options were conceivable. This not-yet-determined or liminal quality is central to my practice. I seek out such places and sometimes they actually find me. The debates being held about them in the political realm, in the press or among particular communities are incorporated into the concept of my work – as is currently the case with the department stores. I believe that art can be a good means with which to think collectively about places and open up new perspectives.

PL: With the presentation at the Musikinstrumenten-Museum, your exhibition includes an external venue you've long been enthusiastic about. What does it mean to you to be showing your work there now – also against the backdrop of your previous works involving unusual historical instruments, as in *Infra Voice*?

PL: Mit dem Musikinstrumenten-Museum stellst du an einem externen Ort aus, von dem du schon lange begeistert bist. Was bedeutet es dir, nun dort auszustellen – auch vor dem Hintergrund deiner bisherigen Beschäftigung mit besonderen historischen Instrumenten wie in *Infra Voice*?

AK: Das Museum ist voll von interessanten Instrumenten, woraus ich noch viel mehr schöpfen könnte. Mittendrin werden im Frühjahr 2026 die Performances *Strings* (2010) und *Alone Together* (2016) aufgeführt. Beide übrigens mit dem Solistenensemble Kaleidoskop, das auch in *A Cashier's Opera* auftritt. Während der gesamten Ausstellungslaufzeit ist dort außerdem die vierte Videoarbeit der Ausstellung zu sehen: *Ganz ungültig, nur ein Versuch* (2024). Eine Szene aus dem Film, der sich mit der ‚Nullten', der ungültigen Sinfonie von Anton Bruckner aus dem 19. Jahrhundert auseinandersetzt, wurde dort sogar gedreht. Da sich meine Ausstellung mit unterschiedlichen Orten und Räumen beschäftigt, passt es gut, dass die Besucher*innen angeregt werden, weitere Orte zu erkunden.

PL: Dazu zählt auch das ganz in der Nähe des Hamburger Bahnhof gelegene Berliner Medizinhistorische Museum der Charité – für mich ein überraschender Satellit. Wie kam es zu dieser Kooperation?

AK: Die Initiative zur Zusammenarbeit kam vom Hamburger Bahnhof, weil sich das Museum im Zuge seines 30-jährigen Jubiläums 2026 stärker mit der Nachbar*innenschaft vernetzen möchte. Aus diesem Anlass entwickle ich eine neue Performance mit dem Titel *zum Sonnendeck* (2026), eigens für das Solistenensemble Kaleidoskop. Sie wird in der beeindruckenden Hörsaalruine aufgeführt, einem heutigen Veranstaltungsraum des Museums. Inhaltlich beschäftigt sich die Arbeit mit Prozessen von Heilung und Veränderung, sowohl auf persönlicher als auch auf gesellschaftlicher Ebene. Was passiert, wenn ein Mensch einen Transformationsprozess durchlebt hat? Und wie sieht das für

AK: The museum is filled with really interesting musical instruments from which I could definitely draw even more inspiration. In spring 2026, my works *Strings* (2010) and *Alone Together* (2016) will be performed in the midst of this collection of instruments. Incidentally, both performances are being presented in collaboration with Solistenensemble Kaleidoskop, who also appear in *A Cashier's Opera*. And for the duration of my exhibition, the fourth video piece – *Ganz ungültig, nur ein Versuch* (2024) – will also be screened at the Musikinstrumenten-Museum. One scene from that film – which focuses on the 19th-century symphony by Anton Bruckner that was declared invalid by the composer and is now known as *Die Nullte* ["No. 0"] – was actually shot in this location. Given that my exhibition is concerned with a range of different places and spaces, it seems appropriate that visitors are being encouraged to explore additional locations.

PL: These include the Medizinhistorisches Museum der Charité [Medical History Museum of the Charité Hospital], which is located very close to Hamburger Bahnhof. I was surprised that you chose this site as a satellite venue. How did that cooperation come about?

AK: This particular cooperation was initiated by Hamburger Bahnhof because, in the context of its 30th anniversary in 2026, the museum is seeking to establish stronger links with neighbouring institutions. With this in mind, I'm currently developing a new performance piece specially for Solistenensemble Kaleidoskop. Entitled *zum Sonnendeck* (2026), it'll be performed in the impressive ruin of the former lecture hall that is now a venue for events at the Medizinhistorisches Museum. Thematically, *zum Sonnendeck* deals with processes of healing and transformation, on both a personal and a societal level. What happens when a person has lived through a process of transformation? And what does that look like for an entire urban community? In this work, I refer among others to the history of the Berlin Wall, which ran directly between Hamburger Bahnhof (then in West

eine ganze Stadtgesellschaft aus? Ich verweise unter anderem auf die Geschichte der Berliner Mauer, die einst direkt zwischen dem Hamburger Bahnhof (damals in West-Berlin) und der Charité (in Ost-Berlin) verlief. Auf dem Dach der Charité befand sich – und befindet sich noch – ein Sonnendeck, das der Erholung von Patient*innen diente. Als die Mauer stand, wurde der Zugang jedoch gesperrt, um den Blick auf den Mauerstreifen und West-Berlin zu verhindern. Über diese historische Dimension hinaus denke ich auch an die Corona-Pandemie als einen kollektiven Einschnitt, den wir gesellschaftlich, so glaube ich, noch gar nicht verarbeitet haben.

PL: Der Kreis zur Kathedrale aus *Le Chant des Maisons* schließt sich, indem du in der Heilige-Geist-Kirche in Moabit eine weitere Live-Performance aufführen wirst. Was passiert dort?

AK: In *the lord loves changes, it's one of his greatest delusions,* 2018 ursprünglich als Videoarbeit konzipiert, pfeift eine Gruppe von Menschen gegen ein Orgelspiel an – eine Ausschöpfung der Dehnbarkeit von Musik, aber auch ein Akt des Widerstands sowie eine Reflektion über Protestkultur. Für die Filmaufnahme hatte ich bewusst keinen sakralen Raum gewählt, sondern die mit einer Konzertorgel ausgestattete Hamburger Laeiszhalle, weil ich religiöse Assoziationen vermeiden wollte. Umso interessanter ist es, die Performance jetzt in einer Kirche neu zu arrangieren, und zu beobachten, inwiefern sich die Arbeit dadurch verändert. Die Performance ist ein sehr intensives akustisches Erlebnis, das für die Performer*innen und das Publikum physisch total erschöpfend ist.

Entstanden ist die Arbeit für eine Ausstellung bei Savvy Contemporary, die sich dem US-amerikanischen Komponisten und Künstler Julius Eastman widmete. In seinem Werk spielen institutionelle Kritik und eine spirituelle Auseinandersetzung mit Religion und Protest eine große Rolle. Sein Musikstück *Gay Guerrilla* (1979) bezieht sich unter anderem auf den Choral *Ein feste Burg ist unser Gott*

Berlin) and the Charité Hospital (in East Berlin). On the roof of the Charité there was – and still is – a sun deck that patients could use as a place to relax. When the Wall was built, however, access to the sun deck was blocked so as to obstruct the view of the "death strip" and of West Berlin. Above and beyond this historical dimension, I am also thinking about the COVID-19 pandemic as a collective caesura that we as a society have surely not yet processed.

PL: You're also tracing a full circle back to the cathedral in *Le Chant des Maisons* by staging a further live performance in the Heilige-Geist-Kirche [Church of the Holy Spirit], a church in the neighbourhood of Moabit. What's going to happen there?

AK: In *the lord loves changes, it's one of his greatest delusions*, which was originally conceived as a video piece in 2018, a group of people whistle in opposition to the sound of an organ being played. This is not only an exploration of the elasticity of music, but also an act of resistance and a reflection on protest culture. When selecting the filming location in 2018, I deliberately chose the Laeiszhalle, a concert hall in Hamburg with a large pipe organ, rather than a sacred space, because I wanted to avoid religious associations. That makes it all the more interesting to be arranging the upcoming performance in a church, and to observe how the work changes as a result. The performance is a very intense and totally exhausting acoustic experience – for the performers, but also for the audience.

I created *the lord loves changes, it's one of his greatest delusions* for an exhibition at Savvy Contemporary in Berlin that was devoted to the American composer and artist Julius Eastman. Institutional critique and a spiritual approach to religion and protest were central to Eastman's practice. His musical composition *Gay Guerrilla* (1979) refers, among other things, to Martin Luther's chorale *Ein Feste Burg ist unser Gott* (A Mighty Fortress Is Our God; written before 1529). This protestant hymn has been appropriated, rearranged and also abused in many different contexts throughout its history – for example during the two world wars. Eastman reinterpreted the

(vor 1529) von Martin Luther. Dieses protestantische Lied wurde in der Geschichte immer wieder angeeignet, umgeformt und auch missbraucht – z.B. in den beiden Weltkriegen. Eastman deutete das Stück zu einem queeren Protestsong um. Mir geht es in meiner Arbeit weniger um eine direkte Auseinandersetzung mit seiner Person oder seinem beeindruckenden Werk, sondern um abstrakte Themen wie Transformation, Protest und die symbolische Kraft von Klang und Stimme.

PL: Räumlich am weitesten vom Hamburger Bahnhof entfernt zeigst du eine Neuauflage der Videoarbeit *how to live in the echo of other places* – nicht in einer Shopping Mall, sondern auf einer Shopping-Meile, dem Kurfürstendamm in Berlin-Charlottenburg. Was hat dich zur Präsentation einer/dieser Arbeit inmitten des geschäftigen Großstadttreibens bewegt?

AK: Ingrid Buschmann hat diesen 104 m² großen LED-Screen am Ku'damm als möglichen Ort für die Videoarbeit entdeckt und die Betreiber waren sofort begeistert, dort auch Kunst zu zeigen. Ich finde es natürlich toll, dass ich diese Arbeit jeden Abend im öffentlichen Raum präsentieren darf. Die ursprüngliche Version entstand im Rahmen eines größeren Projekts in Kooperation mit *Imagine the City* (2022) im Hamburger Hafen und wurde dort auf 14 m Länge von Sonnenuntergang bis Sonnenaufgang auf eine Lagerhalle projiziert. Jetzt gibt es eine speziell für Berlin produzierte Iteration. Jeden Abend unterbricht eines der zwei- bis fünfminütigen Videos die Abfolge der sehr schnellen und kurzen Werbeclips.

Meine Videos zeigen einen digital erzeugten, leuchtenden Sonnenuntergang, in dem Wort für Wort persönliche Erinnerungen erscheinen. Diese stammen von unterschiedlichen Menschen, mit denen ich im Kontext der Ausstellung zusammenarbeite. Die erzählten Geschichten sind kurz, oft nicht länger als drei oder vier Sätze. Durch die Wortabfolge setzen sie sich erst beim Lesen stückweise zusammen. Das verlangt Geduld, aber gerade

piece as a queer protest song. My work is less concerned with directly referencing Eastman as a person or his impressive oeuvre than with exploring abstract themes such as transformation, protest and the symbolic power of sound and the human voice.

PL: In the location furthest away from Hamburger Bahnhof, you are showing a new iteration of your video *how to live in the echo of other places* – not in a shopping mall, but on a shopping mile – the Kurfürstendamm in Berlin's Charlottenburg district. What inspired you to present a work/this work in a bustling city environment?

AK: Ingrid Buschmann discovered the 104 m² LED screen on the Ku'damm as a possible location for the video screening, and the owners were immediately enthusiastic about the idea of showing art on the screen. I am of course delighted to be able to present this work in a public space every evening. The original version was produced as part of a larger project in cooperation with *Imagine the City* (2022), which was staged in Hamburg's HafenCity; my work was shown there on a similar scale, but from sunset to sunrise as a projection onto the front of a warehouse building. An iteration of this piece has now been produced specially for Berlin. Every evening, one of my videos – which last between two and five minutes – interrupts the rapid sequence of very short adverts being shown on the screen.

My videos show a digitally created glowing sunset that serves as a backdrop for personal memories, which appear one word at a time as texts on the screen. These texts were provided by different people I worked with in the context of the exhibition. The stories they tell are short – often no more than three or four sentences long. The sequential presentation means that they come together piece by piece as you watch. This demands patience from the viewer, but that's precisely why I find the idea of presenting it on the Ku'damm so fitting. It's disconcerting or even irritating to watch, which may even lend it a resistant quality.

deswegen finde ich die Präsentation am Ku'damm richtig. Sie irritiert und bekommt vielleicht sogar etwas Widerständiges.

PL: Nach all den konkreten Orten, über die wir gesprochen haben, fällt der Sonnenuntergang aus dem Rahmen: ein Motiv, das uns als globale Gemeinschaft verbindet und dabei romantisch und scheinbar ortlos ist. Welche Intention verfolgst du mit diesem Slow-Motion-Bild?

AK: Trotz der Universalität – wir leben alle unter der gleichen Sonne – verbinden sich mit dem Sonnenuntergang ganz persönliche Geschichten, denen die eingeblendeten Worte Ausdruck verleihen, auch wenn diese nicht unbedingt inhaltlich mit dem Bildmotiv in Verbindung stehen. Vielmehr materialisieren sich mit jedem der aktuell über zwanzig Videos sowohl sehr beiläufige als auch bedeutsame Erinnerungen. Manchmal lässt sich erahnen, an welchen Orten man da ist.

Eine deiner ersten Fragen zielte darauf, wie sehr ich an das Publikum denke. Hier spielt es eine ganz wichtige Rolle. Denn der eigene Rhythmus, der Weg durch die Stadt, gerät kurz ins Stocken, wird verschoben oder gebrochen. Wer sich eigentlich auf dem Weg irgendwohin befindet, nimmt diesen Sonnenuntergang vielleicht wie eine Unterbrechung wahr. Meine Hoffnung ist, dass man sich eine der Geschichten mitnimmt und sich wundert, was das eigentlich war. In Zukunft soll die Arbeit auch an weiteren Orten im Außenraum präsentiert werden. Bei jeder Präsentation kommen neu generierte Sonnenuntergänge und neue Erinnerungen von Personen hinzu, die an der jeweiligen Ausstellung beteiligt sind.

PL: *OFF SCORE* ist deine bisher umfassendste Werkschau. Welche Bedeutung hat diese Ausstellung für dich?

AK: Für mich ist es spannend und wichtig, meine Arbeiten erstmals in diesem Umfang und Zusammenhang zu zeigen. In der Ausstellung zeigt sich, was sich auch in unserem

PL: After all the concrete locations we've been discussing, the sunset stands out: this motif connects us all as a global community, but at the same time it is romantic and seemingly placeless. What's the intention behind this slow-motion image you've created?

AK: Despite its universality – we are all living under the same sun – the sunset is associated with very personal stories that are conveyed by the projected words, even if these do not necessarily have a thematic connection to the visual motif. Instead, the currently over 20 videos evoke some very incidental as well as some very meaningful memories. Sometimes the viewer can guess where these memories were made. One of the first questions you asked related to how much I think about the audience. Here, the audience plays a very important role, because the viewer's individual rhythm, their journey through the city, is briefly interrupted, suspended or broken. A passer-by who is actually on their way somewhere may regard this sunset as an interruption. My hope is that people will take one of the stories with them and wonder, 'What was that?' The work will also be shown in other outdoor locations in the future. Each time it is shown, newly generated sunsets and a new selection of memories contributed by people involved in the respective exhibition will be incorporated into the work.

PL: *OFF SCORE* at Hamburger Bahnhof is the most comprehensive display of your works to date. What does this exhibition mean to you?

AK: It's exciting and important to be showing my work on this scale and in this context for the first time. The exhibition reveals what has also become clear during our conversation: individual elements in my works are frequently interconnected and many aspects are interwoven, even though each work has its own specific aims. It's particularly satisfying that my three main mediums – film, sound installation and performance – are put on an equal footing in this presentation, and also that a whole series of performances

Gespräch klar erkennen ließ: Individuelle Elemente beziehen sich immer wieder aufeinander und Vieles ist miteinander verwoben, obwohl jede Arbeit für sich genommen auf etwas anderes zielt. Besonders schön ist, dass Film, Soundinstallation und Performance als meine drei zentralen künstlerischen Medien gleichwertig präsentiert werden. Und auch dass eine ganze Performance-Reihe 2026 stattfindet. Ich bin sehr dankbar gegenüber dem gesamten Team des Hamburger Bahnhof, gegenüber Sam Bardaouil und Till Fellrath für die Einladung und vor allem Ingrid Buschmann für die inspirierende Zusammenarbeit, die gleichzeitig sehr viel Spaß gemacht hat.

Natürlich gibt es auch Werke, die nicht vertreten sind: Einige, die sich stärker mit naturwissenschaftlichen Aspekten auseinandersetzen – wie *Infra Voice* oder *Gravity's Tune* –, werden stattdessen dieses und nächstes Jahr in anderen Kontexten gezeigt.

Auch nach der Ausstellung wird die Auseinandersetzung mit Orten und ihren Bedeutungen sicherlich weiterhin eine tragende Rolle in meinen Arbeiten spielen. Ich habe das Gefühl, dass es dort noch Vieles zu entdecken und zu bearbeiten gibt. Für mich ist dieses Feld noch lange nicht erschöpft. Meine Herangehensweisen möchte ich in Zukunft noch viel mehr erweitern, und dabei ist noch komplett offen, in welche Richtungen das gehen kann.

PL: Darauf bin ich sehr gespannt! Vielen Dank für das Gespräch – und dafür, dass du akustische Geschichten freilegst, die ansonsten verborgen bleiben.

will take place in 2026. I am very grateful to the entire team at Hamburger Bahnhof – to Sam Bardaouil and Till Fellrath for inviting me, and above all to Ingrid Buschmann for the inspiring and highly enjoyable collaboration. Of course there are works of mine that are not included here: some pieces that specifically address scientific themes – such as *Infra Voice* or *Gravity's Tune* – will be shown in other contexts later this year or in 2026. Even after this exhibition, exploring different places and their meanings will no doubt continue to play a pivotal role in my work. I have a feeling that there is still a lot to be discovered and elaborated in this field, which for me is far from exhausted. I'd like to expand my approaches even further in the future, and it's impossible to say what direction this will take me in.

PL: I'm excited to see where it takes you! Thank you for this conversation – and for uncovering acoustic (hi)stories that would otherwise remain hidden.

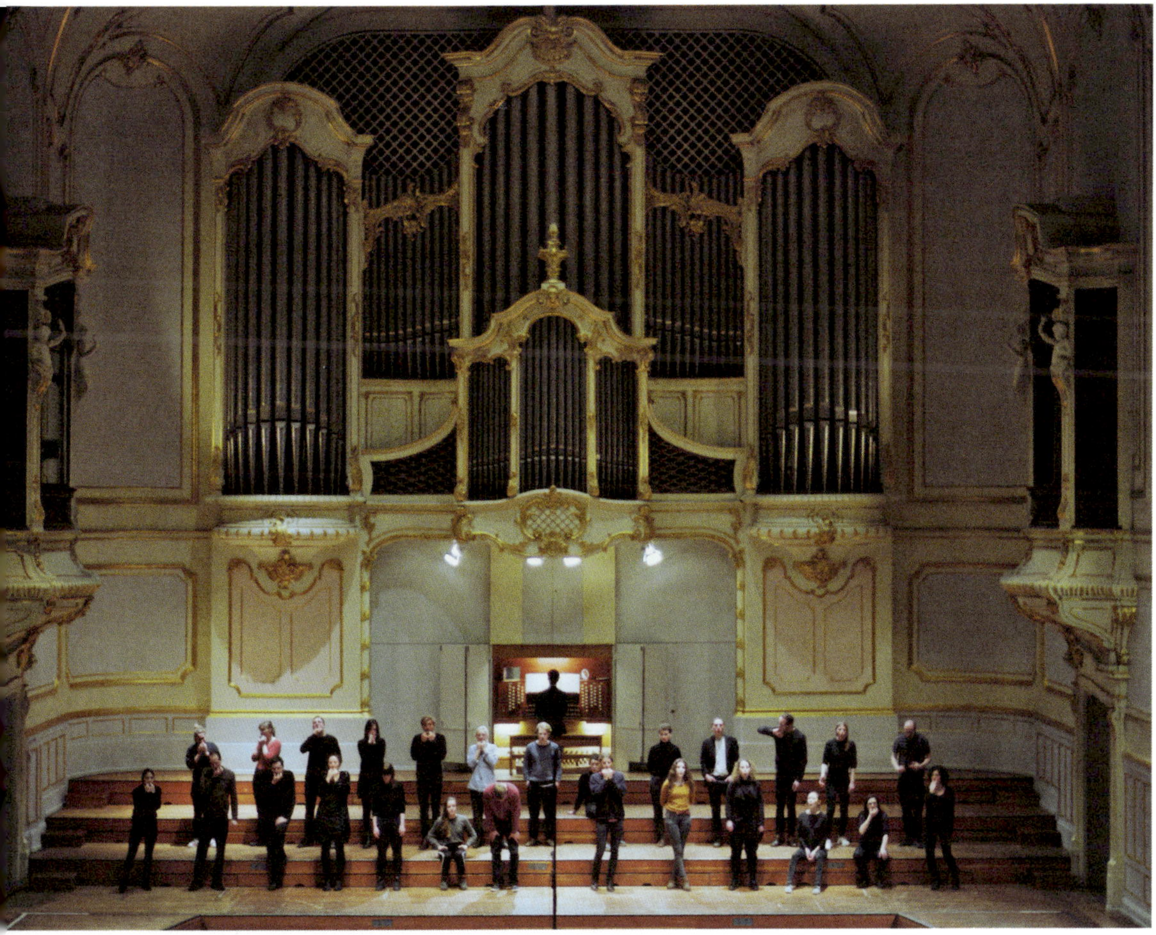

Annika Kahrs, *the lord loves changes, it's one of his greatest delusions,* 2018,
HD Video, Farbe, Ton / colour, sound, 15:49 Min., Videostandbild / video still

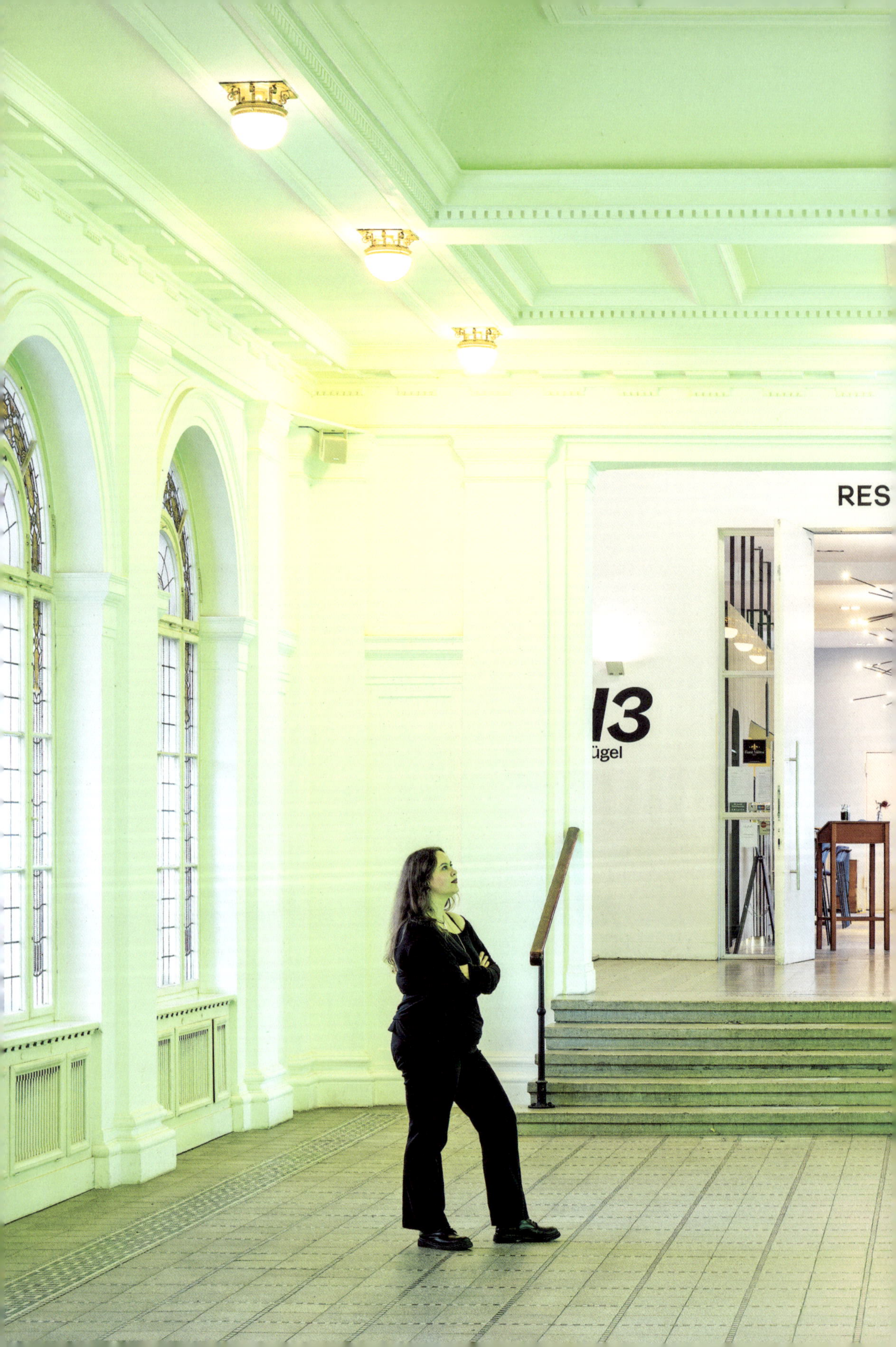
RES
ügel

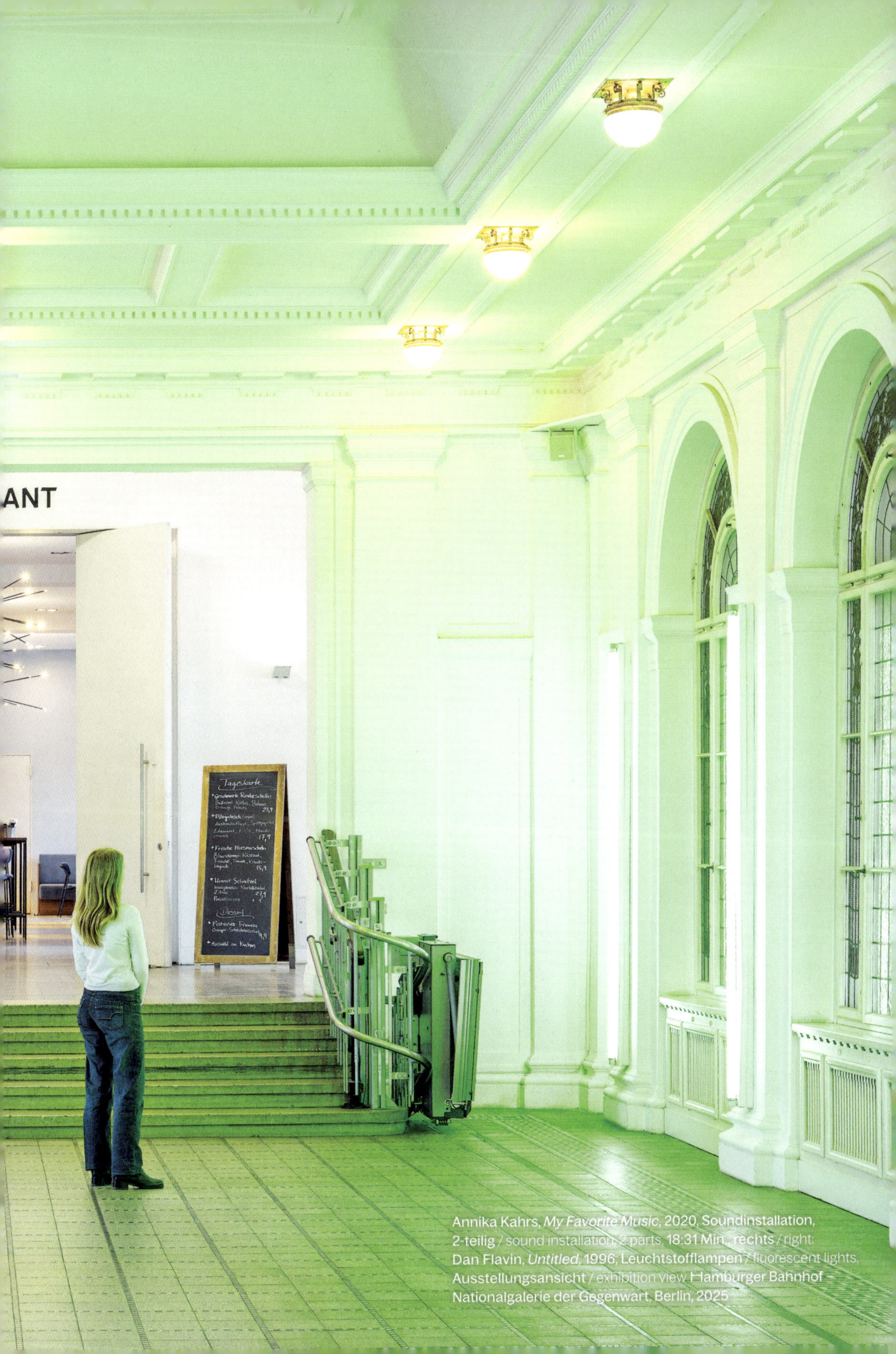

Annika Kahrs, *My Favorite Music*, 2020, Soundinstallation, 2-teilig / sound installation, 2 parts, 18:31 Min., rechts / right: Dan Flavin, *Untitled*, 1996, Leuchtstofflampen / fluorescent lights, Ausstellungsansicht / exhibition view Hamburger Bahnhof – Nationalgalerie der Gegenwart, Berlin, 2025

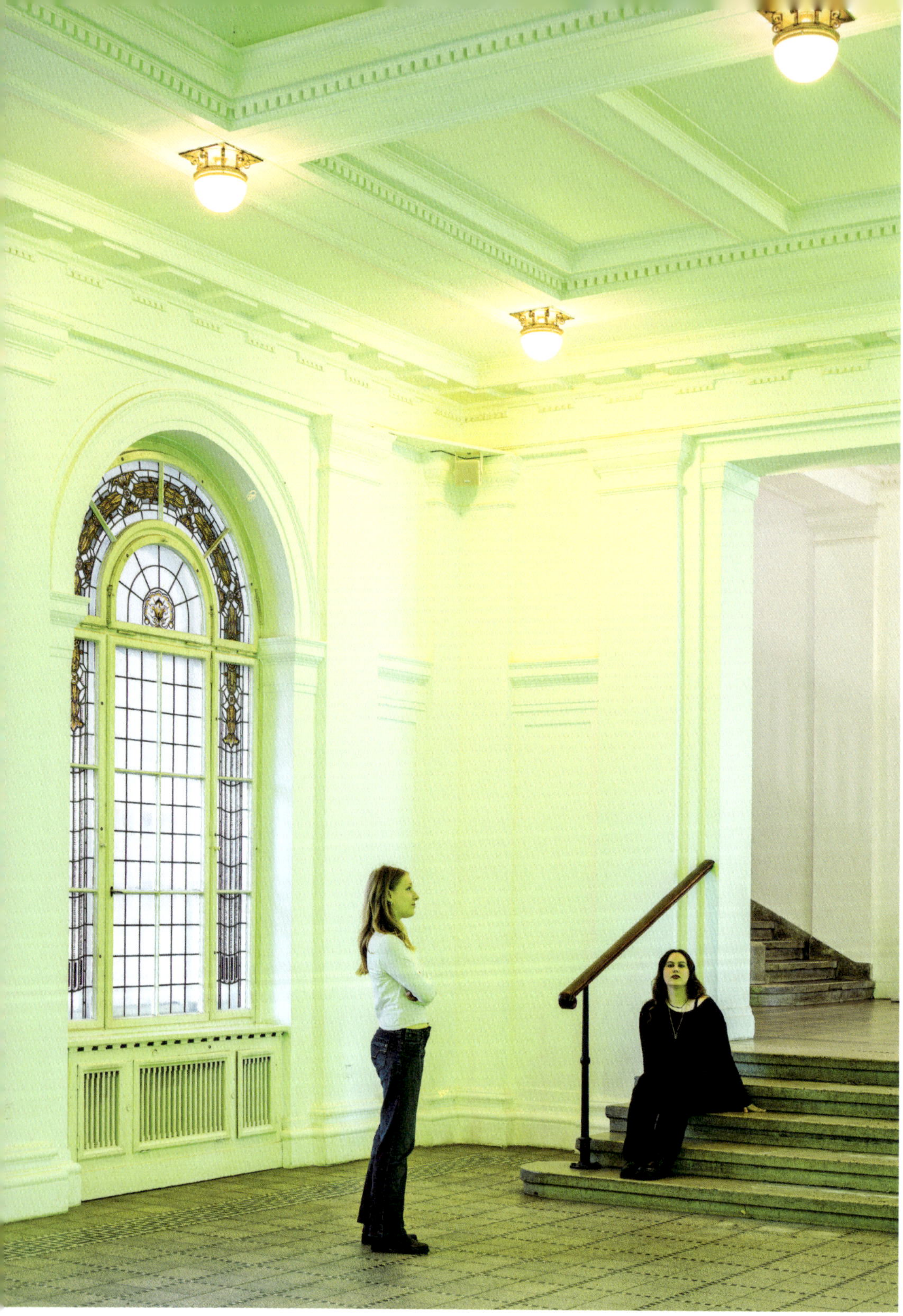

Annika Kahrs, *My Favorite Music,* 2020, Soundinstallation, 2-teilig / sound installation, 2 parts, 18:31 Min., Ausstellungsansicht / exhibition view Hamburger Bahnhof – Nationalgalerie der Gegenwart, Berlin, 2025

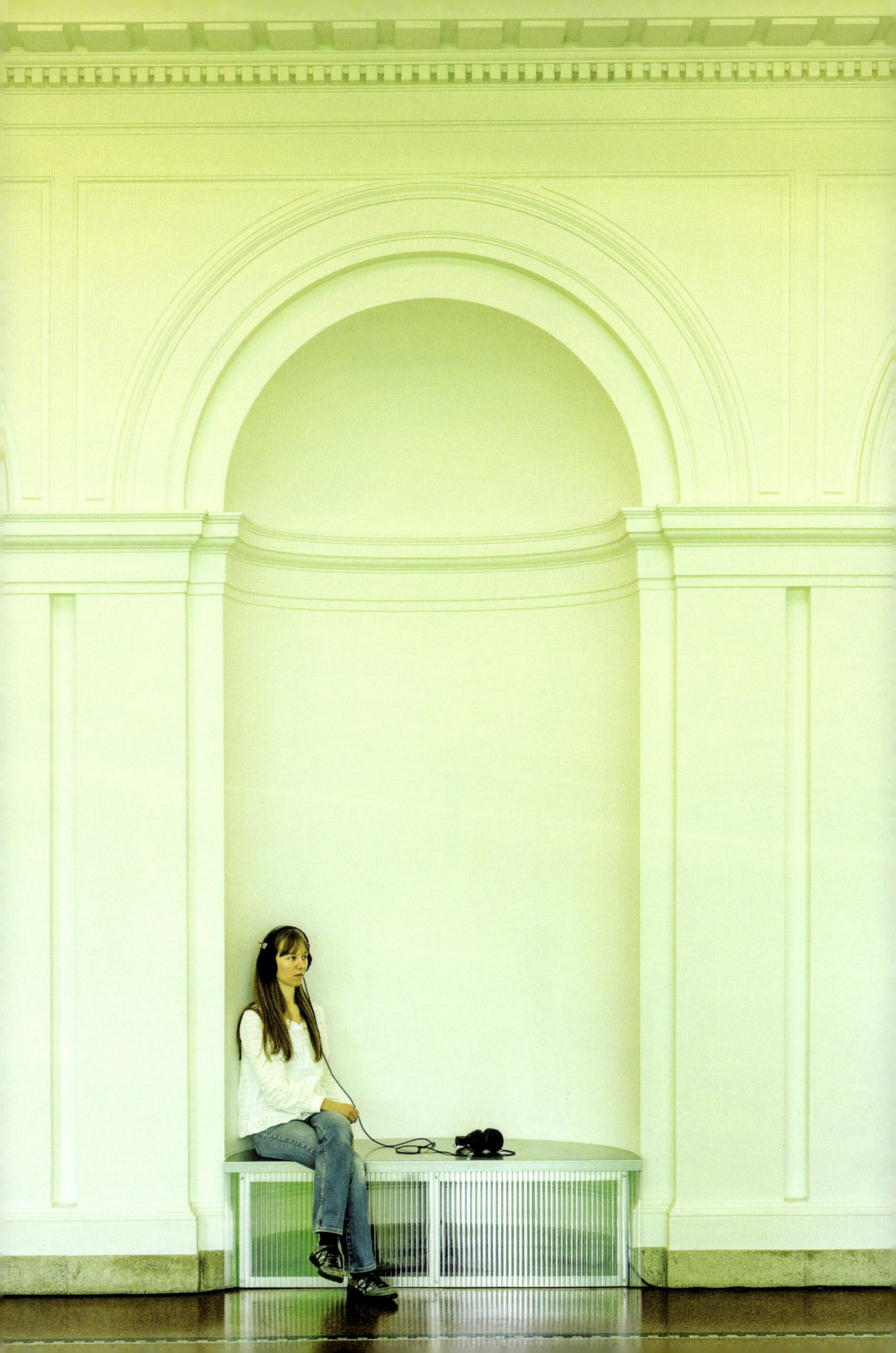

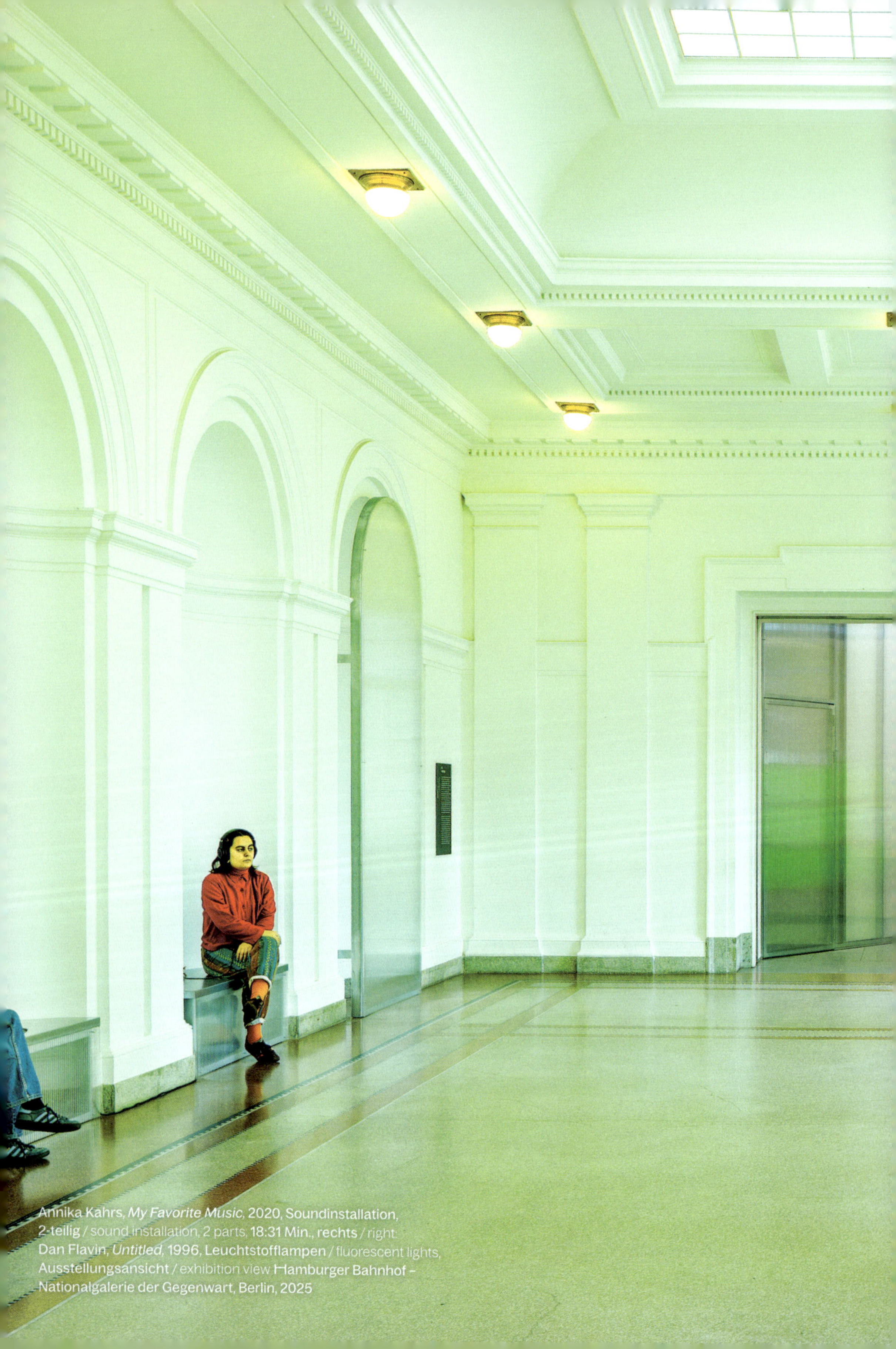

Annika Kahrs, *My Favorite Music*, 2020, Soundinstallation, 2-teilig / sound installation, 2 parts, 18:31 Min., rechts / right: Dan Flavin, *Untitled*, 1996, Leuchtstofflampen / fluorescent lights, Ausstellungsansicht / exhibition view: Hamburger Bahnhof – Nationalgalerie der Gegenwart, Berlin, 2025

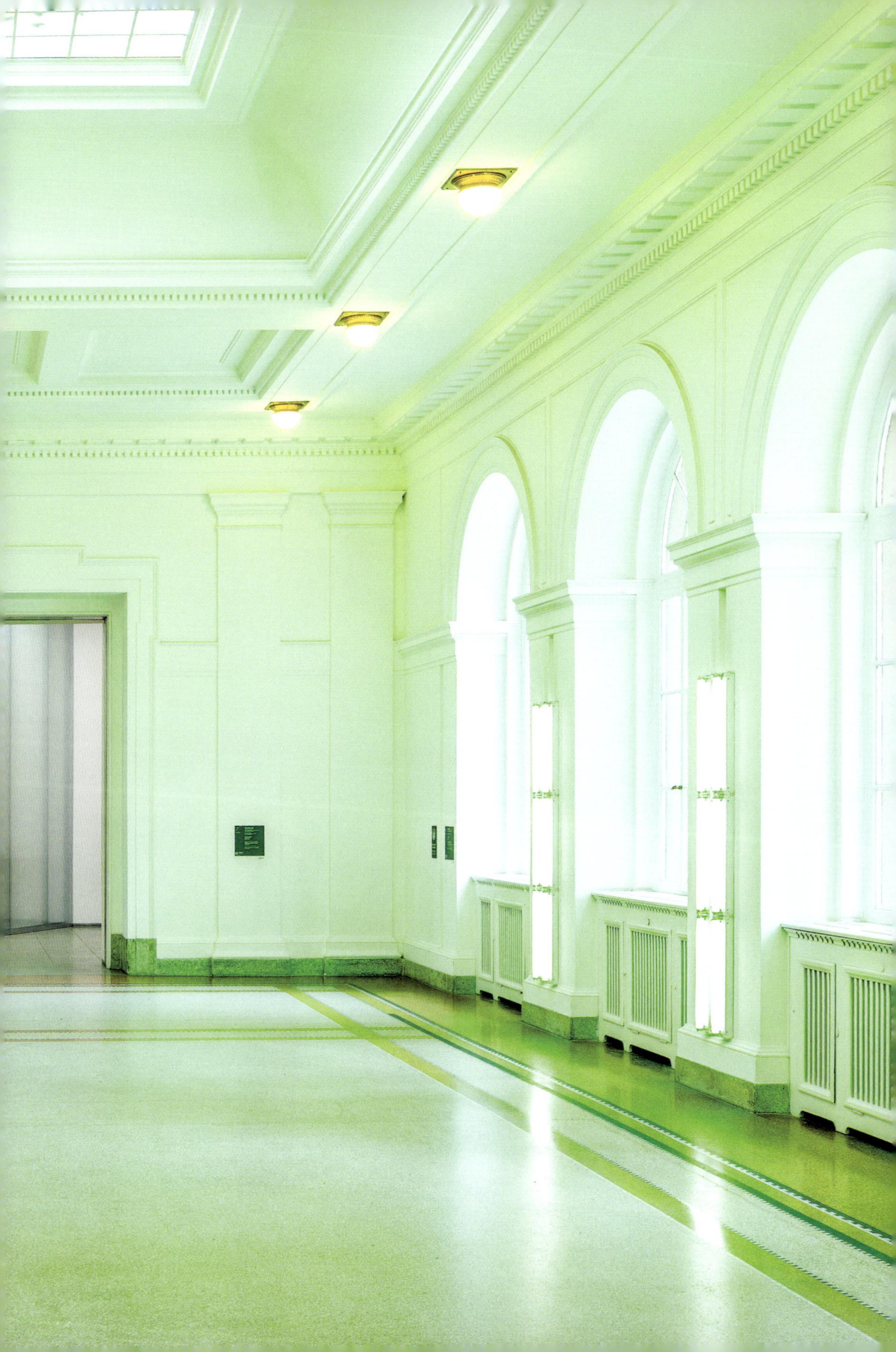

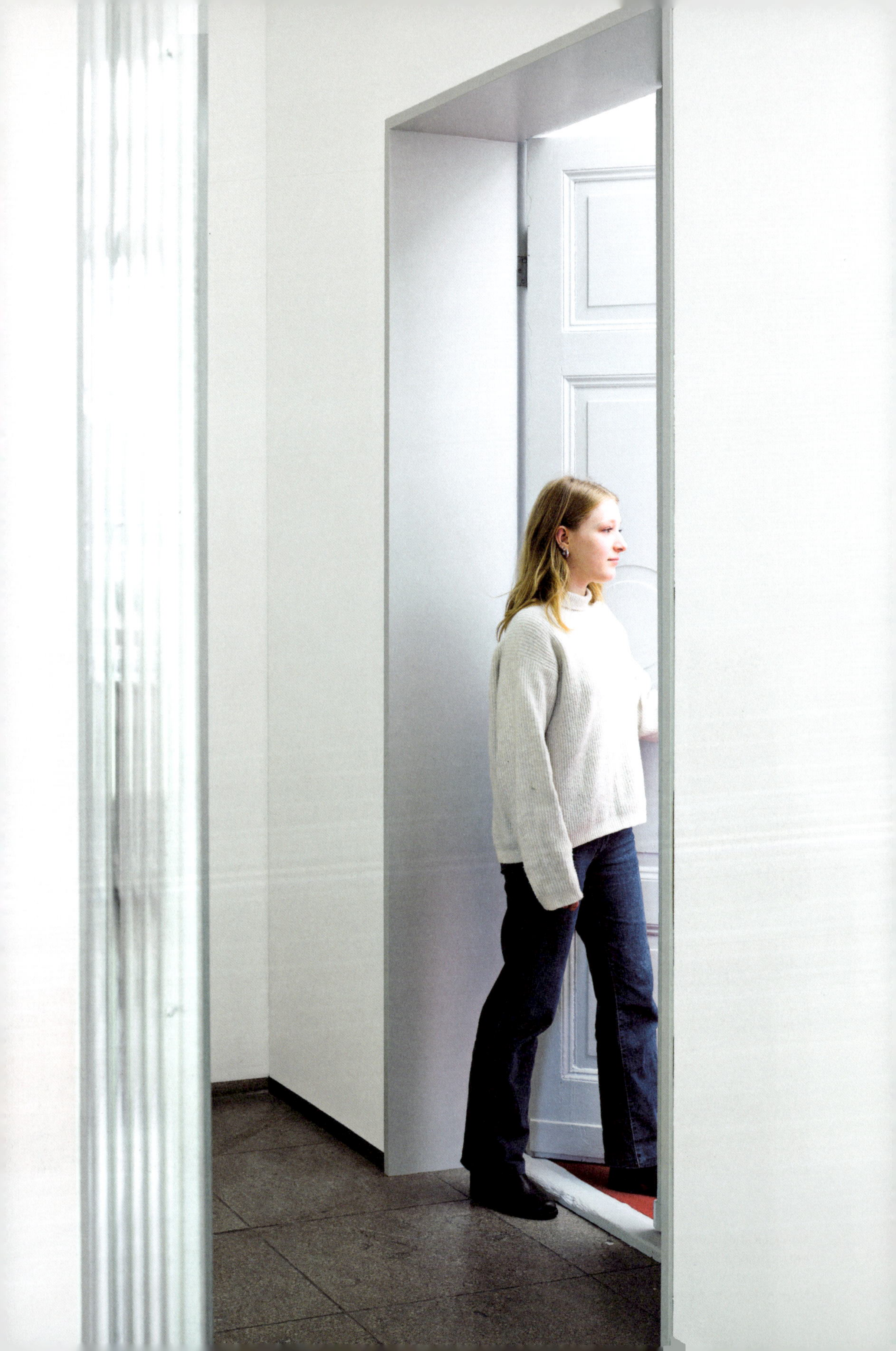

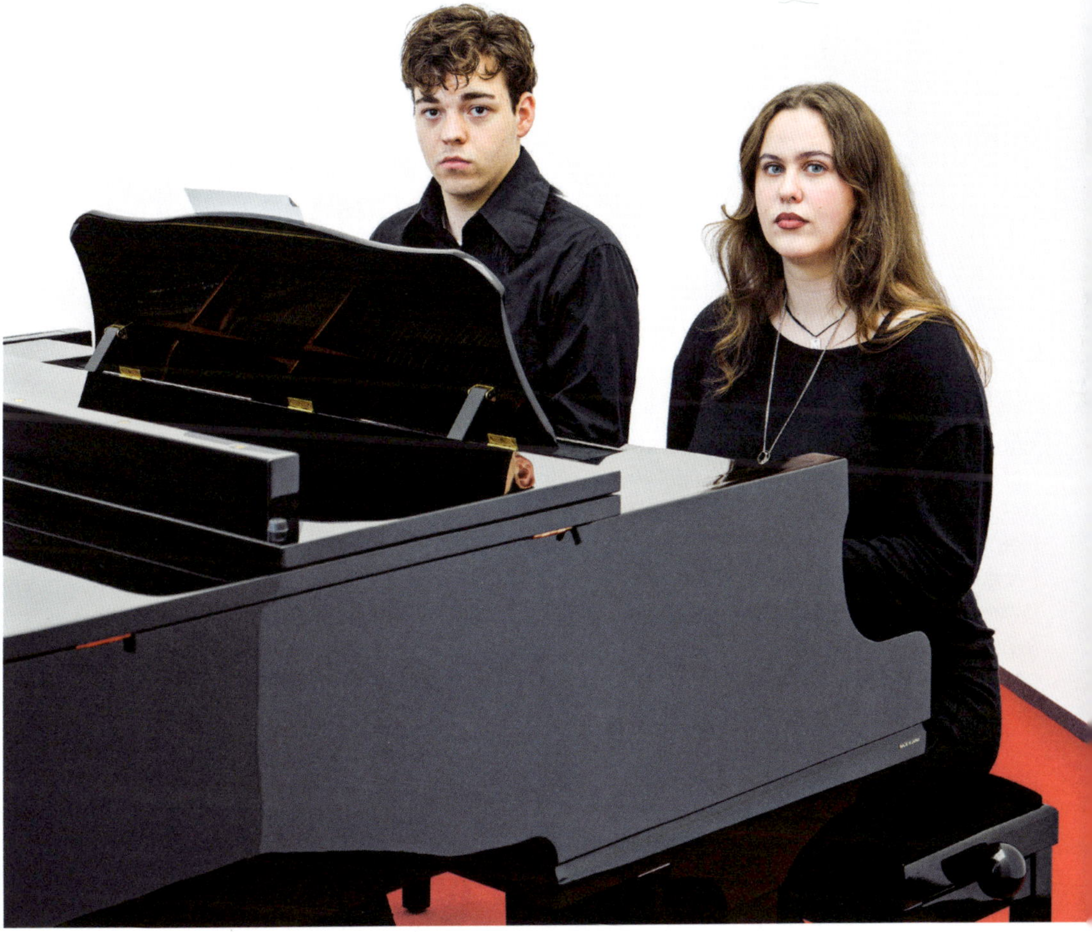

Annika Kahrs, *For Two To Play On One,* 2012, Performance, Installation, Performanceansicht / performance view Hamburger Bahnhof – Nationalgalerie der Gegenwart, Berlin, 2025

Die Schönheit der Unterschiede / The Beauty of Difference

Susanne Pfeffer

Wie klingt ein Quartett, wenn die Musikerinnen reihum die Instrumente wechseln? Wie reagieren Ziervögel auf Franz Liszts *Saint François d'Assise. La Prédication aux Oiseaux* [Vogelpredigt des heiligen Franz von Assisi]? Ist ein Duett komplett, allein zu zweit? Welche tonalen Tiefen, die allein ein Oktobass erzeugen oder eine Giraffe hören kann, bleiben dem menschlichen Ohr verborgen?

Die filmischen Arbeiten von Annika Kahrs gleichen performativen Anordnungen. Klar und präzise, wissenschaftlich fundiert und zugleich widerständig fantastisch. Mittels leichthändig erscheinenden und teils spielerischen Verrückungen legt die Künstlerin die Grundlagen vermeintlicher Ordnungen offen und befreit sie von ihren inneren Logiken. Sie bringt Dinge zusammen, die auf den ersten Blick nicht zusammengehören, und weist zugleich evident nach, dass sie es tun.

How does a quartet sound when the musicians keep swapping instruments in turn? How do songbirds react to Franz Liszt's *Saint François d'Assise. La Prédication aux Oiseaux* [Saint Francis of Assisi's Sermon to the Birds]? Is a duet complete when there are only two players? What tonal depths – which only an octobass can produce or a giraffe can hear – are beyond the audible perception of humans?

Annika Kahrs's filmic works resemble performative arrangements: clear and precise, scientifically sound, and yet defiantly fantastical. Through seemingly effortless and at times playful dislocations, the artist exposes the foundations of supposed orders and liberates them from their inner logic. She brings together things

Stets basieren ihre Arbeiten auf einer tiefen Kenntnis, aber auch großer Empathie für die Themen, die Orte mit ihren jeweiligen Historien sowie den unterschiedlichen Menschen und ihren Kulturen. Dabei ist Kahrs' utopischer Anspruch fröhlich präsent.

Die Empfindsamkeit als auch die Empfindungen der Tiere und Menschen stehen dabei stets im Mittelpunkt und werden sichtbar, nachvollziehbar – wie spürbar. Die Schönheit der Unterschiedlichkeit von Tieren, Menschen, Landschaften und Kulturen tritt in jedem einzelnen Filmbild hervor.

Die Frage, wie wir alle, die hier sind, in all unserer Unterschiedlichkeit gemeinsam miteinander agieren, stellt Annika Kahrs in allen ihren Arbeiten. Eine Frage, die grundlegender nicht sein könnte und gegenwärtig dringender ist denn je.

that at first don't seem to belong together, while simultaneously demonstrating conclusively that they actually do.

Kahrs's works are rooted in a deep knowledge of, but also profound empathy for, her subjects – her themes and the places with their individual histories, as well as the diversity of people and their distinct cultures. Her utopian vision maintains a cheerful presence throughout her creative oeuvre.

The sensitivity and feelings of both animals and humans are always at the centre of her work, which renders them visible and comprehensible – perceptible. The beauty in the diversity of animals, people, landscapes and cultures emerges in every single frame of her films.

In all of her work, Annika Kahrs asks how all of us here, in all our diversity, interact with one another. It is a question that could not be more fundamental or feel more urgent than it does right now.

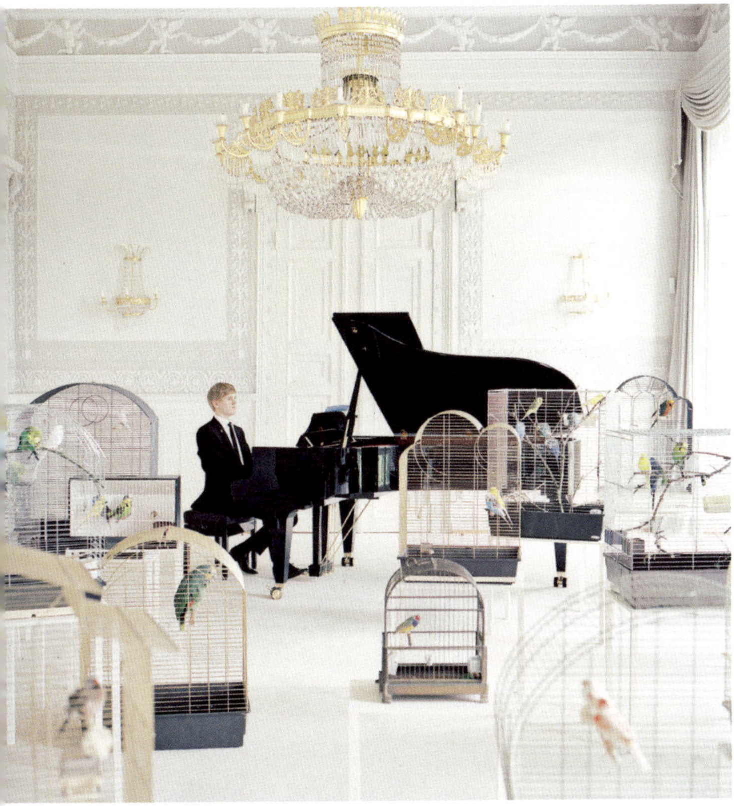

Annika Kahrs, *Playing to the Birds*, 2014, C-Print, 60 × 60 cm

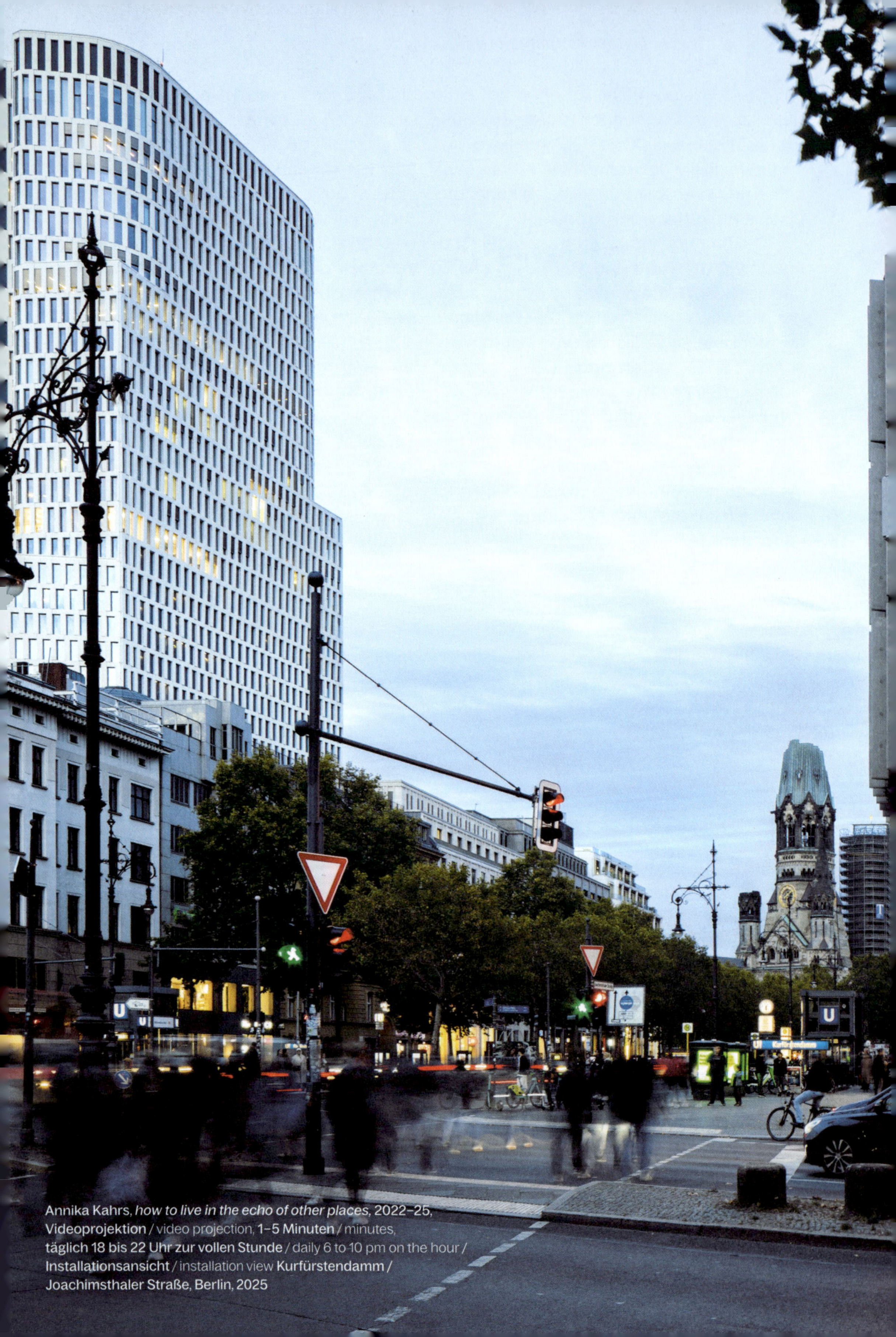

Annika Kahrs, *how to live in the echo of other places*, 2022–25,
Videoprojektion / video projection, **1–5 Minuten** / minutes,
täglich 18 bis 22 Uhr zur vollen Stunde / daily 6 to 10 pm on the hour /
Installationsansicht / installation view **Kurfürstendamm /
Joachimsthaler Straße, Berlin, 2025**

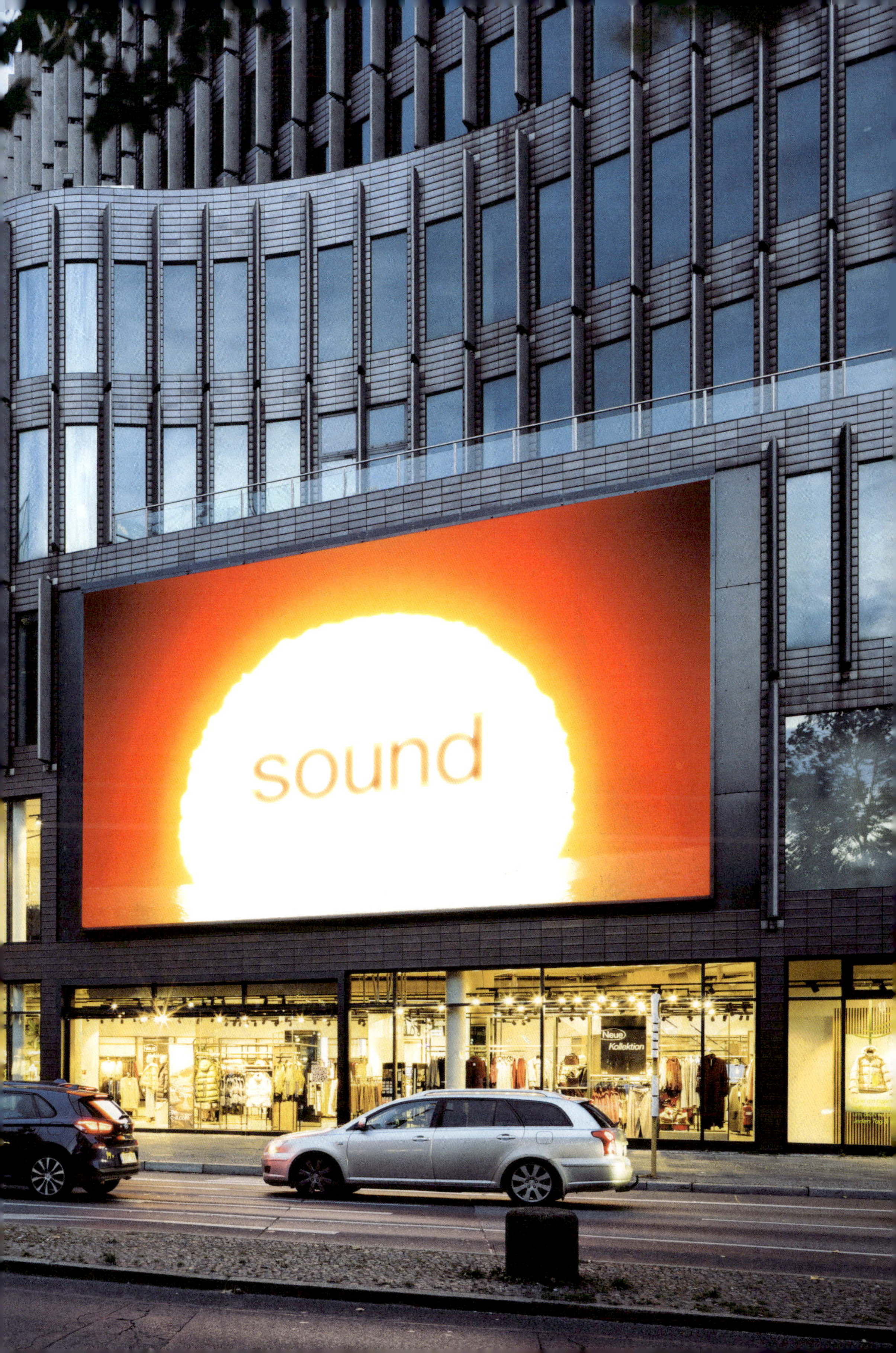
sound
Neue
Kollektion

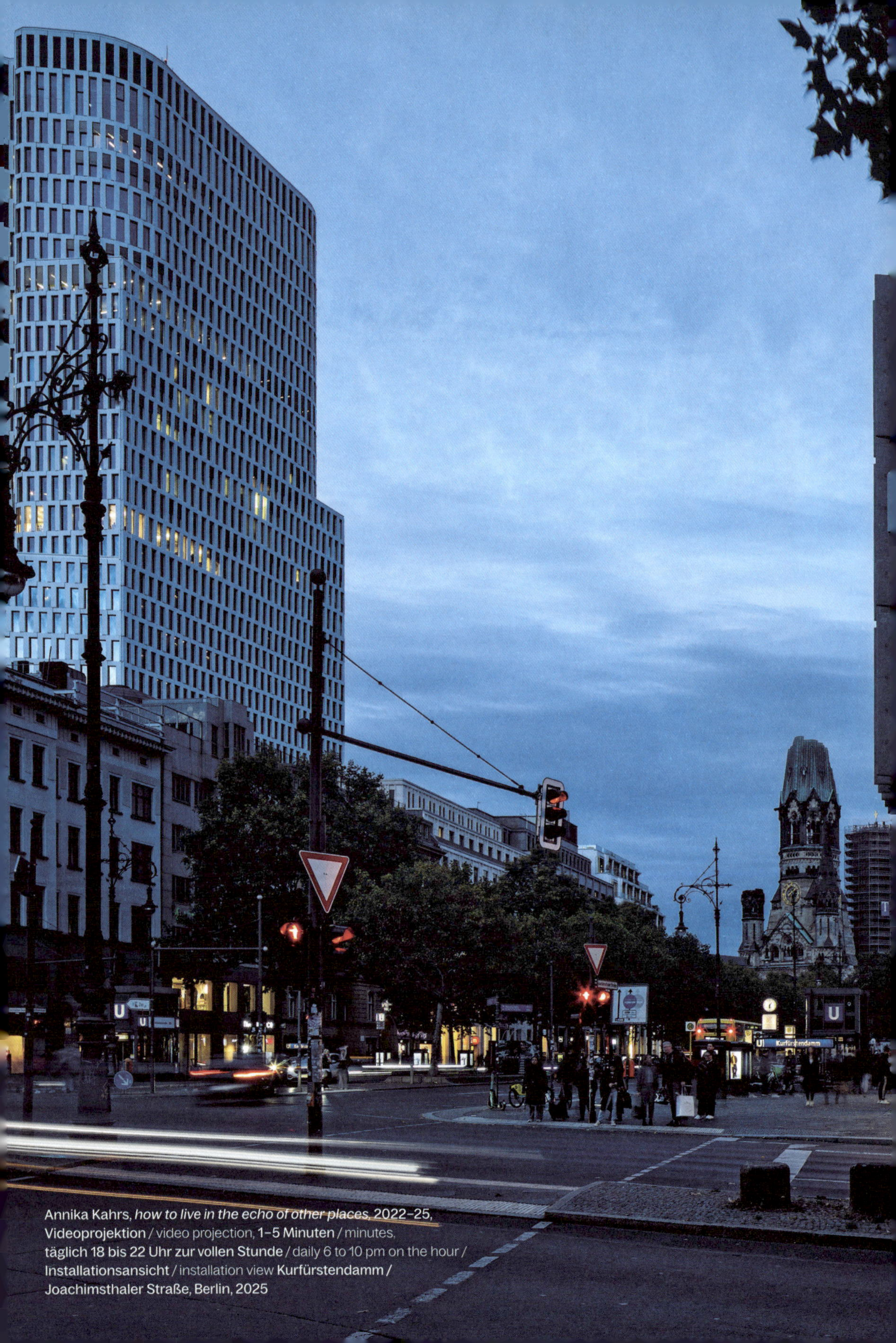

Annika Kahrs, *how to live in the echo of other places*, 2022–25,
Videoprojektion / video projection, **1–5 Minuten** / minutes,
täglich 18 bis 22 Uhr zur vollen Stunde / daily 6 to 10 pm on the hour /
Installationsansicht / installation view **Kurfürstendamm /
Joachimsthaler Straße, Berlin, 2025**

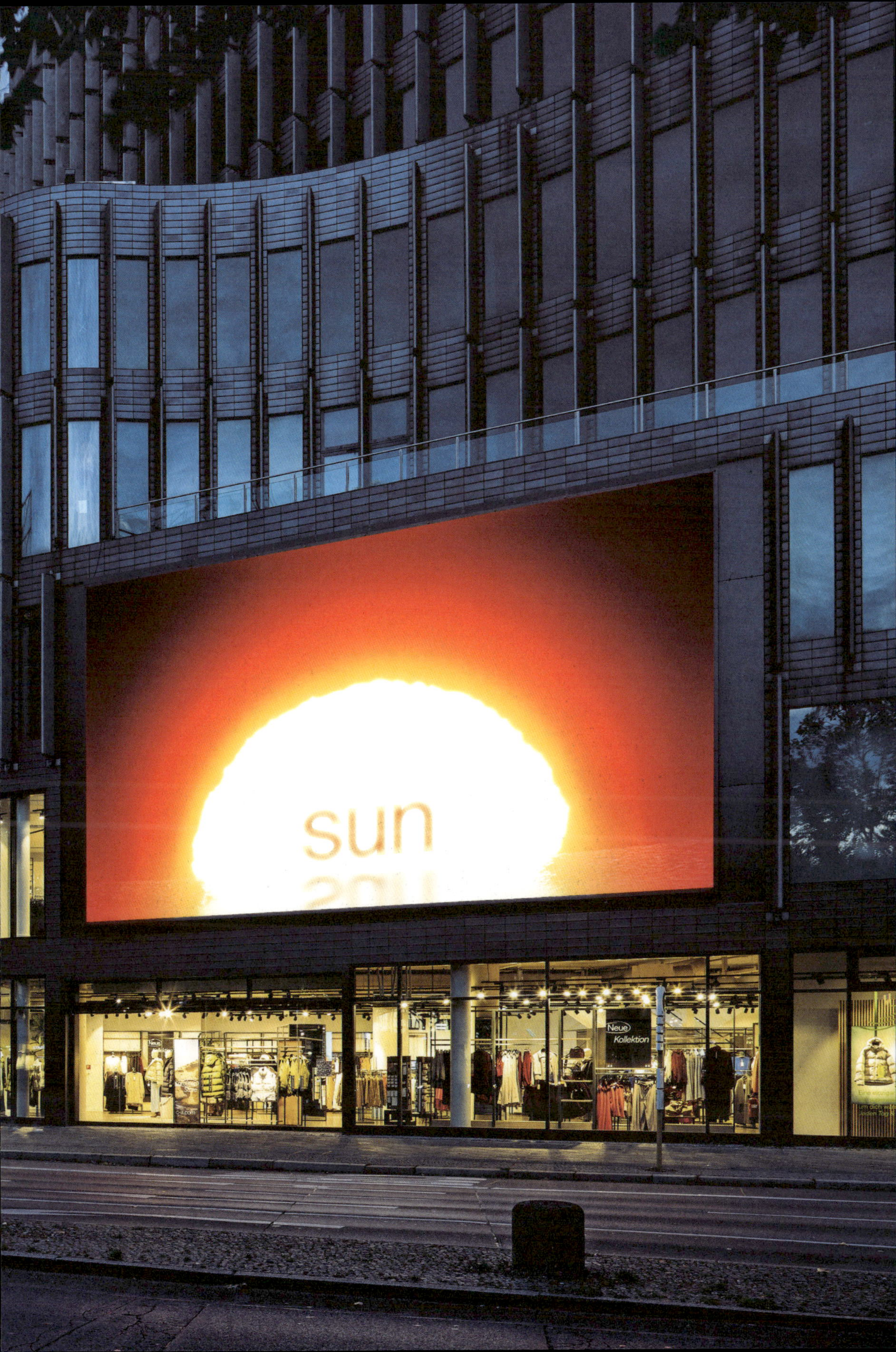
sun
Neue
Kollektion

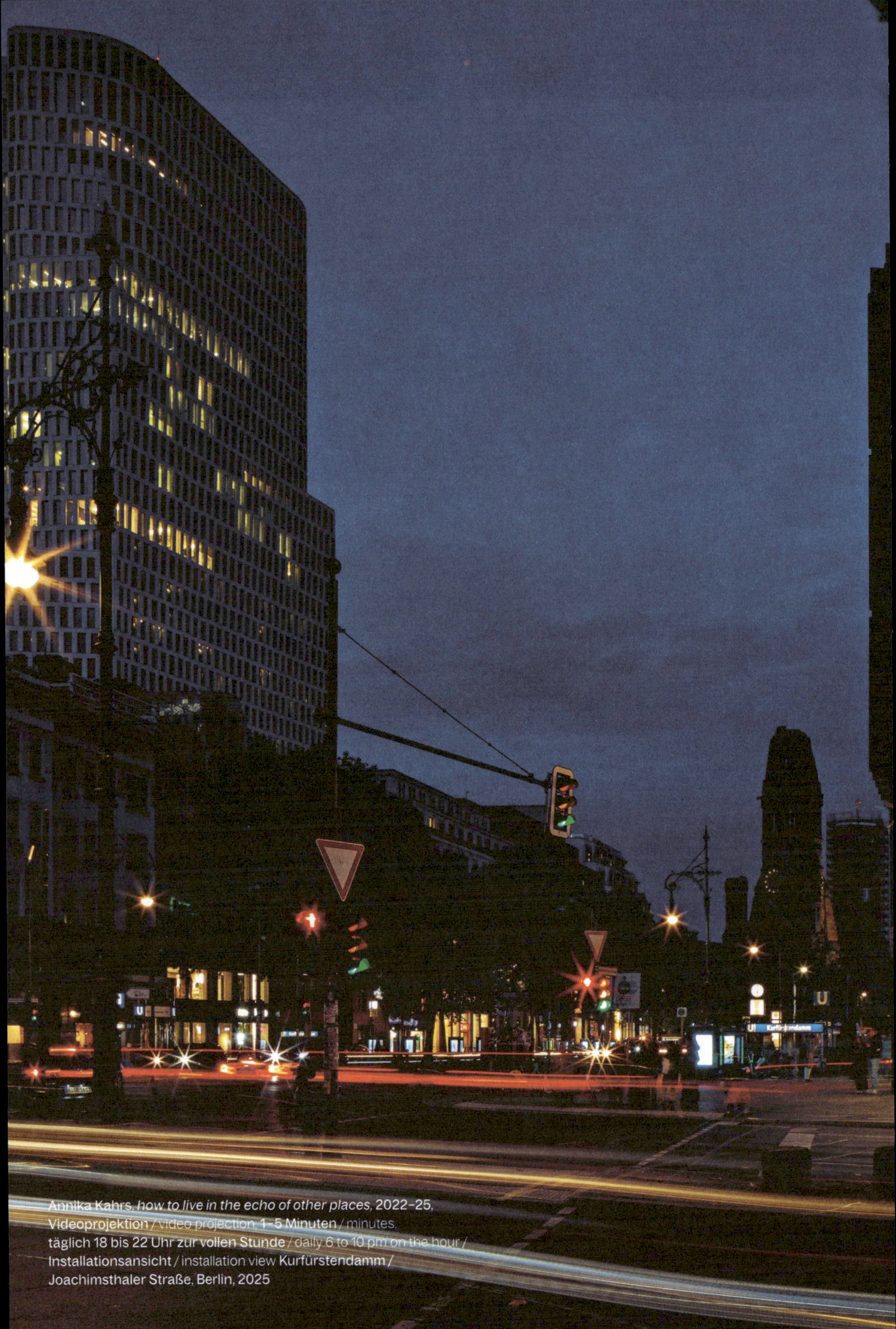

Annika Kahrs, *how to live in the echo of other places*, 2022–25,
Videoprojektion / video projection, **1–5 Minuten** / minutes,
täglich 18 bis 22 Uhr zur vollen Stunde / daily 6 to 10 pm on the hour /
Installationsansicht / installation view **Kurfürstendamm /
Joachimsthaler Straße, Berlin, 2025**

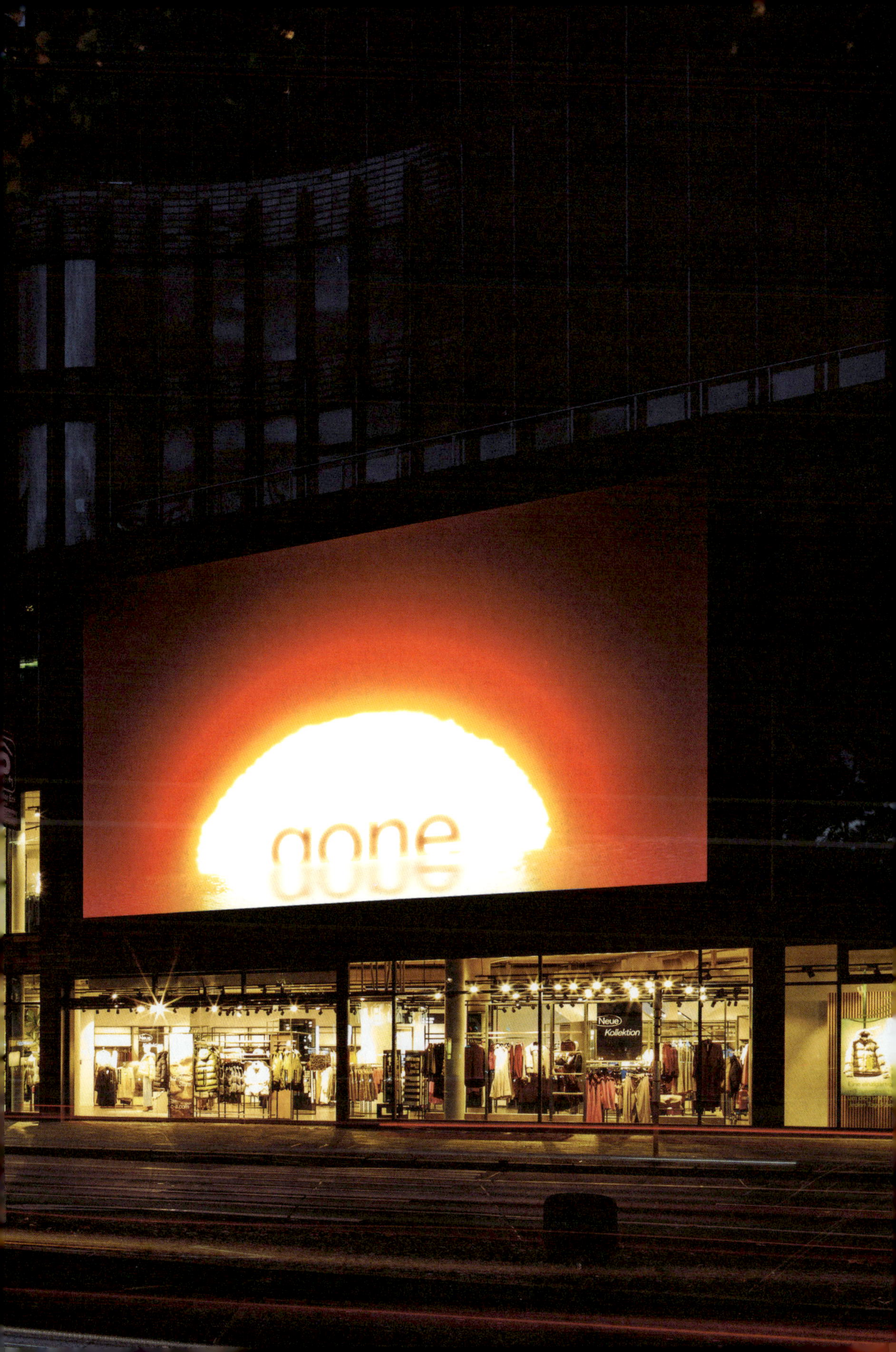
gone
Neue
Kollektion

Annika Kahrs

Geboren / Born **in Achim, DE, 1984**
Lebt und arbeitet / Lives and works **in Berlin, DE**

Ausbildung / Education

2005–12
Studium der Freien Kunst / Visual Arts studies at **Hochschule für bildende Künste, Hamburg, DE, Akademie der bildenden Künste, Wien** / Vienna, **AT & Hochschule für Bildende Künste, Braunschweig, DE**

Ausgewählte Einzelausstellungen / Selected Solo Exhibitions

2025
Annika Kahrs. **Städtische Galerie Nordhorn, Nordhorn, DE (bevorstehend** / forthcoming)

Annika Kahrs: OFF SCORE. **Hamburger Bahnhof – Nationalgalerie der Gegenwart, Berlin, DE; Katalog** / catalogue

2023
Annika Kahrs: Gravity's Tune. **Schering Stiftung, Berlin, DE**
Annika Kahrs: An attempt to prove that what is passionate and pleasing in the art of singing, speaking and performing upon musical instruments, is derived from the sound. **Nassauischer Kunstverein Wiesbaden, Wiesbaden, DE**

2022
Annika Kahrs: how to live in the echo of other places. **IMAGINE THE CITY, HafenCity, Hamburg, DE**

2021
Annika Kahrs: silence is the sound of a missed opportunity. **Yellow Solo, Berlin, DE**

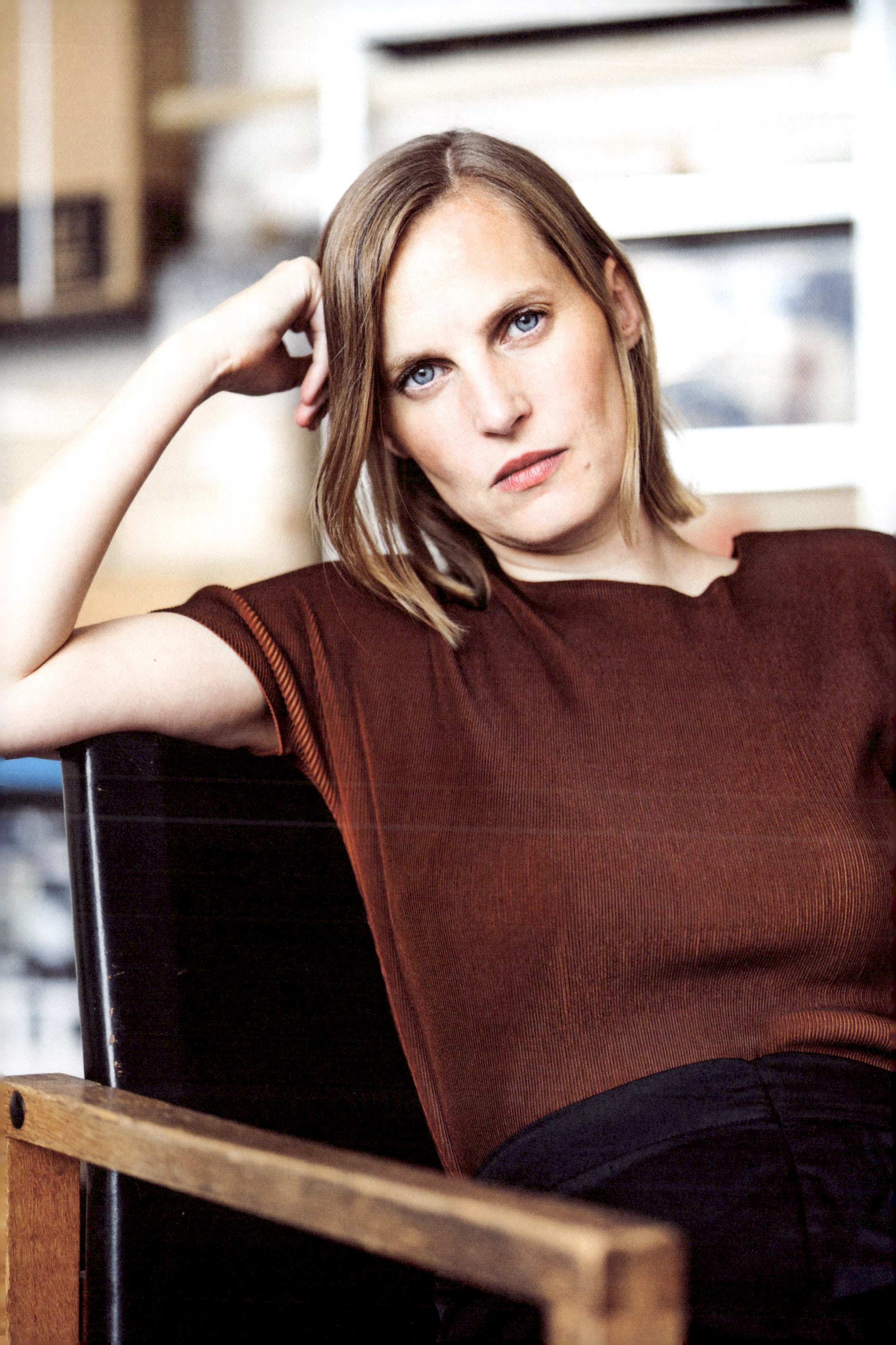

2020
sesin melodim, seslerin yankım benim deine stimme ist mein klang ist dein geräusch ist mein echo. Mit / With Derya Yıldırım, Mind the Gap #2, Bieberhaus, Hamburg, DE
One's Company, Two's A Crowd, Six Is A Party: Fleetstreet Theater Residency. Mit / With Nguyen Phuong-Dan, Fleetstreet Theater, Hamburg, DE

2019
the billion year spree. Flat Time House, London, GB

2018
Staging Realities II. Mit / With Anja Dietmann & Mette Sterre. Kunstverein in Hamburg, Hamburg, DE
Annika Kahrs: Infra Voice. Kasseler Kunstverein, Kassel, DE; Begleitheft / brochure

2016
Annika Kahrs: Playing to the Birds. Franz Marc Museum, Kochel am See, DE

2015
Annika Kahrs: lines. Kunsthalle Bremerhaven, Bremerhaven, DE
Annika Kahrs: Playing to the Birds. Kunsthal 44Møen, Møen, DK

2014
Annika Kahrs: A Concert for the Birds. Situations, The Lord Mayor's Chapel, Bristol, GB
Annika Kahrs: Chim Cảnh. Stipendiatenausstellung Neue Kunst in Hamburg, Hamburg, DE

2013
Annika Kahrs: Playing to the Birds. Kunstraum München, München / Munich, DE; Katalog / catalogue

2012
Annika Kahrs: George Maciunas Förderpreis. TANAS, Berlin, DE

Ausgewählte Gruppenausstellungen / Selected Group Exhibitions

2025
Biennale Son, Sion, CH
*Cine*ami*es.* ICAT – Institute for Contemporary Art & Transfer at HFBK, Hamburg, DE
Für die Vögel. Museum für Gegenwartskunst Siegen, Siegen, DE; Begleitheft / brochure
Activating! Handlungsvorstellung als Werk. Kunsthaus Baselland, Basel, CH
Why look at animals. EMΣT, National Museum of Contemporary Art Athens, Athen / Athens, GR; Katalog / catalogue
Vom Himmel gefallen. Overbeck-Gesellschaft, Kunstverein Lübeck, Lübeck, DE
Herausgeforderte Gemeinschaft. Kunstmuseum Magdeburg, Magdeburg, DE

2024
October Salon, Belgrad / Belgrade, RS
Pauli Preis 2024. Kunsthalle Bremen, Bremen, DE; Katalog / catalogue
Wie alles begann: Bruckners Visionen. Stift St. Florian, Sankt Florian, AT

2023
It's Human Nature? Kunstverein Harburger Bahnhof, Hamburg, DE
Räume mit Aussicht: Crossatlantic Narratives – Stipendiat:innen 2022 der Villa Aurora. Haus Kunst Mitte, Berlin, DE
Gezwitscher: Kunst aus der Vogelperspektive. Kunsthalle Wilhelmshaven, Wilhelmshaven, DE (weitere Station / travelled to: House of Arts, Ústí nad Labem, CZ); Katalog / catalogue

TONO Festival, Mexico City, MX
Nam June Paik: I Expose the Music. Museum Ostwall, Dortmunder U, Dortmund, DE; Katalog / catalogue

2022
Manifesto of Fragility. Biennale de Lyon, Lyon, FR; Katalog / catalogue
something new, something old, something desired. Hamburger Kunsthalle, Hamburg, DE

2021
Villa Aurora & Thomas Mann House: all the lonely people. silent green Kulturquartier, Berlin, DE (weitere Station / travelled to: LAXART, Los Angeles, CA, US)
Für Dieter Roth. Internationales Sommerfestival, Kampnagel, Hamburg, DE
Listen Deeply. MONA FOMA, Tasmanien / Tasmania, AU
Le juste Prix. Fondation d'entreprise Ricard, Paris, FR
Sound and Silence. Kunstmuseum Bonn, Bonn, DE; Katalog / catalogue
The Architecture of Confinement. BNKR, München / Munich, DE; Katalog / catalogue
So Close / So Far. Hyper Cultural Passengers, Hamburg, DE
Denken wie ein Oktopus, oder: Tentakuläres Begreifen. Rudolf-Scharpf-Galerie, Wilhelm-Hack Museum, Ludwigshafen, DE; Katalog / catalogue
The Poetry of Translation. Kunst Merano arte, Meran / Merano, IT; Katalog / catalogue
VideoKunstNächte. Kunsthalle Recklinghausen, Recklinghausen, DE

2020
Corona Sound System. Kunstverein in Hamburg, Hamburg, DE

2019
Concerto para pássaros. Goethe-Institut, Salvador da Bahia, BR
Max-Pechstein-Preis. Max-Pechstein-Museum, Kunstsammlungen Zwickau, Zwickau, DE; Broschüre / brochure
Fuzzy Dark Spot: Videokunst aus Hamburg. Sammlung Falckenberg, Deichtorhallen Hamburg, Hamburg, DE; Katalog / catalogue
Scheitern. BLECH – Raum für Kunst Halle, Halle, DE
Act. Q18, Köln / Cologne, DE
MOVES#200 – 202, a Calendar, a Performance, a Concert, and Films by. Image Movement, Berlin, DE
StoryWorks. Kunstmuseum Magdeburg, Magdeburg, DE

2018
La Nuit de l'instant. Les Ateliers de l'image, Centre Photographique Marseille, Marseille, FR
We Have Delivered Ourselves From the Tonal: Of, With, Towards, On Julius Eastman. SAVVY Contemporary, Berlin, DE; Katalog / catalogue
/me followed by an action. Vierte Welt, Berlin, DE
Gastspiele. Städtische Galerie Nordhorn, Nordhorn, DE
AMBITUS: Kunst und Musik heute. Kunstmuseum Magdeburg, Magdeburg, DE; Katalog / catalogue
Nordwest Zeitgenössisch. Kunstmuseum Bremerhaven, Bremerhaven, DE
Anders. Kunstmuseum Bremerhaven, Bremerhaven, DE

2017
wieder und wider. Hamburger Kunsthalle, Hamburg, DE
Zur See: Werke aus der Sammlung der Kunsthalle Bremerhaven. Städtische Galerie Delmenhorst, Delmenhorst, DE
Cinéma. Kunsthalle Lingen, Lingen, DE
VG Stipendium 2017. Kestner Gesellschaft, Hannover / Hanover, DE
Was wir sehen wollen. Kunstverein Grafschaft Bentheim, Neuenhaus, DE; Katalog / catalogue

2016
Schule der Distanz. Gropius Bau, Berlin, DE
Paula Modersohn-Becker Kunstpreis 2016. Große Kunstschau Worpswede, Worpswede, DE; Katalog / catalogue

Ein Knacks im Leben: Wir scheitern… und wie weiter? Vögele Kultur Zentrum, Pfäffikon, CH
Fragile Strength. Cité Internationale des Arts, Paris, FR

2015
Lexus Hybrid Art, Moskau / Moscow, RU
Thessaloniki Biennale of Contemporary Art, Thessaloniki, GR; Katalog / catalogue
Raumstationen: 87. Herbstausstellung niedersächsischer Künstlerinnen und Künstler. Kunstverein Hannover, Hannover / Hanover, DE; Katalog / catalogue
Vom Verbergen. Museum Angewandte Kunst, Frankfurt a.M., DE
Home Work. Open Forum, Berlin, DE
Und weg mit den Minuten: Dieter Roth und die Musik. Hamburger Bahnhof – Nationalgalerie der Gegenwart, Berlin, DE; Katalog / catalogue
Das Geheimnis der Vögel. Höhenrausch, Linz, AT; Katalog / catalogue
Dazwischentreten. Künstlerhaus Bremen, Bremen, DE
Sound in Motion: Internationale Video- und Performancekunst. Kunstmuseum Stuttgart, Stuttgart, DE
Sammlungspräsentation / Collection presentation, Museum Weserburg, Bremen, DE

2014
On The Road / En el camino. Santiago de Compostela, ES; Katalog / catalogue
Im Frühling, Darling. Kunstverein in Hamburg, Hamburg, DE
Artdate Festival di Arte Contemporanea. The Blank, Bergamo, IT
Felix & Foam, Foam, Amsterdam, NL
Hamburger Arbeitsstipendium: Stipendianten 2013. Kunstverein Harburger Bahnhof, Hamburg, DE
Shift. Basurto, Mexico City, MX

2013
The Unanswered Question: İskele 2. TANAS & Neuer Berliner Kunstverein, Berlin, DE; Katalog / catalogue
Bienal International de Curitiba, Curitiba, BR
Besser scheitern. Hamburger Kunsthalle, Hamburg, DE (weitere Station / travelled to: Internationale Tage Ingelheim, Ingelheim a.R., DE); Katalog / catalogue

2012
One on One. KW Institute for Contemporary Art, Berlin, DE; Katalog / catalogue
+6|2012: Shortlist Columbus-Förderpreis für aktuelle Kunst. Kunsthalle Ravensburg, Ravensburg, DE; Katalog / catalogue

Ausgewählte Performances und Screenings / Selected Performances and Screenings

2026
Annika Kahrs: Strings. Städtische Galerie Nordhorn, Nordhorn, DE (bevorstehend / forthcoming)
Annika Kahrs: Strings. Musikinstrumenten-Museum, Berlin, DE (bevorstehend / forthcoming)
Annika Kahrs: Alone Together. Musikinstrumenten-Museum, Berlin, DE (bevorstehend / forthcoming)
Annika Kahrs: zum Sonnendeck. Hörsaalruine, Berliner Medizinhistorisches Museum, Berlin, DE (bevorstehend / forthcoming)
Annika Kahrs: the lord loves changes, it's one of his greatest delusions. Heilige-Geist-Kirche, Berlin, DE (bevorstehend / forthcoming)

2024
Alone Together. Fleetinsel Festival, Hamburg, DE

2023
Videoart at Midnight. Babylon, Berlin, DE
Annika Kahrs: Strings. Nassauischer Kunstverein Wiesbaden, Wiesbaden, DE

2020
Annika Kahrs: the lord loves changes, it's one of his greatest delusions. Double Feature, Schirn Kunsthalle, Frankfurt a.M., DE

2019
Annika Kahrs: the lord loves changes, it's one of his greatest delusions. Festival des Cinémas Différents et Expérimentaux de Paris, Paris, FR
Annika Kahrs: the lord loves changes, it's one of his greatest delusions. Internationale Kurzfilmtage Festival Oberhausen, Oberhausen, DE
Annika Kahrs: Strings. Flat Time House, London, GB
Annika Kahrs: Strings. Concerto para pássaros, Goethe-Institut, Salvador da Bahia, BR

2018
THIS IS A LOVE SONG. Klosterfelde Edition, Berlin, DE
Alone Together. Staatsoper Hannover, Hannover / Hanover, DE
THIS IS A LOVE SONG. Kunstverein in Hamburg, Hamburg, DE
Annika Kahrs: Strings. Staatsoper Hannover, Hannover / Hanover, DE

2016
the announcement. Hamburger Kunsthalle, Hamburg, DE
Annika Kahrs: Strings. Fragile Strength, Cité Internationale des Arts, Paris, FR

2015
Annika Kahrs: Strings. Artissima, Turin, IT

2014
études cliniques ou artistiques. KW Institute for Contemporary Art, Berlin, DE

2013
Strings. HAU Hebbel am Ufer, Berlin, DE

Auszeichnungen und Stipendien / Awards and Residencies

2024
Pauli Preis, Kunsthalle Bremen, Bremen, DE (Shortlist)
Artist-in-Residence, Mercedes-Benz Art Scope & Arts Initiative Tokyo, Tokio / Tokyo, JP
Artist-in-Residence, Deutsche Akademie Rom Villa Massimo, Casa Baldi, Olevano Romano, IT

2023
Artist-in-Residence, Villa Aurora, Los Angeles, CA, US

2022
Stipendium / Scholarship, Stiftung Kunstfonds, Bonn, DE

2021
Sonderstipendium / Special Grant, INITIAL, Akademie der Künste Berlin, Berlin, DE

2020
Stipendium / Scholarship, Stiftung Kunstfonds, Bonn, DE
Artist-in-Residence, Fleetstreet Theater, Hamburg, DE
Heitland Honneur, Heitland Foundation, Celle, DE

2019
Internationaler Wettbewerb / International Competition, Festival des Cinémas Différents et Expérimentaux de Paris, Paris, FR
Max-Pechstein-Stipendium, Max-Pechstein-Museum, Kunstsammlungen Zwickau, Zwickau, DE
Kunststipendium / Art Scholarship, ZEIT-Stiftung Bucerius, Hamburg, DE
Artist-in-Residence, VILA SUL, Salvador da Bahia, BR

2018
Stipendium / Scholarship, **Stiftung Kunstfonds, Bonn, DE**

2017
VG Stipendium / Scholarship, **Kestner Gesellschaft, Hannover** / Hanover, **DE**

2015–16
Artist-in-Residence, Cité Internationale des Arts, Paris, FR

2014
Bremerhaven Stipendium / Scholarship, **Bremerhaven, DE**

2013
Arbeitsstipendium für bildende Kunst der Freien und Hansestadt Hamburg, Hamburg, DE

2012–14
Atelierstipendium / Studio Grant, **GSM, Hamburg, DE**

2012–13
Reisestipendium / Travel Grant, **Neue Kunst in Hamburg e.V., Hamburg, DE**

2012
George Maciunas Förderpreis, Berlin, DE

2011
Hauptpreis / Main Award, **20. Bundeskunstwettbewerb des Bundesministeriums für Bildung und Forschung „Kunststudentinnen und Kunststudenten stellen aus", Bonn, DE**
Jahresstipendium / Annual Grant, **Freundeskreis der HFBK e.V., Hamburg, DE**

Ausgewählte Publikationen / Selected Publications

Ellen Blumenstein (Hg. / ed.), *The City Imagined mit / with Annika Kahrs*, Hamburg: Imagine the City – Kunst und Kultur in der HafenCity e.V., 2023.

Janine Mackenroth & Bianca Kennedy (Hg. / eds.), *I [love] Women in Art*, München / Munich: Pool Positions, 2020.

Annika Kahrs: Shifting Sounds, Hamburg: Verlag der Fachbuchhandlung Sautter + Lackmann, 2019.

Produzentengalerie Hamburg (Hg. / ed.), *Annika Kahrs: Star-filled Skies*, Eigenverlag / self-published, 2014.

Jakob Schillinger (Hg. / ed.), *Annika Kahrs & Nguyen Phương-Dan: Hanoi View*, Hamburg: Textem Verlag & Neue Kunst in Hamburg e.V., 2014.

Susanne Pfeffer & Brigitte Oetker (Hg. / eds.), *Jahresring #057: My Work and Me*, Köln / Cologne: Buchhandlung Walther König, 2010.

Öffentliche Sammlungen / Public Collections

Hamburger Kunsthalle, Hamburg, DE
Kunsthalle Bremen / Der Kunstverein in Bremen e.V., Bremen, DE
Kunstmuseum Bremerhaven / Kunstverein Bremerhaven von 1886 e.V., Bremerhaven, DE
Kunstmuseum Magdeburg, Magdeburg, DE
Musée d'art contemporain de Lyon, Lyon, FR
Museum Weserburg Bremen / Sammlung Dominic und Cordula Sohst-Brennenstuhl, Bremen, DE
Nationalgalerie, Staatliche Museen zu Berlin, Berlin, DE

OÖ Landes-Kultur GmbH, Linz, AT
Sammlung LBBW, Landesbank Baden Württemberg, Stuttgart, DE
Sammlung Zeitgenössische Kunst des Bundes, DE
Vehbi Koç Foundation Contemporary Art Collection, Istanbul, TR

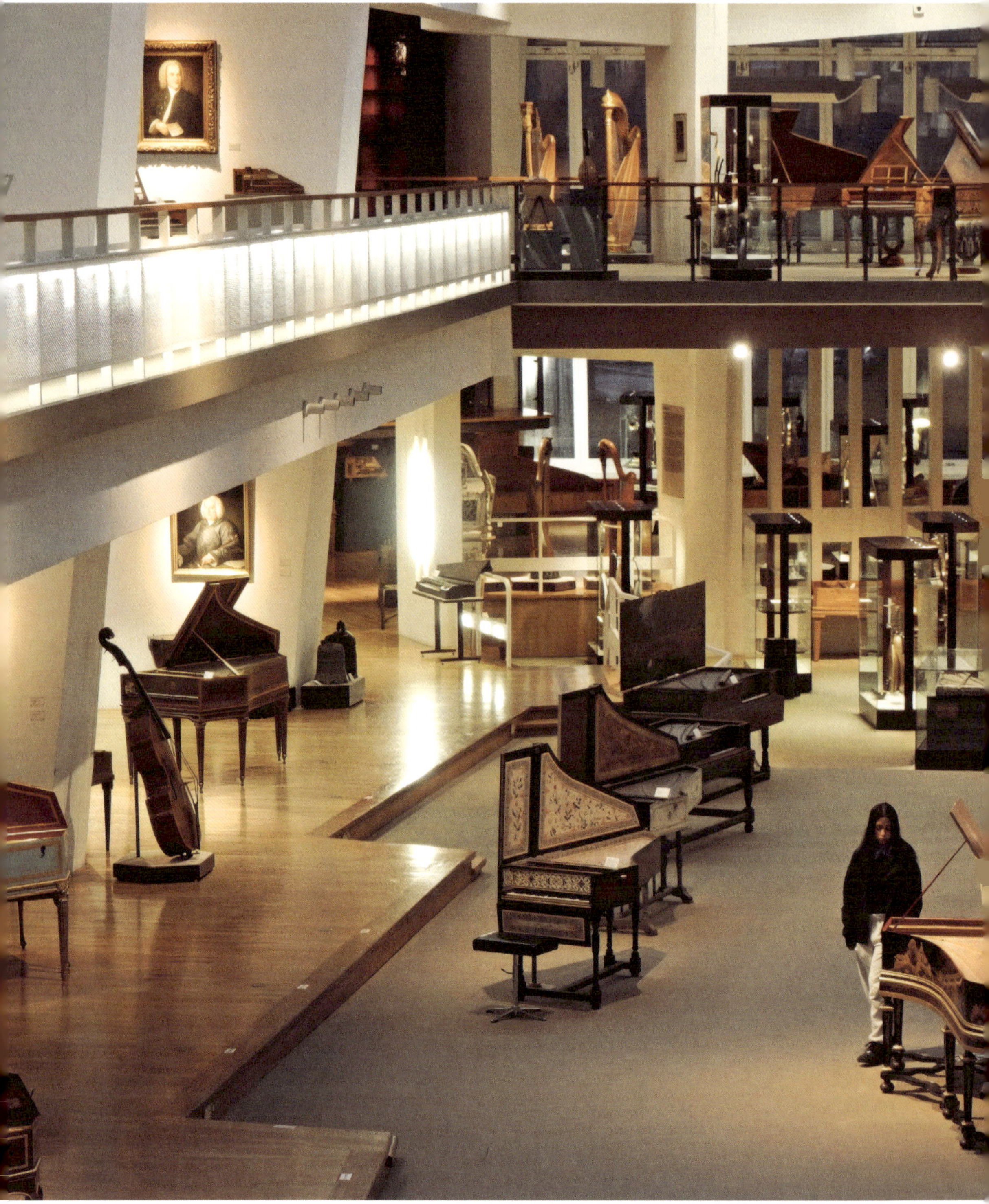

Annika Kahrs, *Ganz ungültig, nur ein Versuch,*
2024, 4K Video, Farbe, Ton / colour, sound,
22 Min., Videostandbild / video still

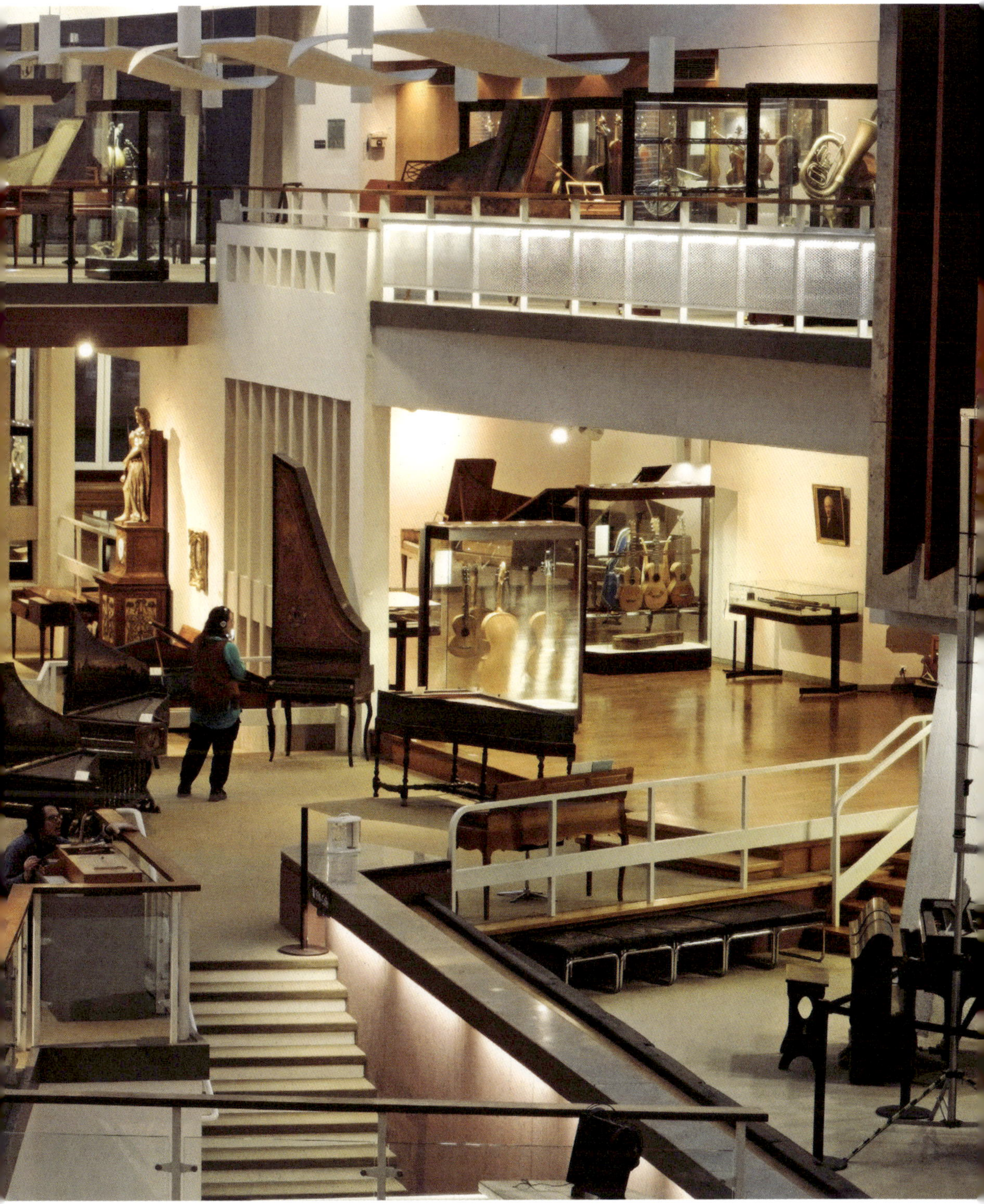

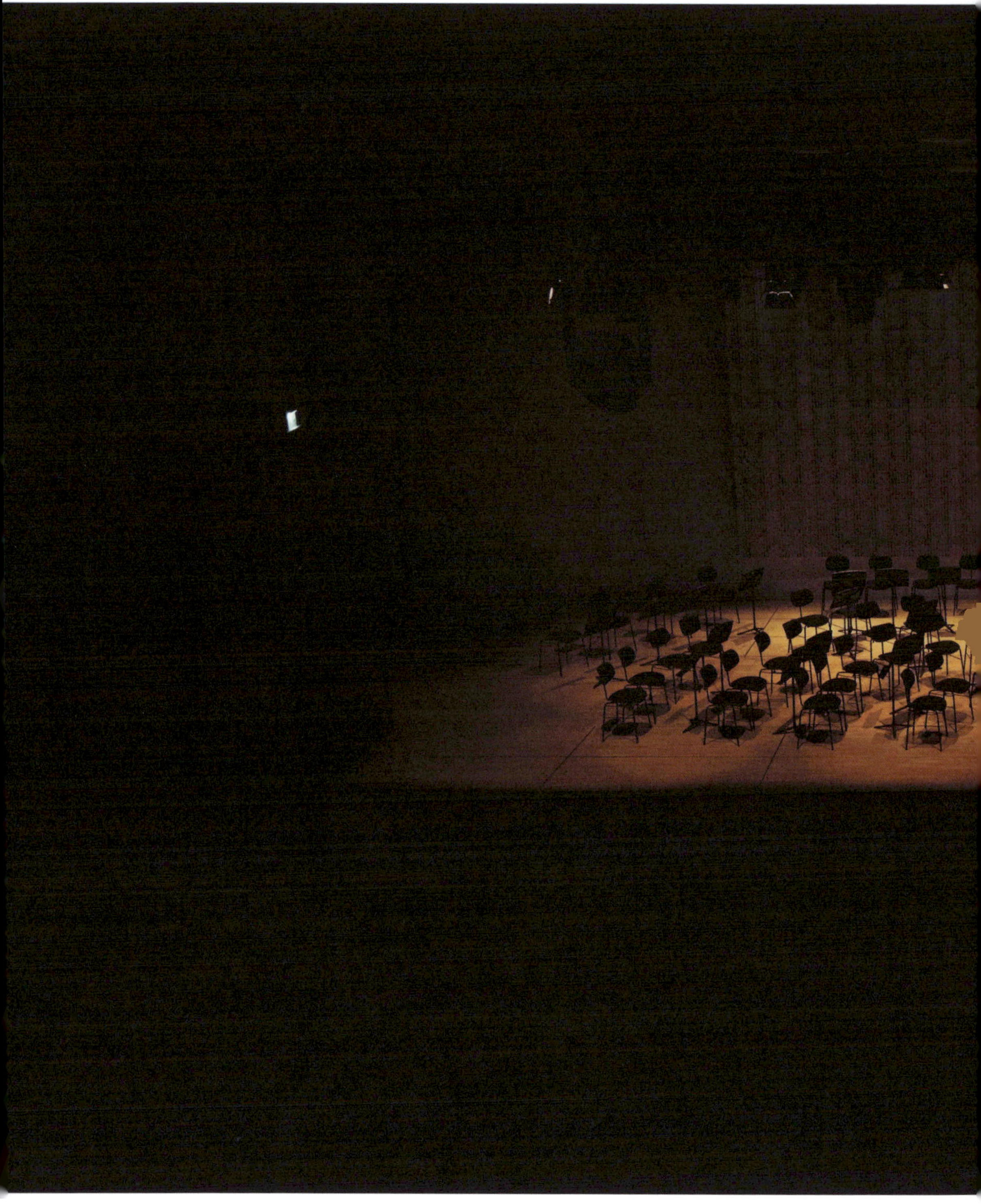

Annika Kahrs, *Ganz ungültig, nur ein Versuch,*
2024, 4K Video, Farbe, Ton / colour, sound,
22 Min., Videostandbild / video still

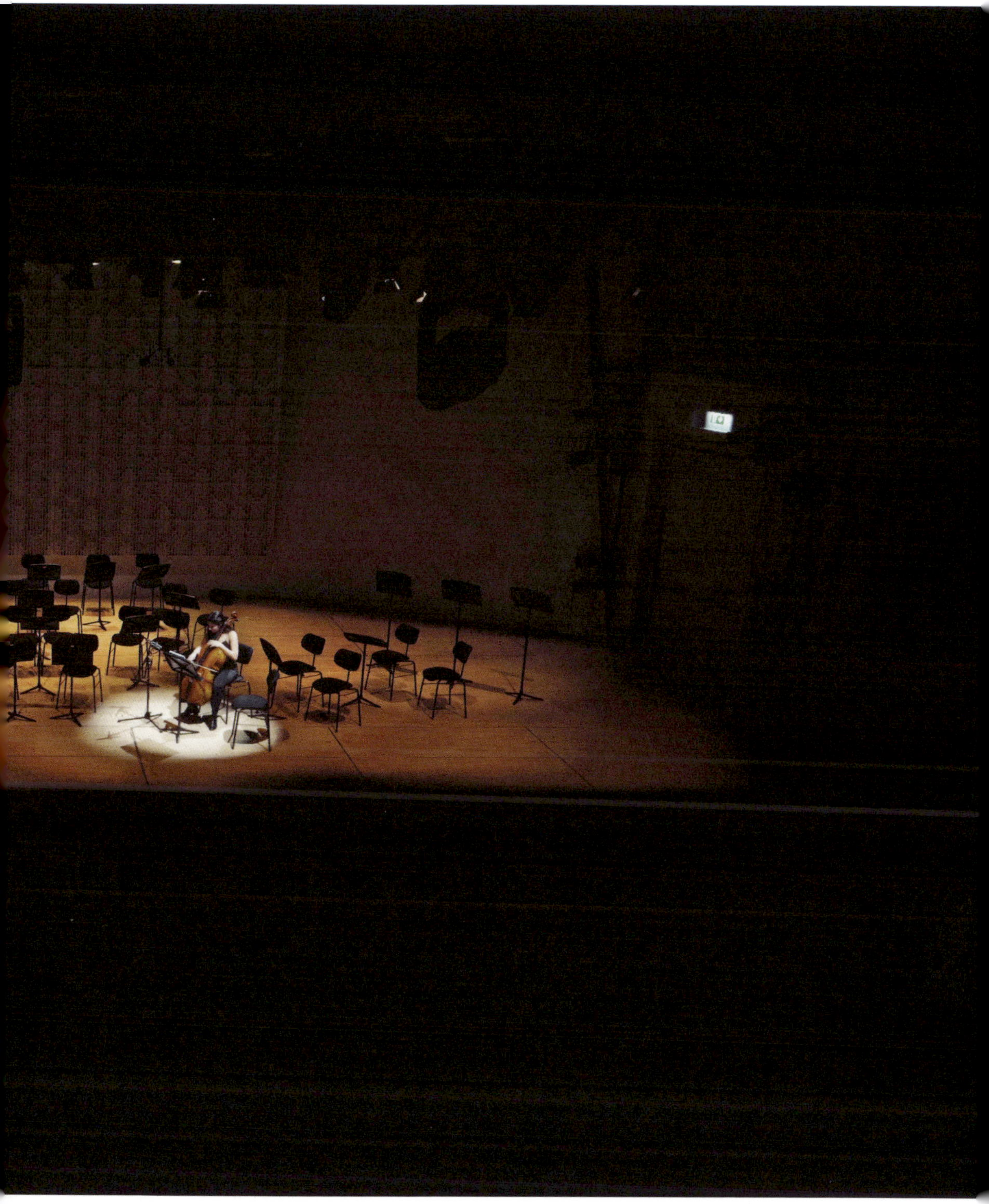

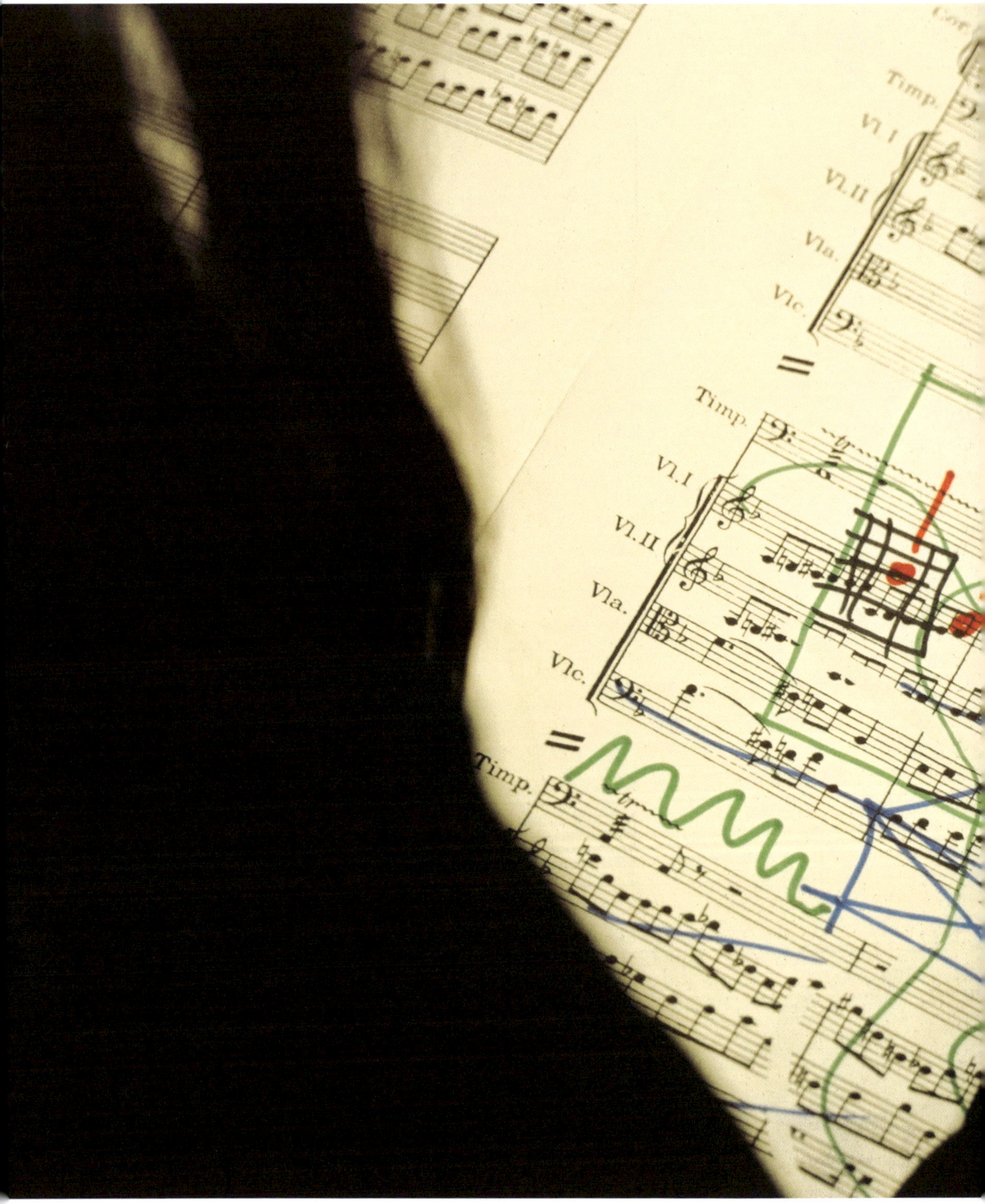

Annika Kahrs, *Ganz ungültig, nur ein Versuch,*
2024, 4K Video, Farbe, Ton / colour, sound,
22 Min., Videostandbild / video still

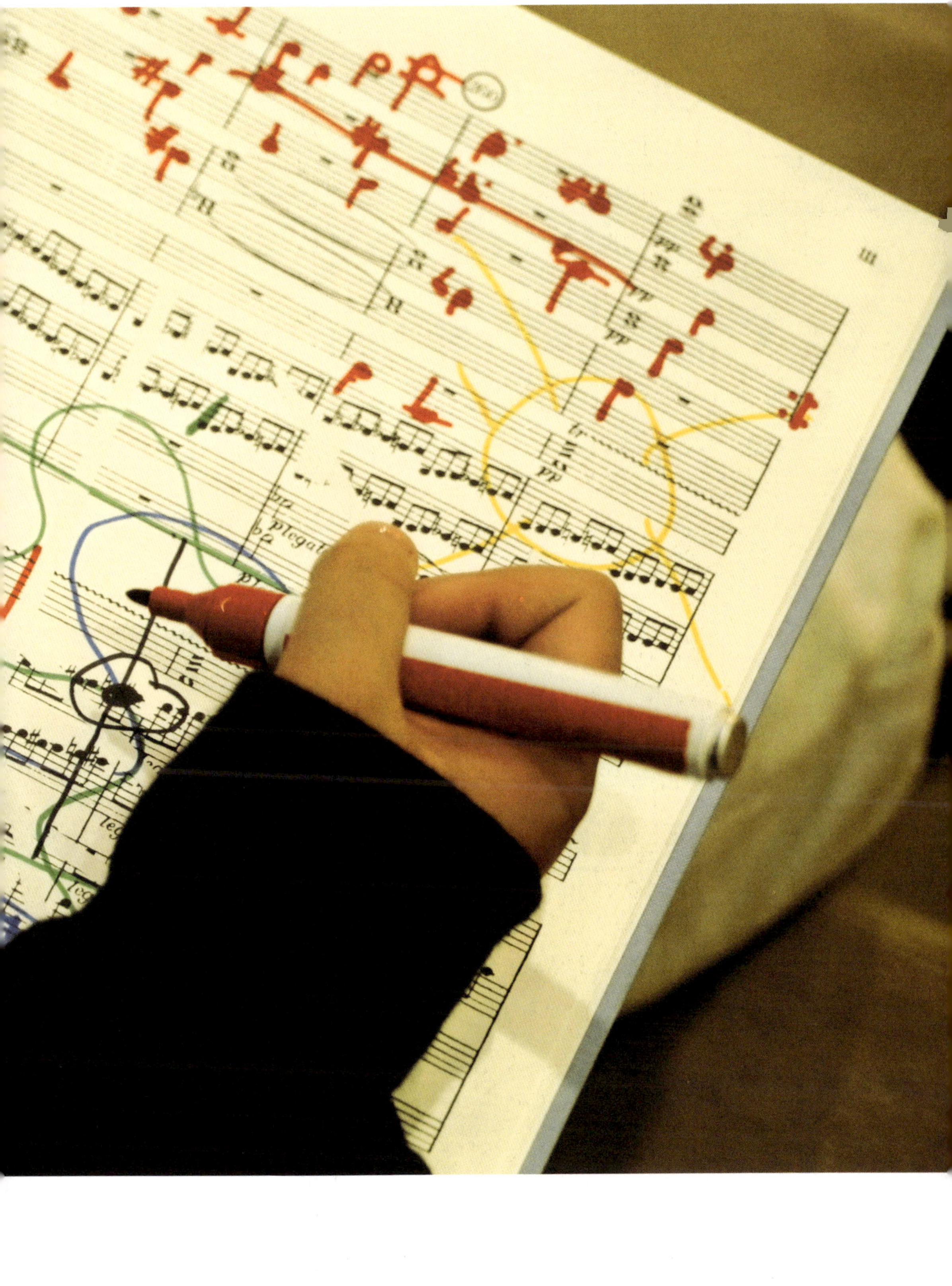

Standorte /
Locations

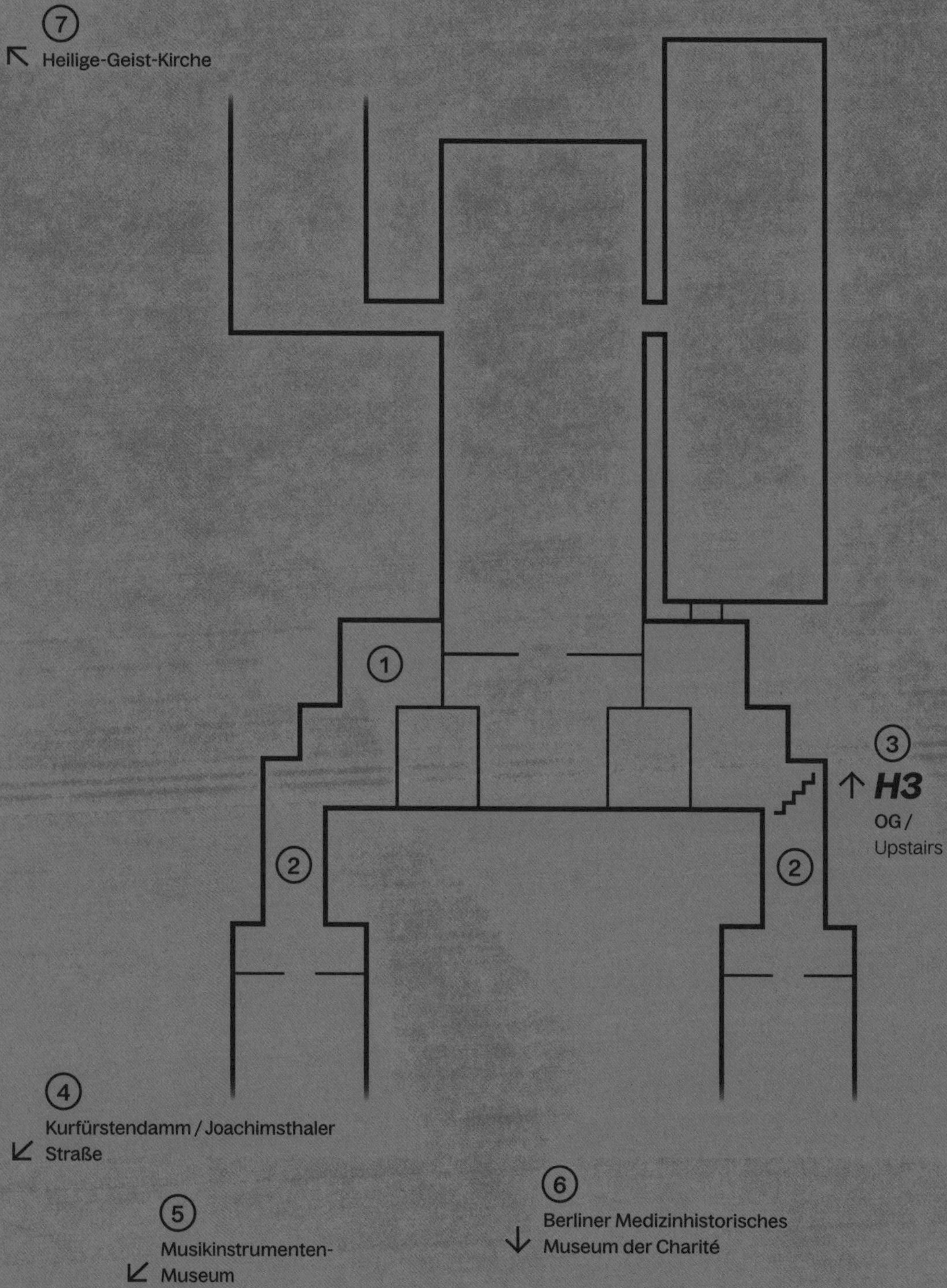

1. Forum, Hamburger Bahnhof – Nationalgalerie der Gegenwart

   For Two To Play On One, 2012

2. Historische Übergänge / Historical passageways, Hamburger Bahnhof – Nationalgalerie der Gegenwart

   My Favorite Music, 2020

3. ***H3***, Hamburger Bahnhof – Nationalgalerie der Gegenwart

   yellow orange then red and blue, 2024
   La Banda, 2024
   Le Chant des Maisons, 2022
   A Cashier's Opera, 2025

4. Kurfürstendamm / Joachimsthaler Straße, Berlin, täglich 18 bis 22 Uhr zur vollen Stunde / daily 6 to 10 pm on the hour

   how to live in the echo of other places, 2022–25

5. Musikinstrumenten-Museum, Berlin, Tiergartenstraße 1, 10785 Berlin

   19. Februar 2026 / 19 February 2026
   Strings, 2010
   Alone Together, 2016
   Performances

   19. Februar – 1. März 2026 / 19 February – 1 March 2026
   Ganz ungültig, nur ein Versuch, 2024
   Videoinstallation / Video installation

6. Berliner Medizinhistorisches Museum der Charité Hörsaalruine, Virchowweg 16, 10117 Berlin

   18. März 2026 / 18 March 2026
   zum Sonnendeck, 2026
   Performance

7. Heilige-Geist-Kirche Perleberger Straße 36, 10559 Berlin

   15. April 2026 / 15 April 2026
   the lord loves changes, it's one of his greatest delusions, 2018
   Performance

Ausgestellte Werke / Exhibited Works

Annika Kahrs
A Cashier's Opera, 2025

4K Video, Farbe, Ton / colour, sound, **36 Min.,**
Edition Nr. / no. **1 von** / of **5 + 2 AP**
Staatliche Museen zu Berlin, Nationalgalerie
2025 erworben durch / acquired by
FREUNDE der Nationalgalerie
Komposition / Composition: **Louis d'Heudières**
Kamera / Camera:
Karsten Krause, Levente Pavelka, Goscha Steinhauer
Tonaufnahmen / Sound Recording:
Patrick Dadaczyński, Miguel Murrieta Vásquez
Produktionsleitung / Production Manager:
Rosanna Graf
Unterstützung / Support: **Kenna Capalbo**
Koordination / Co-ordination: **Ozan Maral**
Maske / Make-up:
Rosanna Graf, Kenna Capalbo, Marit Blossey
Kostümbild / Costume Design: **Rosanna Graf**
Sound Design & Sound Mixing: Ariel Schlichter
Colour Grading: Tim Liebe
Title Design: Laurens Bauer
Mit / With:
Boram Lie, Mari Sawada, Anna Faber, Ildiko Ludwig, Isabelle Klemt, Zheni Rafailova, Shihab Eltahir, Mohammad El-Asmar, Marylou Guerra, Fanny Hucht, Jara Lutz, Lenja Tull, Carla Rentschler, Naê Flor Selka de Paiva, Glenn Lax, Jonathan Kiebel, Flint Schmidt, Sergej Iwanaga, Max Onno, Achim Schlak, Nina Guo

Produziert von / Produced by:
FREUNDE der Nationalgalerie

Ausgestellt / Exhibited:
***H3*, Hamburger Bahnhof – Nationalgalerie der Gegenwart**

Annika Kahrs
La Banda, 2024

4K Video, Farbe, Ton / colour, sound, **22 Min.,**
Edition von / of **5 + 2 AP**
Courtesy Annika Kahrs & Produzentengalerie Hamburg
Komposition / Composition: **Louis d'Heudières**
Kamera / Camera: **Karsten Krause, Lorenzo Huskamp**
Tonaufnahmen / Sound Recording:
Patrick Dadaczyński
Set-Koordination / Set Co-ordination:
Annalisa Piersanti
Produktionsleitung / Production Manager:
Lorenzo Huskamp
Sound Design & Sound Mixing: Ariel Schlichter
Colour Grading: Levente Pavelka
Title Design: Laurens Bauer
Mit / With:
L'Associazione Banda Musicale di Olevano Romano: Maria Carla De Pisa, Aurora Cerini, Carolina Rocchi, Martina Rischia, Lara Rocchi, Chiara De Giusti, Maria Alessandra Stoica, Maria Teresa Ferrari, Claudia Cerini, Beatrice Carletti, Erica De Persio, Giulia Mattei, Matteo Renzi, Giulia Rocchi, Clara Proietti, Anita Sterbini, Bianca Eleonora Cecchetto, Francesco Proietti, Augusto Carletti, Vittorio Arceri, Sara Martini, Cecilia Carletti, Stefano Pratesi, Federico Eusepi, Roberto Ciani, Mario Tabolacci, Arnaldo Mampieri, Flavio Proietti, Davide Baldi

Ermöglicht durch Annika Kahrs' Stipendium der Deutschen Akademie Rom Casa Baldi, gefördert von der Beauftragten für Kultur und Medien (BKM), und unterstützt von Raum für Kunst Hamburg e.V. / Made possible by Annika Kahrs's scholarship at Deutsche Akademie Rom Casa Baldi, funded by the Federal Government Commissioner for Culture and the Media (BKM), and supported by Raum für Kunst Hamburg e.V.

Ausgestellt / Exhibited:
***H3*, Hamburger Bahnhof – Nationalgalerie der Gegenwart**

Annika Kahrs
Le Chant des Maisons, 2022

4K Video, Farbe, Ton / colour, sound, 24:30 Min.,
Edition von / of 5 + 2 AP
Courtesy Annika Kahrs &
Produzentengalerie Hamburg
Komposition / Composition: Louis d'Heudières
Kamera / Camera: Karsten Krause, Levente Pavelka
Tonaufnahmen / Sound Recording: Karsten Krause
Technische Assistenz / Technical Assistance:
Bastien Bereta & Alexis Seul
Sound Design & Sound Mixing: Ariel Schlichter
Colour Grading: Levente Pavelka
Title Design: Andrés Serantes
Mit / With:
Héloïse Anfreville, Vincent Augier, Clarisse Cagnat, Ombeline Chanial, Jules Chanial, Elvire Gardon, Thelma Lamy, Noémie Lancon, Daphné Leblanc, Léandre Godin, Muriel Avet, Michel Bourgeay, Bernadette Chavanel, Madeleine Lucet, Brigitte Migeon, Mireille Pignaud, Lorene Reymond, Cathy Walther, Jeannine Durieux, Théo Faure, Anthony Galinier, Alexandre Rannou, Marie Liotard, Stéphane Kohn, Guillaume Bernard, Rémi Barberon, Pascal Fraisse, Michel Gaillard, Théo Degantho, Frédéric Fontimpe, Julien Jay, Maxime Noel

Produziert von La Biennale de Lyon im Rahmen der 16e Biennale D'Art contemporain 2022 kuratiert von Till Fellrath & Sam Bardaouil mit freundlicher Unterstützung von ifa-Institut für Auslandsbeziehungen, Goethe-Institut Lyon, Produzentengalerie Hamburg & Raum für Kunst Hamburg e.V. /
Produced by La Biennale de Lyon on occasion of the 16e Biennale D'Art contemporain 2022 curated by Till Fellrath & Sam Bardaouil with the kind support of ifa-Institut für Auslandsbeziehungen, Goethe-Institut Lyon, Produzentengalerie Hamburg & Raum für Kunst Hamburg e.V.

Ausgestellt / Exhibited:
H3, Hamburger Bahnhof – Nationalgalerie der Gegenwart

Annika Kahrs
yellow orange then red and blue, 2024

Set aus 6 handgeätzten Antikglasscheiben /
Set of 6 hand-etched antique glass plates
Je / Each 11,5 × 20,5 cm
Courtesy Annika Kahrs &
Produzentengalerie Hamburg

Ausgestellt / Exhibited:
H3, Hamburger Bahnhof – Nationalgalerie der Gegenwart

Annika Kahrs
My Favorite Music, 2020

Soundinstallation, 2-teilig / Sound installation, 2 parts,
18:31 Min., Edition von / of 5 + 2 AP
Courtesy Annika Kahrs &
Produzentengalerie Hamburg
Produktionsleitung / Production Management:
Nina Kuttler
Sound Design & Sound Mixing: Ariel Schlichter
Mit / With:
Alexandra, Jan Sjoerds, Jörg Peter Petersen, Thomas Golembiewski

In Auftrag gegeben von / Commissioned by
Kunstverein in Hamburg
In Zusammenarbeit mit / In collaboration with
Hinz&Kunzt

Ausgestellt / Exhibited:
Historische Übergänge /historical passageways, Hamburger Bahnhof – Nationalgalerie der Gegenwart

Annika Kahrs
For Two To Play On One, 2012

Performance für 2 Pianist*innen /
Performance for 2 piano players,
Edition von / of 3 + 2 AP
Courtesy Annika Kahrs & Produzentengalerie
Hamburg
Mit / With:
Hakim Azmi, Christoph Böhm, Mia Bodet,
Sophie Braun, Telmo Carvajal Díe, Kyrylo Chynchevyi,
Boris Hadzija, Imyeon Han, Joe Houston,
Anastasiia Husak, Angelina Kalachenkova,
Yoonji Kim, Yuhan Liu, Steven Mainka,
Akihito Maruyama, Viktoriia Mashyka, Dohi Moon,
Tanja Niiranen, Shion Ota, Chloe Pak, Jared Redmond,
Helena Röhn, Katharina Scheidemantel,
Anastasiia Schykyrynska, Ruiqi Shi, Ruiliu Xu

In Auftrag gegeben von KW Institute for
Contemporary Art Berlin im Rahmen der Ausstellung
ONE ON ONE, 2012. /
Commissioned by KW Institute for Contemporary Art
Berlin on occasion of the exhibition ONE ON ONE, 2012.

Ausgestellt / Exhibited:
Forum, Hamburger Bahnhof – Nationalgalerie
der Gegenwart

Annika Kahrs
how to live in the echo of other places, 2022–25

Videoprojektion / Video projection,
1–5 Minuten / minutes
Courtesy Annika Kahrs & Produzentengalerie
Hamburg
3D-Künstler / 3D artist: Alexander Trattler
Produziert für / Produced for Imagine the City /
Kunst und Kultur in der HafenCity e.V.

Ausgestellt / Exhibited:
Kurfürstendamm / Joachimsthaler Straße, Berlin,
täglich 18 bis 22 Uhr zur vollen Stunde /
daily 6 to 10 pm on the hour

Annika Kahrs
Ganz ungültig, nur ein Versuch, 2024

4K Video, Farbe, Ton / colour, sound, 22 Min.,
Edition von / of 5 + 2 AP
Courtesy Annika Kahrs & Produzentengalerie
Hamburg
Kamera / Camera: Levente Pavelka
Tonaufnahmen / Sound Recording:
Patrick Dadaczyński
Musikalische Beratung / Musical Consultation:
Louis d'Heudières
Produktionsleitung / Production Management:
Nina Kuttler
Sound Design & Sound Mixing: Ariel Schlichter
Colour Grading: Levente Pavelka
Titel- & Buchdesign / Title Design & Book Design:
Laurens Bauer
Mit / With:
Alexander Fahima, Peru Odriozola Marquet,
May Metika Fischer, Sebastian Felix Lampert,
Paris Tutera Kyriakopoulos, Maria Cárdenes Torres,
Lina Gómez, Baran Mohammadbeigi, Alex Heide,
Clara Pérez Campuzano

In Auftrag gegeben von / Commissioned by
OÖ Landes-Kultur GmbH

Ausgestellt / Exhibited:
Musikinstrumenten-Museum, Berlin, 19. Februar –
1. März 2026 / 19 February – 1 March 2026

Performances

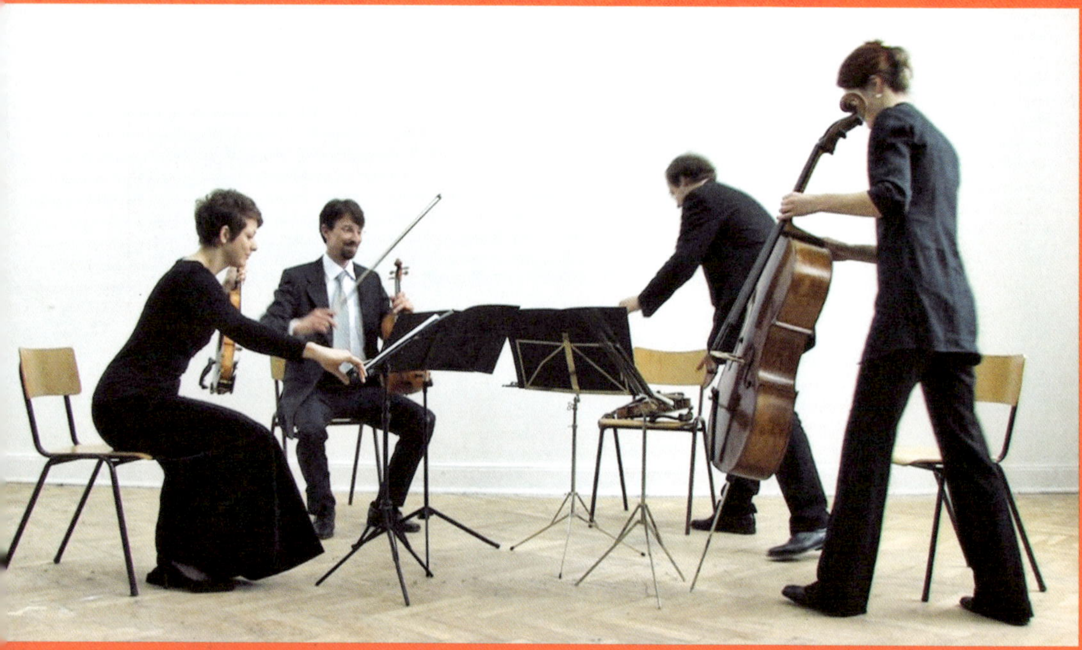

Annika Kahrs, *Strings*, 2010, HD Video, Farbe, Ton / colour, sound, 8:20 Min., Videostandbild / video still

19. Februar 2026 / 19 February 2026
Musikinstrumenten-Museum

Annika Kahrs
Strings, 2010

Streichquartett / String quartet, **10 Min.,**
Solistenensemble Kaleidoskop

Annika Kahrs
Alone Together, 2016

4 Performer*innen / Sänger*innen /
4 performers / singers, **30 Min.,**
Solistenensemble Kaleidoskop
Musikalische Bearbeitung /
Musical Arrangement:
Louis d'Heudières

Entwickelt im Rahmen von /
Developed within the framework of
***Immersion: Schule der Distanz No. 1,* als Teil von /**
as part of **Berliner Festspiele im /** at **Gropius Bau,**
Berlin, 2016

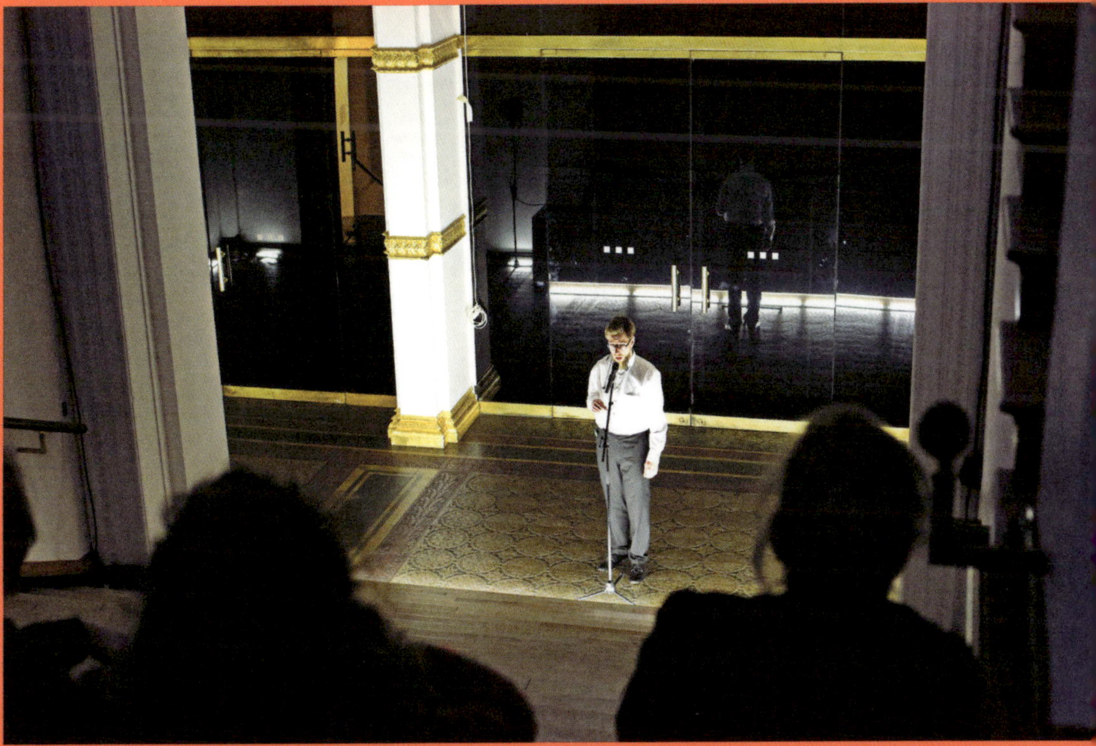

Annika Kahrs, *Alone Together,* 2016, Performance, 30 Min.,
Performanceansicht / performance view **Gropius Bau, Berlin, 2016**

18. März 2026 / 18 March 2026
Berliner Medizinhistorisches Museum
Hörsaalruine / Lecture hall ruin

Annika Kahrs
zum Sonnendeck, 2026

7 Performer*innen / 7 performers, **30 Min.**,
Solistenensemble Kaleidoskop
Komposition / Composition: **Louis d'Heudières**

In Auftrag gegeben von Freunde* Guter Musik Berlin e.V. im Rahmen von *Hamburger Bahnhof On Tour* / Commisioned by Freunde* Guter Musik Berlin e.V. as part of *Hamburger Bahnhof On Tour*, **2026**

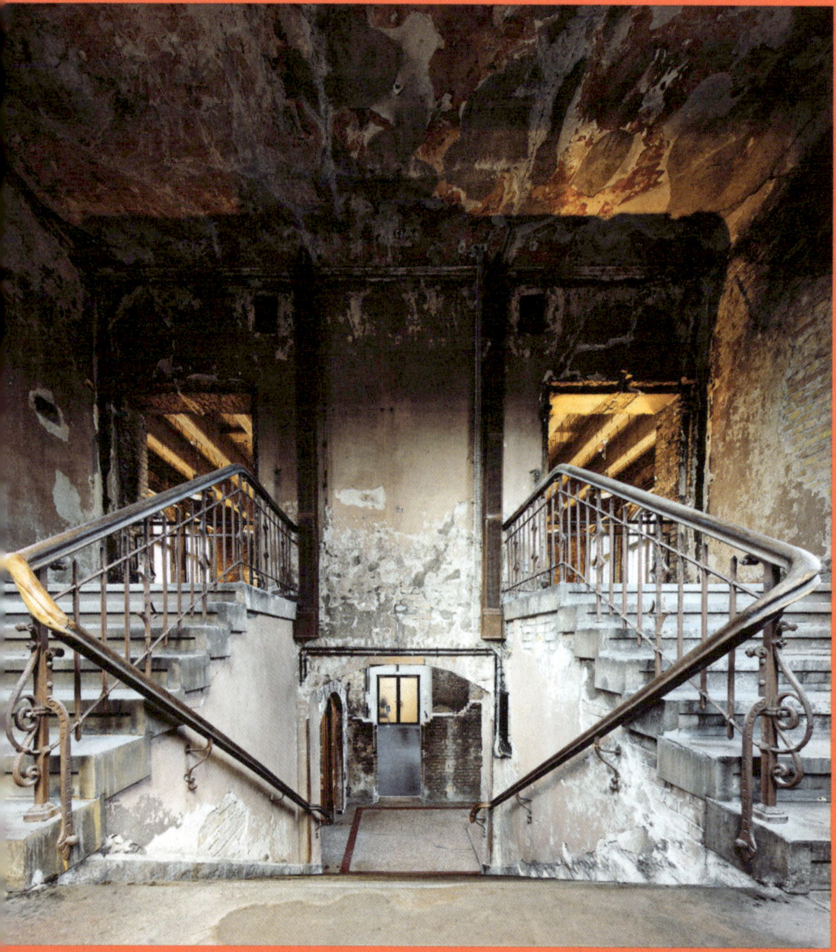

Hörsaalruine / Lecture hall ruin, **Berliner Medizinhistorisches Museum** / Museum of Medical History, **Berlin**

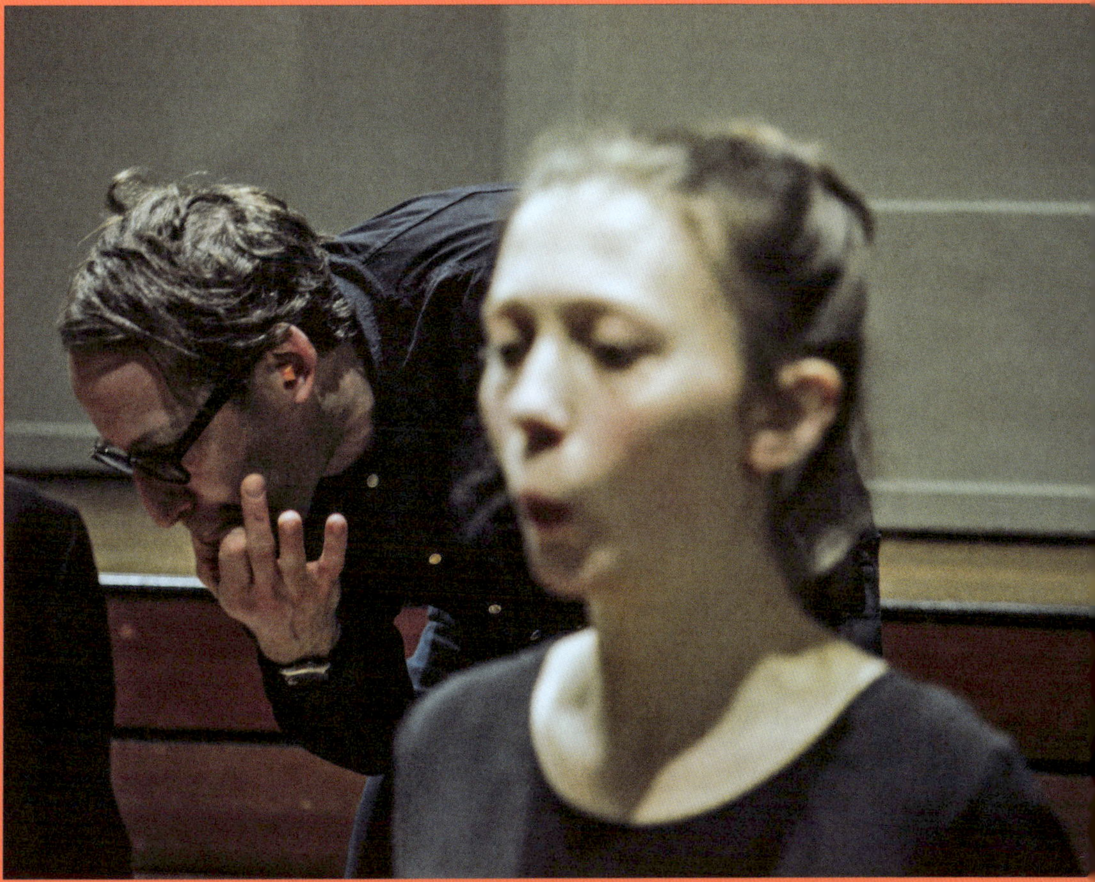

Annika Kahrs, *the lord loves changes, it's one of his greatest delusions,* 2018, HD Video, Farbe, Ton / colour, sound, 15:48 Min., Videostandbild / video still

15. April 2026 / 15 April 2026
Heilige-Geist-Kirche

Annika Kahrs
the lord loves changes, it's one of his greatest delusions, 2018

Pfeif-Chor und Orgel / Whistle choir and organ, **30 Min.,**
Solistenensemble Kaleidoskop
Orgel / Organ: **Alexander Moosbrugger**
Komposition / Composition: **Louis d'Heudières**

In Auftrag gegeben von SAVVY Contemporary, koproduziert von MaerzMusik – Festival für Zeitfragen / Commissioned by SAVVY Contemporary, co-produced by MaerzMusik – Festival for Time Issues

Impressum / Imprint

Diese Publikation erscheint anlässlich der Ausstellung /
Published on the occasion of the exhibition
Annika Kahrs. OFF SCORE
14. November 2025 – 3. Mai 2026 /
14 November 2025 – 3 May 2026
im / at Hamburger Bahnhof – Nationalgalerie der Gegenwart, Staatliche Museen zu Berlin
Direktoren / Directors: Sam Bardaouil & Till Fellrath
smb.museum/hbf

Ausstellung / Exhibition

Kuratorin / Curator: Ingrid Buschmann
Restauratorische Betreuung / Conservation: Elisa Carl
Ausstellungskoordination / Exhibition Co-ordination: Elena Montini, Sophie Schattner
Kommunikation / Communication: Fiona Geuß, Anna Nike Sohrauer, Paul Angermeyer, Lorenz Dünges, Nada Hussein, Theo Lemaire
Kunstvermittlung / Mediation: Claudia Ehgartner, Sonja Azizaj, Miriam Elisa Heidenreich
Sekretariat / Office: Katrin Berendsen, Katherine Israel-Koedel
Sammlungsverwalter / Collection Management: Jörg Lange, Thomas Seewald
Hauselektrik / Inhouse Electrics: Garry Rogge
Haustechnik / Maintenance: Dirk Wagner, Stefan Gösche, Frank Wloka
Praktikant*innen / Interns: Mara Hock, Hyunkyung Kim, Paulina Köberle, Florian Mojem

Ausstellungsarchitektur / Exhibition Architecture: klaud Koepf Lechthaler Architecture & Urban Design
Ausstellungsbau / Exhibition Construction: MWB Theater- und Veranstaltungsdesign
Art Handling: Abrell & van den Berg
Medientechnik / Audiovisuals: visionb Kunstservice, LIMES Media GmbH
Licht / Lighting: LICHTblick Bühnentechnik
Ton / Sound Design: NOUS Audio GmbH
Kirchenbänke / Church benches: Ev. Heilige-Geist-Gemeinde Berlin Moabit
Malerarbeiten / Painting: LIQUID PAINT
Ausstellungsgrafik / Exhibition Graphics: Eps51
Produktion Ausstellungsgrafik / Production of Exhibition Graphics: Annette Herwegh

STUDIO ANNIKA KAHRS
Studio: Kenna Capalbo
Ausstellungston / Exhibition Sound Design: Ariel Schlichter
Koordination / Co-ordination: Ozan Maral
Musikkomposition & -arrangement / Music Composition & Arrangement: Louis d'Heudières
Produktionsleitung Film / Production Manager Film: Rosanna Graf

HAMBURGER BAHNHOF ON TOUR
Ein Performanceprogramm von / A performance programme organised by Freunde* Guter Musik Berlin e.V. in Zusammenarbeit mit / in co-operation with Hamburger Bahnhof – Nationalgalerie der Gegenwart, Musikinstrumenten-Museum SIM PK, Berliner Medizinhistorisches Museum der Charité & Ev. Heilige-Geist-Gemeinde
Konzept / Concept: Ingrid Buschmann, Gabriele Knapstein

Publikation / Catalogue

Für die / For the **Nationalgalerie – Staatliche Museen zu Berlin**
herausgegeben von / edited by
Sam Bardaouil & Till Fellrath
Autor*innen / Authors:
Ingrid Buschmann, Annika Kahrs, Philipp Lange, Susanne Pfeffer
Redaktion / Editing: **Lisa Hörstmann**
Übersetzungen / Translations:
Anne Diestelkamp, Jacqueline Todd

Visuelles Konzept und Design /
Visual Concept and Design: **Eps51**
Druck und Bindung / Printing and Binding:
Tipostampa, Moncalieri
Papier / Paper: **Fedrigoni Arena White Rough**
Schriften / Fonts: **HB Bagoss (Displaay)**

Cover:
Annika Kahrs, ***A Cashier's Opera*****, 2025,**
4K Video, Farbe, Ton / colour, sound, **36 Min.,**
Videostandbild / video still

Erschienen bei / Published by
Silvana Editoriale S.p.A., Cinisello Balsamo
www.silvanaeditoriale.it

Silvana Editoriale

Hauptgeschäftsführung / Chief Executive:
Michele Pizzi
Verlagsleitung / Editorial Director: **Sergio Di Stefano**
Art Director: Giacomo Merli
Redaktionskoordination / Editorial Coordinator:
Maria Chiara Tulli
Korrektorat / Copy Editor: **Cristina Pradella**
Produktionskoordination / Production Coordinator:
Antonio Micelli
Redaktionsassistenz / Editorial Assistant:
Giulia Mercanti
Bildredaktion / Photo Editor: **Silvia Sala**
Pressestelle / Press Office: **Lidia Masolini**

Die Deutsche Nationalbibliothek verzeichnet diese Publikation in der Deutschen Nationalbibliografie; detaillierte bibliografische Daten sind im Internet über http://dnb.dnb.de abrufbar. /
The German National Library lists this publication in the German National Bibliography. Detailed bibliographic data are available at http://dnb.dnb.de.

Printed in the EU
ISBN: 9788 83666 076 6

FSC www.fsc.org
MISTO
Carta | A sostegno della gestione forestale responsabile
FSC® C173858

Abbildungsverzeichnis / Photo Credits

Foto S. / Photo pp. **4–19, 68–75, 78–83:**
© Staatliche Museen zu Berlin,
Nationalgalerie / Jacopo La Forgia
Foto S. / Photo p. **50: © Helge Mundt**
Foto S. / Photo pp. **54, 55:**
© Hamburger Kunsthalle / Hans Wulf Kunze
Foto S. / Photo p. **60: © Jens Ziehe**
Foto S. / Photo p. **85: © Rosanna Graf**
Foto S. / Photo p. **105: © Jens Franke**
Foto S. / Photo p. **106: © Sven Geißler**

Dank / Acknowledgements

Die Ausstellung wird ermöglicht durch /
The exhibition is made possible by:
FREUNDE der Nationalgalerie
Mit Unterstützung von / With support from:
LIMES Media GmbH

Die Publikation wurde ermöglicht durch /
The publication was made possible by:
Katharina Schulenberg-Leduc & Thierry Leduc
Hamburger Bahnhof International Companions e.V.
Mit Unterstützung von / With support from:
Raum für Kunst Hamburg e.V.

Das ausstellungsbegleitende Performanceprogramm /
The performance programme accompanying the exhibition,
Hamburger Bahnhof On Tour
wird gefördert von / is funded by:
Hauptstadtkulturfonds

Der Hamburger Bahnhof dankt für die enge Zusammenarbeit mit dem Studio der Künstlerin und Produzentengalerie Hamburg. /
Hamburger Bahnhof would like to thank the artist's studio and Produzentengalerie Hamburg for their close collaboration.